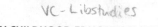

EARLY CHILDHOOD EDUCATION SERIES

Leslie R. Williams, Editor
Millie Almy, Senior Advisor

Making Friends in School: Promoting Peer Relationships in Early Childhood
PATRICIA G. RAMSEY

Play and the Social Context of Development in Early Care and Education
BARBARA SCALES, MILLIE ALMY, AGELIKI NICOLOPOULOU, & SUSAN ERVIN-TRIPP, Eds.

The Whole Language Kindergarten
SHIRLEY RAINES ROBERT CANADY

Good Day/Bad Day: The Child's Experience of Child Care
LYDA BEARDSLEY

Children's Play and Learning: Perspectives and Policy Implications
EDGAR KLUGMAN
SARA SMILANSKY

Serious Players in the Primary Classroom: Empowering Children Through Active Learning Experiences
SELMA WASSERMANN

Child Advocacy for Early Childhood Educators
BEATRICE S. FENNIMORE

Managing Quality Child Care Centers: A Comprehensive Manual for Administrators
PAMELA BYRNE SCHILLER
PATRICIA M. DYKE

Multiple Worlds of Child Writers: Friends Learning to Write
ANNE HAAS DYSON

Young Children Continue to Reinvent Arithmetic—2nd Grade: Implications of Piaget's Theory
CONSTANCE KAMII

Literacy Learning in the Early Years: Through Children's Eyes
LINDA GIBSON

The Good Preschool Teacher: Six Teachers Reflect on Their Lives
WILLIAM AYERS

A Child's Play Life: An Ethnographic Study
DIANA KELLY-BYRNE

Professionalism and the Early Childhood Practitioner
BERNARD SPODEK, OLIVIA N. SARACHO, & DONALD L. PETERS, Eds.

Looking at Children's Play: The Bridge from Theory to Practice
PATRICIA A. MONIGHAN-NOUROT, BARBARA SCALES, JUDITH L. VAN HOORN, & MILLIE ALMY

The War Play Dilemma: Balancing Needs and Values in the Early Childhood Classroom
NANCY CARLSSON-PAIGE
DIANE E. LEVIN

The Piaget Handbook for Teachers and Parents
ROSEMARY PETERSON
VICTORIA FELTON-COLLINS

Teaching and Learning in a Diverse World: Multicultural Education
PATRICIA G. RAMSEY

The Early Childhood Curriculum: A Review of Current Research
CAROL SEEFELDT, Ed.

The Full-Day Kindergarten
DORIS PRONIN FROMBERG

(Continued)

Promoting Social and Moral
Development in Young Children
CAROLYN POPE EDWARDS

A Teacher at Work: Professional
Development and the Early Childhood
Educator
MARGARET V. YONEMURA

Today's Kindergarten
BERNARD SPODEK, Ed.

Supervision in Early Childhood
Education
JOSEPH J. CARUSO
M. TEMPLE FAWCETT

Visions of Childhood: Influential Models
from Locke to Spock
JOHN CLEVERLEY
D. C. PHILLIPS

Starting School: From Separation
to Independence
NANCY BALABAN

Young Children Reinvent Arithmetic:
Implications of Piaget's Theory
CONSTANCE KAMII

Ideas Influencing Early Childhood
Education
EVELYN WEVER

Diversity in the Classroom:
A Multicultural Approach
FRANCES E. KENDALL

The Joy of Movement in Early Childhood
SANDRA R. CURTIS

Island of Childhood: Eduation in the
Special World of Nursery School
ELINOR FITCH GRIFFIN

Moral Classrooms, Moral Children

Creating a Constructivist Atmosphere in Early Education

Rheta DeVries and Betty Zan

TEACHERS COLLEGE PRESS

Teachers College, Columbia University
New York and London

Published by Teachers College Press, 1234 Amsterdam Avenue, New York, N.Y. 10027

Library of Congress Cataloging-in-Publication Data

DeVries, Rheta.
  Moral classrooms. moral children: creating a constructivist
atmosphere in early education / Rheta DeVries and Betty Zan.
      p.   cm.
  Includes bibliographical references and index.
  ISBN 0-8077-3342-3.—ISBN 0-8077-3341-5 (paper)
    1. Moral education (Early childhood) 2. Constructivism
(Education) 3. Moral development. I. Zan, Betty. II. Title.
LB1139.35.M67D48 1994
370.11'4—dc20   93-44317

ISBN 0-8077-3341-5 (paper)
ISBN 0-8077-3342-3

Printed on acid-free paper
Manufactured in the United States of America
01 00 99 98 97 96 95 94   8 7 6 5 4 3 2 1

Contents

Acknowledgments   *ix*

Introduction   1

1   **What Do We Mean by "Moral Classrooms?"**   **7**

Vignettes from Three Classrooms   7
Sketches of the Sociomoral Atmospheres in
    Three Classrooms   10
Components of the Sociomoral Atmosphere   22
Research on Sociomoral Atmosphere and
    Children's Sociomoral Development   23
The Sociomoral Atmosphere as Hidden Curriculum   25
So What Is the Constructivist Sociomoral
    Atmosphere?   26

2   **What Do We Mean by "Moral Children?"**   **28**

What We Do Not Mean by "Moral Children"   28
How Children Think About Moral Rules   31
How Children Think About Others   32
Observing Moral Children in the Classroom   38
Summary   41

3   **How the Sociomoral Atmosphere Influences the**   **43**
    Child's Development

Social Interaction and Construction of the Self   44
The Teacher-Child Relationship   45
Peer Relationships   52
Summary   57

4   Establishing a Constructivist Sociomoral Atmosphere   **58**

Classroom Organization 58
Activities 62
The Teacher's Role 70
Summary 78

5   Conflict and Its Resolution   **79**

The Role of Conflict in Development 79
Sociomoral Atmosphere and Conflict Resolution 81
Conflict Between Teacher and Child 101
Summary 102

6   Grouptime   **104**

Objectives for Grouptime 104
The Role of the Teacher 106
Conducting Grouptime 108
Grouptime Lost, Grouptime Regained 122
Summary 123

7   Rule Making and Decision Making   **125**

Objectives 125
Rule Making 126
Decision Making 139
Summary 144

8   Voting   **145**

Objectives 145
Guidelines for Voting 146
Summary 161

9   Social and Moral Discussions   **162**

What Is "Social," "Moral," and "Sociomoral?" 162
Moral Judgment Theory 164
Moral Dilemmas 166
Objectives of Sociomoral Discussions 168
Guidelines for Conducting Hypothetical Sociomoral
    Discussions 168
Real-Life Moral Discussions 174
Hypothetical Dilemmas Drawn from Real-Life
    Experiences 175
Summary 177

10   Cooperative Alternatives to Discipline   **178**

The Role of Personal Experience in Social and
    Moral Development 179
Two Types of Sanctions 180
Guidelines for Implementing Constructivist
    Alternatives to Discipline 185
Summary 190

11   Activity Time *learning, environment*   **192**

Objectives and Rationale 193
Three Categories of Knowledge Reflected in
    Activities 193
Planning for Activity Time 197
Implementing Activity Time 201
Three Sources of Difficulty in Implementing
    Activity Time 216
Summary 216

12   Clean-Up Time   **218**

Objectives 218
How to Present Clean-up to the Class 219
Problems with Clean-up 221
Solutions to Clean-up Problems 222
Summary 232

13   Lunch Time   **233**

Objectives 234
Guidelines for Lunch Time 234
Summary 242

14   Nap Time/Rest Time   **243**

Problems of Nap Time 243
Guidelines for a Less Stressful Nap Time 244
Summary 249

15   Academics ?   **250**

The Sociomoral Context for Teaching Academics 251
The Conditions for Promoting Academics 252
The Constructivist Integration of Academics 254
Summary 262

16   The Difficult Child   **264**

The Behaviorist Approach 265
Integration of Psychodynamic and Constructivist
    Theories 268
Guidelines for Working with the Difficult Child 270
Summary 278

17   The Sociomoral Atmosphere of the School   **279**

Kohlberg and Colleagues' Work on Assessing
    Moral Culture 279
Children's Experience of the School Atmosphere 281
The Teacher's Experience of the School Atmosphere 283
Principles for Principals 284
The Sociomoral Atmosphere of the State
    Department of Education 289
Summary 290

Appendix   293
References   297
Index   301
About the Authors   310

Acknowledgments

This book is the result of collaboration with many teachers over a number of years. In particular, we draw from videotapes made in the Human Development Laboratory School (HDLS) at the University of Houston. We videotaped once each week during 1989–1990 in Peige Fuller's classroom, and twice each week during 1990–1991 in Coreen Samuel's classroom. Other videotaped resources were collected less systematically from the classrooms of Karen Capo, Stephanie Clark, Carol Olson, Angie Quesada, Kathryn Saxton, Mary Wells, and Marti Wilson.

To Ms. Lorraine Bradley Goolsby we express appreciation for help in developing social and moral dilemma discussion stories that provided the basis of Chapter 9.

We want to express our appreciation to the Limited-Grant-in-Aid Program at the University of Houston for support of the classroom videotape research, to the Harry S. and Isabel C. Cameron Foundation for support of program development reflected in the book, and to the Spencer Foundation for support of the research described in chapter 1 that serves as the inspiration for this work.

We owe special thanks to Ms. Deborah Murphy, Dr. Juanita Copley, and Dr. Hermina Sinclair who reviewed the entire manuscript and offered many helpful suggestions. We also thank our editor, Ms. Susan Liddicoat at Teachers College Press for her faith in the idea for the book and for all her help throughout the publication process.

We want to express our deep appreciation to all the children and teachers whose efforts have contributed so much to our understanding and formation of constructivist education.

Introduction

The first principle of constructivist education—that a sociomoral atmosphere must be cultivated in which respect for others is continually practiced—is the basis for this book. By "sociomoral atmosphere" we refer to the entire network of interpersonal relations in a classroom. These pervade every aspect of the child's experience in school. The term *sociomoral atmosphere* implies our conviction that all interactions between and among children and their caregivers/educators have an impact on children's social and moral experience and development. This book addresses the question of how to establish and maintain an interpersonal classroom atmosphere that fosters children's intellectual, social, moral, emotional, and personality development.

Readers of the first author's previous books will not be surprised to learn that our work on sociomoral atmosphere is grounded in the research and theory of Jean Piaget. Others may be surprised because Piaget's own main focus was genetic epistemology—the origins and development of knowledge. However, Piaget (1948) emphasized that social life among children is a necessary context for the development of intelligence, morality, and personality. While Piaget did not continue in the direction of his early work on moral judgment (Piaget, 1932/1965), he is consistent in later works in emphasizing the indissociability of intellectual, social, moral, and affective development. In this book, we try to follow the direction indicated by Piaget (1954/1981) when he hypothesized parallel structures and functions for the child's construction of knowledge of the physical and the social world.

The theoretical foundation for our work on sociomoral atmosphere and sociomoral development rests on three parallels in Piaget's theory of sociomoral and cognitive development. The first parallel is that just as knowledge of the object world is constructed by the child, so too must psychosocial knowledge be constructed. That is, sociomoral thought and sociomoral understanding in action undergo qualitative transformations. The second parallel is that just as affect is an indissociable motivational element in intellectual development, socioaffective bonds (or their lack) motivate social and moral development. The third parallel is that an equilibration (or self-regulating) process can be described for social and moral development as for cognitive development. For example, this equilibration involves affirmation of the self and conservation of the other as a desired partner. In particular, we emphasize how decentering to become conscious of different points of view is necessary for reciprocal adjustments, mutual comprehension in shared systems of meaning, and social coordination. In addition, intrapersonal and interpersonal conflict play crucial roles in the development of self-regulation in both intellectual and sociomoral domains. By "self-regulation," Piaget referred to an internal system that regulates thought and action. These parallels suggest that the conditions for sociomoral development are the same conditions for intellectual development.

This book extends the definition and articulation of constructivist education offered in previous publications. Overviews (DeVries & Kohlberg, 1987/1990; Kamii & DeVries, 1975/1977) emphasized the educational goal of cognitive development, as did books on group games (Kamii & DeVries, 1980), physical knowledge activities (Kamii & DeVries, 1978/1993), and arithmetic (Kamii, 1982, 1985, 1989, 1994). In this book we argue that constructivist education is not just physical-knowledge activities, group games, arithmetic debates, pretend play, blockbuilding, whole language literacy activities, and so forth. Implementing constructivist education in its most essential aspect involves more than activities, materials, and classroom organization. In earlier publications the importance of socioemotional and sociomoral development was outlined. In *Constructivist Early Education: Overview and Comparison with Other Programs* (DeVries & Kohlberg, 1987/1990), Piaget's view of the necessary role of social life in the development of intelligence was elaborated. In one chapter of that book, Kohlberg and Lickona advocated social and moral discussion, rule making, capitalizing on conflict, and an emphasis on community and responsibility. They pointed out that children must construct their moral understandings from the raw material of their day-to-day social interactions. Our book takes off from this idea. We provide a constructivist rationale for a particular type of sociomoral atmosphere and describe the practical ways in which teachers can cultivate it.

Our perspective on sociomoral atmosphere is influenced by the ideas of Jackson (1968) and Kohlberg (Power, Higgins, & Kohlberg, 1989) on the "hidden curriculum" of moral education in schools. The hidden curriculum consists of the norms and values embedded in the social structure of schools, especially those related to discipline. Kohlberg's "Just Community" approach to education of high school students emphasizes democratic principles as well as caring relationships. These are also part of our view of the sociomoral atmosphere. However, our own conception of the constructivist sociomoral atmosphere as it applies to younger children encompasses more than democratic principles of justice and care. We emphasize the cooperative nature of the constructivist teacher-child relationship and the influence of the child's entire school experience on the child's development.

One unifying theme of this book is that of development as the aim of constructivist education. Therefore, the most desirable school atmosphere is one that optimally promotes the child's development—social, moral, and affective, as well as intellectual. Unfortunately, the sociomoral atmosphere of most schools and child care institutions so emphasizes intellectual development that sociomoral and affective development are negatively influenced. This leads to a second unifying theme of this book, the conception of the constructivist teacher-child relationship as one of mutual respect in which the teacher minimizes the exercise of unnecessary authority in relation to children. In previous publications cited above we emphasized the theoretical importance of a cooperative teacher-child relationship. Here we flesh out this general guideline with specific principles of teaching and examples drawn from videotapes of classrooms.

The aim of our book is decidedly practical. However, practicalities are rooted in theoretical rationales based on child development research. We are aware that many educators have been disappointed with the lack of practical help offered by much research and theory in child development. Yet we are committed to contributing to the development of a science of educational practice that has theoretical coherence and empirical validity. Without such a steadying framework, educators' convictions swing with the pendulum. Open to the appeals of one bandwagon or fad after another, the field does not progress but stumbles along.

We are encouraged to continue in our efforts to travel a two-way street between theory and practice by the responses of teachers with whom we have worked. The theory is useful to them. Convictions about what they do are anchored in knowing why they teach as they do. Peige Fuller, the director of an infant and toddler program, expresses this attitude in the following way.

> Theory has a negative connotation in education. Teachers seem to say, "Give us a bag of tricks." I say, "Give us a foundation for being able to figure it out ourselves." You're not giving teachers a pre-packaged thing. You're trusting them and encouraging them to grow and learn as teachers and as people. Not to give that to teachers is a grave disrespect. Just giving teachers a bag of tricks is like giving teachers a worksheet. That's exactly an analogy. Not to give teachers theory is just to give them worksheets. If you don't understand the theory, even all the good ideas that come from constructivism—all the good activities—amount to a sophisticated bag of tricks. Every good method, if it isn't backed up by knowledge of why you're doing it, is going to reach limitations. If teachers don't understand the why of teaching in a particular situation, the next situation will be different, and they won't be able to go into their understanding of children and their understanding of what it means to facilitate children's learning, in order to know what to do next. (Personal communication, June 1992)

In this book, we try to provide the theory and rationales that will enable teachers to "go into their understanding" and make professional educational decisions. We believe that teachers should not be technicians but theoretically sophisticated professionals.

In chapter 1, we address the question, What do we mean by moral classrooms? Drawing from research on teacher-child interactions in three kindergarten classrooms in mostly black, urban, public schools for children from low-income families (DeVries, Haney, & Zan, 1991; DeVries, Reese-Learned, & Morgan, 1991a), we describe three very different sociomoral atmospheres that illustrate conflicting educational paradigms.

In chapter 2, we answer the question, What do we mean by moral children? first by saying what we do not mean. When we speak of "moral children," we do not mean children who are merely obedient or who simply know moral rules of others, act in prosocial ways, conform to social conventions of politeness, have certain character traits, or are religious. Instead, we refer to moral children as people grappling with interpersonal issues that are a natural part of their lives. We examine children's judgments about right and wrong, good and bad, as characterized by moral realism and limited perspective-taking.

In chapter 3 we turn to the question, How does the sociomoral atmosphere influence the child's development? Here we present perhaps the most important aspect of Piaget's theory with regard to the sociomoral atmosphere: the distinction between two types of adult-child relationships that result in very different effects on the child's development. We also talk about the role of social interaction in the construction of the self and discuss the benefits of peer interaction in a constructivist classroom.

Chapter 4 focuses on how to establish a constructivist sociomoral atmosphere. This begins by organizing the classroom to meet children's needs, then by organizing the environment for peer interaction and child responsibility. Respect for children leads to a program based on interest, experimentation, and cooperation.

A unique feature of constructivist education is conflict resolution, the topic of chapter 5 in which we discuss the role of conflict in development. We present the constructivist teacher's approach toward children's conflicts and discuss the issue of conflict between teacher and child.

Four chapters are devoted to grouptime and its activities. In chapter 6 we discuss objectives, the role of the teacher, and general principles on conducting grouptime, including formal aspects, management strategies, and content of grouptime. In chapter 7 on rule making and decision making, we talk about objectives and how constructivist teachers foster children's self-regulation by allowing them to make the rules by which the class lives. Chapter 8 on voting presents objectives and guidelines for conducting voting. Chapter 9 on social and moral discussions presents moral judgment theory, defines dilemmas, and points to sources of good dilemmas for discussion.

Chapter 10 is devoted to cooperative alternatives to discipline. The constructivist emphasis on children's self-regulation does not mean that teachers are permissive. Constructivist teachers do develop cooperative strategies for managing a classroom of children and coping with inevitable breakdowns in cooperation.

Activity time is the subject of chapter 11 in which we discuss objectives and rationale, planning in terms of three kinds of knowledge, and general categories of activities having constructivist rationales.

Clean-up time is the subject of chapter 12 in which we present constructivist objectives and talk about how to promote children's feelings of necessity about clean-up.

Chapter 13 on lunch time emphasizes that this period of the day is important for the development of children's shared peer relationships, especially shared experience.

Chapter 14 on nap time/rest time addresses problems in managing nap time in ways consistent with constructivist education.

In chapter 15 we focus on academics, addressing the sociomoral atmosphere for academics, the conditions for promoting academics, and the constructivist integration of academics.

We focus on approaches to working with the difficult child in chapter 16. Finally, in chapter 17 we discuss the sociomoral atmosphere of the school for children and teachers. Appendix A provides constructivist rationales for general categories of activities.

One caveat concerns our use of the term *constructivist*. This word refers to a psychological, not an educational theory. Therefore, when we say *constructivist education* and *constructivist teacher,* we are using a convenient shorthand to refer to an educational approach.

The children described and quoted in this book are diverse in many ways, representing many ethnicities, social classes, parent education levels, and family incomes. The teachers we describe are also ethnically diverse.

Readers may wish to compare our approach with others, including Thomas Lickona's books *Raising Good Children* (1985) and *Educating for Character: How Our Schools Can Teach Respect and Responsibity* (1991); JoAnn Shaheen and Lisa Kuhmerker's book *Free to Learn, Free to Teach* (1991); and Myra Shure's *I Can Problem Solve (ICPS): An Interpersonal Cognitive Problem Solving Program* (1992).

What Do We Mean by "Moral Classrooms?"

When we speak of *moral classrooms,* we are talking about classrooms in which the sociomoral atmosphere supports and promotes children's development. The sociomoral atmosphere is the entire network of interpersonal relations that make up a child's experience of school. This experience includes the child's relationship with the teacher, with other children, with academics, and with rules. Moral classrooms are characterized by a certain kind of sociomoral atmosphere. Our entire book addresses the question given in the title of this first chapter. Right away, however, we want to say that we are not referring to classrooms characterized by a program of indoctrination such as lessons on character or the "value of the week."

VIGNETTES FROM THREE CLASSROOMS

To illustrate different types of sociomoral atmosphere, we begin with brief vignettes from three kindergarten classrooms in lower-income neighborhoods of a large urban public school district. Our accounts are taken from videotapes made of 2 days in each classroom at the end of the school year. Consider what it is like to be a child in the classrooms described below.

Classroom 1: The Boot Camp

Twenty-two kindergarten children sit at desks arranged in rows. The teacher stands in front of the class, frowning and speaking in a stern tone.

Listen, my patience is not going to last very long with you today. Sit down (yelling and pointing her finger at a child)! Three, 6, get ready. (As the teacher claps once for each number, children and teacher chant in unison.) Three, 6, 9, 12, 15, 18, 21, 24, 27, 30. Fives to 100. Get ready. Five, 10 . . . 100. Tens to 100. . . . It's a close call between row 2 and row 4. Excellent job. Good counting by 3s and 5s. We're going to do some problems here. Those of you who did not finish this part of your work today, you're out of luck right now (erases arithmetic homework assignment). Eyes up here. Our first problem is 6 + 3 (writes on board). We don't know what 6 plus 3 equals, but we do know what 6 plus 1 equals. Remember, when we plus one, we say the next number. (Children chant 6 + 1 = 7.) I'm seeing which row can answer me. Get ready. Six + 1 = 7 (children chant in unison as the teacher stabs the numbers on the board with a yardstick to direct the chant). (Same procedure for 6 + 2 = 8 and 6 + 3 = 9.) Eyes on the board, T. I wonder why row 3 (T's row) is losing. A lot of people aren't paying attention. Let me see everyone answering. Get your hands folded and your eyes up here. Now it's time for the teacher game. Listen carefully. I bet I can beat you at this game. I'm going to say some facts. If you get the fact right, you get a point. If I get the fact before you get it, or if I hear a lot of wrong answers, I get the point. If you're misbehaving, I'm going to give myself a point. I'm going to add a new rule to it. Okay, 5 + 2 = (signals for children to respond with downward motion of hand). (Some children say 6 and some say 7.) I thought I heard a wrong answer. I'm going to give myself a point. R, want to give me a behavior point? (The teacher scowls at R.)

We see this teacher as a "Drill Sergeant" and characterize the sociomoral atmosphere of this classroom as an academic "Boot Camp."

Classroom 2: The Community

Twenty kindergarten children and their teacher sit in a circle on a rug. The teacher speaks in a concerned tone.

M's mom was going to bring us a snack today, but her mom didn't get here in time, so she'll bring us something tomorrow.

The only food in the room is some boxes of raisins. Our problem is that we don't have enough to give each person a whole box. (M raises her hand.) M has an idea. What should we do, M? (M suggests opening the box and giving children raisins on plates). That's an idea. If everybody had a plate, how many plates would we need (smiles expectantly)? (E says 17, but L points out that the adult (B) videotaping, N [who chose not to come to grouptime], and two sleeping children had not been counted.) Oh, we didn't count enough. (Children and teacher discuss the count. One child concludes there are 20, and one concludes there are 22.) How many kids are usually in our room? (E says 21.) And who's missing today? (L says J is missing.) So 21 minus 1, J, is how many? (L and E say 20.) If you count B (adult videotaping) and myself, it will be 20 plus 2. So how much will that be? (H answers 22.) So we need 22 sets of raisins. (D suggests, "How about we give two people the boxes and take them out on the plate?") That's an idea! What if each person had a partner and shared? That's a good idea, D. (Several children spontaneously approve, saying, "Yeah.") Okay, everyone find a partner. (Children pair up, some hugging each other in anticipation.) I'm coming around (with the plates). When you get this, how are you going to decide with your partner how much you get? (A child says, "Count 1, 1, 2, 2," putting a raisin on each plate with each number.) Okay, that's an idea. Make sure you do it in a fair way so you get the same amount. D, this was a good idea. (Children break into pairs, divide their box of raisins, and chat while they eat.)

We see this teacher as the friendly "Mentor" and characterize this classroom sociomoral atmosphere as the "Community."

Classroom 3: The Factory

Twenty kindergarten children sit on a rug in rows, looking up at their teacher who stands in front of them at a blackboard, speaking in a calm but serious tone.

Let's zip this up (makes zipping motion across mouth) because we're going to be listening and looking. Those people who want to learn, sit up and listen. If you want to play, you'll have to do it another time. OK, E, have a seat. (Child asks to get some water.) No, I'm sorry, we're ready for you to sit down. Yesterday, we worked in our workbooks on a big word, *subtraction* (writes word on board). We had a lot of turtles swimming together (draws 3 turtles). We had a big set of turtles (draws circle around the turtles). Remember, we took the little one out, and you put him in a box (partially erases one turtle but leaves its broken outline, then draws a turtle outside the circle). Okay, how many did we have in the circle when we started? (All children say 3.) And then how many went away? (Some children say 2 and some say 1.) We took 1 away, and then how many did we have left? (Almost all children say 3.) Two. We had only 2 left. We call that subtraction. We really had two sets inside a great big set. We kept this set, and we took this one away. (The teacher writes several other subtraction problems. Children give many wrong answers, sometimes adding instead of subtracting and sometimes calling the minus sign "equals.") Okay, we're going to go to our tables and turn to page 120. Do I have everybody's eyes up here? I hear some people talking. Shhh, I don't want your mouth up here.

We see this teacher as the "Manager" and characterize this classroom sociomoral atmosphere as the "Factory."

SKETCHES OF THE SOCIOMORAL ATMOSPHERES IN THREE CLASSROOMS

Now let us sketch in more detail children's sociomoral experiences in the three classrooms described above. We focus on the children's experience of the teacher, of arithmetic, of the larger program, and of peers. We then summarize the overall emotional tone of each classroom and raise questions concerning possible effects of the three sociomoral atmospheres on children.

The Boot Camp

In classroom 1, the pervasive sociomoral atmosphere is strong pressure for obedience. Children follow the Drill Sergeant teacher's directions, not only for arithmetic but for exactly how to sit and where to put their hands. Analysis of the videotape of this 33-minute session shows that the children are kept under strict teacher control. During this time the teacher

- Asked 87 test questions and made 157 demands.
- Issued 21 threats, such as:
  "This will just go into our art time today."
  "I'll give myself another point if I hear it again."
  "Do you need to leave? You'd better not be faking today" (about needing to go to the bathroom).
  "You can stand in the corner the rest of the afternoon."
- Made 36 criticisms, such as:
  "I see some people that aren't sitting the right way. Sit with your back up against the chair."
  "Your pencil's not where it should be. Pick up your pencil and write it. Then I want to see your pencil hit the table."
  "You're acting silly."
  "K, that's the kind of behavior that gets you in trouble."
- Administered three arbitrary punishments, such as:
  "I'm going to give myself a point."
  "Give me your paper and you're going to do it in Ms. S's office" (school counselor who, along with the principal, functions as feared disciplinarian who spanks children).
  "We have a daily note going home."
- Lost control twice and intimidated children emotionally by yelling at them.

Such continuous regulation by the teacher leaves the children little or no opportunity for autonomous self-control. Children experience praise for right answers and threats or punishments for deviations in behavior. Their regulation seems to come from outside themselves, from the Drill Sergeant who tells them what to do and what to think.

The children's experience of arithmetic is that learning arithmetic means reciting "facts" or using a crutch procedure to get the right answer (for example, *"when you plus 1, you say the next number")*. The mindlessness of the recitation is manifested by frequent wrong answers despite hours of drilling over the course of the past year. Mathematical truths for these children come from the teacher, not from their own reasoning.

The vignette from classroom 1 is typical of the children's experience of their teacher during 2 whole days of videotaping in this teacher-centered direct-instruction program (considered to be an exemplary classroom by the principal). Small group lessons in reading are conducted in the same fashion as the arithmetic lesson. Children not participating in a small group lesson sit at their desks doing worksheets or assignments written on the chalkboard. Throughout the day, children are exhorted to work, be quiet, and refrain from interactions with classmates. On the whole, children are very compliant, though eyes may drift or glaze, and some children "misbehave" by restlessly shifting in their seats or surreptitiously communicating with a classmate.

Besides the large- and small-group lessons in reading, arithmetic, and language, the Boot Camp teacher reads stories to the class and leads discussions. These activities are also conducted in the same stern manner as lessons. For example, discussion of things found on a poultry farm is the occasion to "see which row knows the most." Children leave the classroom to go to the library, the computer room, physical education, and lunch, supervised by other teachers. Occasional opportunities for a period of outdoor recess depend on whether children are "good." The teacher imposes and strictly enforces rules.

Children's emotional and physical needs are often unmet in classroom 1. Toileting is at set times, and the bathrooms in the school are locked 30 minutes before children leave. Children who ask to go to the bathroom are viewed as suspect. For example, when V asks, "Can I go to the bathroom? I have to go," the teacher accuses, "No, 'cause you're lying." V insists, "No, I'm not," but the teacher replies, "You're telling me a story, V." Later, she allows him to go, but sends another child along, saying, "You're going to go with V to the restroom right now, and (to V) I want a report on you. Young man, you'd better not be faking today. (To other child) Come back and tell me, and (to V) you have one minute in the restroom." To another child, the teacher says, "Do you have to go, or do you just want to get out of your seat? Tomorrow I think I'm going to have to come in the restroom and make sure we're all going when we're supposed to."

Even with so much time spent sitting, opportunities for physical exercise are limited and rationed as rewards for good behavior. The threat of losing playground time is used frequently by the teacher:

> Since you were good this morning and if you can promise to behave, I'll see if we can go out on the playground for a little while.
>
> Everyone must be finished with their work if they're going to go outside today. (To one child) You're going to be doing it when we go outside.

The people who are not finished, I'm going to collect your work now, and you'll be doing it when we go outside later.

(During arithmetic lesson) I want to hear everyone. Remember, we're going for points here. We have 20 minutes outside if you win.

After lunch, children rest for 15 minutes by putting their heads on their desks. When some children have difficulty waking up, the teacher pulls them out of their seats and makes them stand up.

Few open conflicts among children occur in this classroom because of the teacher's rigid control. When a child seems to be on the verge of communicating or aggressing, she says, "Mind your own business and no one else's. Ignore him, and that will help you be good." When one child complains that, "L kicked me in my nose," the teacher "solves" the problem by advising, "Then sit at the end, and nobody will be able to." One conflict does occur during a story when children are sitting on the floor. C protests, "He pinched me," and the teacher asks why. T replies, "She wouldn't give me something I want." Rather than exploring the root of the problem, the teacher upbraids T. "Come here. What have we talked about with you? This is the fourth time in 2 weeks. You got in trouble for this last week, didn't you? When someone does something to you, what do you do? You do what? (T says, "Tell the teacher.") You tell the teacher. You don't do anything yourself. You apologize to her right now. (Child mumbles something.) You say it again, nicer."

Competition rather than community is promoted among children. Nevertheless, children manage to relate to each other with silent looks and conspiratorial illicit whispering. This shared experience occurs outside the teacher-child relationship and despite the teacher.

In order to find out whether the regulation of children's behavior is internal or whether it comes from external teacher control, we asked the teacher to leave the room while children do assigned seatwork. Our videotape shows that most children in Boot Camp do not go on with their work. Instead, they engage in talk, "acting out" (such as running around the room, chasing each other, grabbing others' belongings, and physically aggressing), and "sneaky" behavior (such as looking out the window to see if the teacher is coming, then committing some kind of rule violation). This experiment shows that behavioral regulation comes from the Drill Sergeant's coercion and not from children's autonomous self-regulation.

The overall sociomoral atmosphere of this direct-instruction classroom is one of oppression, anger, anxiety, and social isolation. Children's energy, rather than being expressed, seems pent up and frustrated. Children in this class go to the teacher with more physical complaints than children in either of the other classrooms. This may be due to classroom stress and/or to the fact that the only time this teacher expresses personal concern for children is when they say they do not feel well. In a nutshell, we can say that children in this authoritarian classroom have to suppress their personalities, feelings, and interests in order to meet the teacher's demands and avoid punishment.

What are the effects of such a controlling sociomoral atmosphere on children? First, children feel themselves powerless. Only if they submit completely to the will of the teacher can they "control" what happens to them. However, the teacher's will (that is, the exact behavior she deems unacceptable) is not always predictable, and the most eager-to-please child also elicits criticism and punishment. Further, the expectation that young children can control their behavior to meet such rigid standards makes children's failures inevitable.

Are these children paying too high a price for academic achievement? Is it possible that the results of this heavily academic Boot Camp will be manifested later in rebellion against a system unsympathetic to children's needs and interests? Or will they become calculating by pretending to go along but violating school/societal rules when not under surveillance? Or will they give up their will to the control of others? What happens to the development of children's social and moral competence in this atmosphere? Will they develop this competence outside the school? What happens to initiative and active reasoning?

The Community

In classroom 2, the sociomoral atmosphere is one of respect. The teacher respects children by consulting them about how to solve the snack problem and following their suggestions. Children's ideas are valued, and the Mentor teacher affirms them and encourages their pride in having good ideas. She takes a "we" attitude, frequently identifying with the children as a group member. She facilitates children's interactions among themselves. Fairness is upheld as the goal of interaction with others. The attitude of the group is positive and reflects a feeling of community.

Analysis of the videotape of this classroom during a 30-minute period including the vignette reveals that the Mentor

- Never threatened or punished children
- Asked only 4 test questions and made 23 demands
- Made only 1 criticism.

Instead, her interactions with children are characterized by 151 uses of persuasive strategies such as making suggestions, elaborating on children's ideas, reminding of reasons for rules, offering choices, encouraging the generation of ideas, and upholding the value of fairness. Such persuasive strategies are respectful because they take into account the child's perspective and appeal to cooperative tendencies. In contrast, the Sergeant used only 11 persuasive strategies, and the Manager only 7 in their 30-minute segments.

Children's experience of arithmetic in the vignette is that its purpose is to solve the problem of limited snack. They actively think about the calculation involved in determining how many people need snack. Although answers are not always correct, no one is criticized. The teacher guides children in pursuing two different procedures for figuring out the number of people who need snack. She challenges them to figure out a fair method of division, with the goal of equal portions for all. A child suggests a logical way to be sure both partners have the same amount of raisins, that is, to count systematically 1 (for the self), 1 (for the partner), 2 (another for the self), 2 (another for the partner), and so on. The arithmetic in this activity is embedded in children's purposes and is integrated with a social aim (to negotiate with a peer so both are satisfied) and a moral aim (to achieve equality in the distribution of raisins so as to be fair to both partners).

The vignette from classroom 2 is typical of children's experience of their teacher during 2 days of videotaping in this child-centered constructivist program. In other shared experiences, the class as a whole sings together (and children suggest what to sing as, for example, they take turns naming animals in Old MacDonald's farm), plan and recall a trip to the zoo, enact the story of *The Three Bears,* and discuss common concerns (such as what to do for a classmate who has chicken "pops" and how to solve the problem of the messy pretend center).

In the rather noisy Community classroom, the curriculum is integrated, and children interact with each other, choosing among activities such as:

- Making boats and experimenting by testing them in water to see if they float.
- Pretending in a center furnished as house, restaurant, etc., by creating symbols and negotiating and coordinating with others.
- Writing names and telephone numbers of classmates in order to call them during the summer.
- Dictating a story for the teacher to write by thinking of an unfolding of events in time.
- Exploring the possibilities of PlaDoh in order to create representations of animals seen at the zoo.
- Inventing ways to use black strips of construction paper in art by reasoning about spatial relations (as in creation of paper sculptures).
- Playing board games by taking account of others' perspectives, and inventing strategies to win.
- Making balanced structures with blocks by taking account of a system of weight relationships.

In addition to indoor classroom activities, children engage daily in outdoor play (often involving extensions of classroom activities such as flying kites and catching air with adul- and child-made parachutes).

The Community is organized to meet children's physical and emotional needs. In addition to ample opportunity for physical activity, children nap for at least an hour each day. Although the communal toilet facility is down the hall, bathroom needs are met on an individual basis. Children simply let the teacher know when they want to go. The only rule is that children go one at a time.

Conflicts do arise among children in this classroom, and the teacher takes a great deal of time to help children work through their conflicts. Conflicts are taken seriously as opportunities to help children think about others' points of view and figure out how to negotiate with others. The Mentor says to children:

> Use your words.
> If you don't tell people, they don't understand.
> What could you say to him?
> Can you talk to her yourself, or do you need my help?

Sometimes, the teacher gives children words to say (for example, "Say, 'B, that hurts my feelings.' Say, 'Tell me in words.'"

When children complain that C is monopolizing the PlaDoh, the teacher asks, "Is that fair, C, to have more? Think they like it when you have more?" (J and M say, "No.") "They say no, C. It doesn't seem fair to me for you to have more."

In an argument among three boys over how many marbles each child should have to use in a marble rollway, the Mentor patiently solicits the children's ideas, asks each child if he likes each idea, and supports them through a long procedure of negotiation to decide who should distribute the marbles.

This constructivist Mentor is a companion guide who organizes a program of activities designed to stimulate children's reasoning and provide them with a supportive environment in which to explore and experiment, to make inevitable errors in reasoning, and to invent new ways of reasoning.

Children vote to make many group decisions, and rules are made together by children and teacher. When problems arise, children often suggest making new rules. For example, when some children handle the guinea pig roughly, the children create a set of rules to regulate playing with the guinea pig. In an interview on life in the classroom, children from the Community clearly express a feeling of ownership of classroom rules. When asked, "Who makes the rules in your class?" they say the children make the rules.

When we ask the Mentor to leave the room, children in the Community simply go on with their activities. They work with a balance game, model clay, play cards, and draw and write. Because they pursue their own purposes, they have no desire to become rebellious or sneaky. This experiment shows that Community children are self-regulating rather than being regulated by the teacher.

The emotional tone of this constructivist classroom is friendly and cooperative, reflecting a feeling of community. Children feel comfortable about speaking their minds to the teacher and to each other. Conversations between teacher and children focus on the many shared experiences and negotiations that concern participants in the Community. Humor is expressed. Expressions of affection are abundant in the Community as children often spontaneously hug the teacher, and she returns their affection with a hug or a kiss. While sometimes intense conflicts do arise, children can also be observed expressing affection toward each other. Children actively engage with one another, sharing experiences and negotiating. The teacher fosters children's interactions and friendships with one another. In a nutshell, we can say that children are free to be themselves in the constructivist Community atmosphere, with all their egocentricities, honest feelings, and genuine interests.

What are the effects of such an accepting, respectful, and stimulating sociomoral atmosphere on children? First, children have the opportunity to feel effective in acting on their world. They exercise their will and initiative by acting on objects and people and observing the results of their actions. They begin to modulate the exercise of will in the context of clashes with the wills of others. With teacher assistance in conflicts, children's interpersonal understanding evolves from impulsive, self-centered actions to negotiations that respect the rights and feelings of others.

Do children from the Community become respectful of one another? Do they come to restrain their impulses as a result of experience in mediated conflicts? Do they become more socially and morally competent? Will children get enough academic foundation for later schooling?

The Factory

In classroom 3, the sociomoral atmosphere is pressure for obedient production of class work. However, it is neither as negative as that in the Boot Camp, nor as positive as in the Community. Children seem more willingly obedient, more docile, than those in the Boot Camp. In the vignette, they listen quietly to the teacher and watch as she and a few classmates write answers to subtraction problems on the chalkboard. The teacher speaks to children calmly, but seems emotionally disengaged. Analysis of the videotape of this classroom during a 30-minute period shows that the teacher asked 91 test questions and made 51 other demands. The children in this class, like those in classroom 1, are kept under strict teacher control throughout and have little opportunity for autonomous self control. As in the Boot Camp, children are praised for right answers, but in the videotaped segment the Manager teacher offers only 12 criticisms, and the tone of this classroom is generally much more positive.

Like the Drill Sergeant, this teacher believes strongly in the value of the right answer and corrects all errors. She clearly tries to appeal to children's interests with the turtles in the math lesson. However, children are confused by the fact that they can still see 4 turtles (when one is redrawn out of the circle and the broken outline of the "subtracted" turtle remains). Later, when children sit at their tables, the teacher "walks" them through every step of the worksheet, instructing them to put 3 turtles (loose cutouts) at the top of their page, take 2 away, write 3 - 2 = 1, and glue 1 turtle in the "pond." Again, children seem to be confused by the fact that while they take the turtles out of the pond, they still have them. The second and final problem is 4 - 2 = 2. After telling children what to do and what the answers are, the teacher retires to her desk to check children's work as they come to show it to her. When approved, a child's page is imprinted with the stamp of a nickel.

Children's experience of arithmetic in this Factory classroom is one of uncertainty. Faced with puzzling stories and formalisms they do not understand, children seem very unsure of themselves and rely on the Manager to tell them what to do at every step. The experience of many children seems to be of isolated steps that are not understood as a coherent whole.

Once during the 2 days of videotaping the Manager lost control. A child standing in line at the teacher's desk was being crowded and said, "Stop pushing!" Rather than responding to the child's problem, the teacher impulsively pushes the complaining child out of line and says, "You sit down 'til you can stop all that noise in the line." Other than this incident, she did not threaten or punish children in our 2 days of videotaping. However, children reported in interviews that she punished children by having them put their heads on their desks and shutting them in the bathroom, and that she threatened them with spanking in front of the class.

The Factory vignette is typical of instruction in this eclectic classroom. We call this classroom "eclectic" because that is the teacher's own term, and because this program shares some characteristics of both the direct-instruction and constructivist programs. After Factory children complete their assigned academic work, they can pretend in a housekeeping center, paint at an easel, slide down a small slide, feed gerbils and fish, water plants, do an art activity (although children are to follow the teacher's model), or play dominoes. Before the formal beginning in the morning, they can build with Legos and other construction toys. Children leave the classroom for physical education, library, music, lunch, and outdoor play, supervised by other teachers. Book reading by the teacher that we recorded focuses on informing children about dinosaurs.

Emphasis in this classroom Factory is on production. In addition to worksheets, children paste white paper "bones" on black paper just like the teacher showed them, to represent a dinosaur skeleton. They follow the teacher's model of how to make dinosaur footprints and how to draw a scene with blue water, green plants, purple mountain (she explains, "People use purple because that's a good color for showing distance"), and yellow sun. They use the dinosaur stamp to put a dinosaur in the picture, and write the word "Brontosaurus." The Manager shows how to draw a vicuna (explaining that it is something like a camel), color it light brown, and write the letter *V*, lowercase and uppercase. During rest time, children are called individually to a table and tested on whether they can count to 10; say the days of the week and months of the year; recite their birthday, telephone number, and address; say the name of their school; write their names; identify circle, square, triangle, and rectangle; order numerals to 20 and read the ones the teacher points to; and name their city, state, and country. As they pass groups of these tests, children are rewarded with red, blue, and gold medals posted by their pictures on the bulletin board.

When the teacher plays dominoes with children, she takes charge and directs the game so no mistakes are made. However, she does take the role of a player in the game, alongside children.

The teacher occasionally visits the pretend center, but takes a critical tone. For example, when a child offers her a drink, she replies, "That's okay, but I'd rather have coffee. Haven't you got some coffee in this place? Dump that out and give me some coffee, please. Oh, it's hot. Who made this so hot? I'll just have to sip it. Pretty good, though. Sure is messy in your house. Who keeps house around here? I think when your house is cleaned, I'll come back."

Despite the teacher's impersonal and sometimes critical relation with children, she does appeal to children's interests in feeding gerbils and fish and looking at a live snail and a dead dragonfly. She shares friendly conversations with children, as one child tells her that "My daddy bought me some perfume," and another, "I know where a bird nest is."

This classroom is not so rigidly controlled that conflicts do not occur. Generally, the teacher responds to conflicts between children by forcing an apology, sermonizing, and exhorting children to be more careful in the case of physical harm. She tends to "gloss over" situations without taking children's feelings seriously. She ignores S who complains, "G called me an ugly coon." The teacher frequently "blames the victim." For example, when L complains, "P hit me on the head," she replies, "Why was she doing that? Are you meddling her? I want you to stay clear of L, okay? When I get through here, I'm going to see how nicely you all have settled." In another instance, L complains, "He step on my hand." The teacher replies,

"What are you gonna say? Say 'Excuse me.' Next time, L, let's put our hands in our lap. Be careful to look if you're going to put them on the floor to stand up."

In the most serious conflict when B bit A several times, and A bit B once, the Manager responds without strong feeling. She jokes, "Were you hungry, B?" and sermonizes, "I think little babies bite sometimes, but we're big people, and we're able to say if we don't like something. Are you going to bite anymore, B? I'll be so glad if you don't bite. Are you through biting? Now I want you and A to be friends. Say to A, 'I'm not going to bite anymore.' (Child does not respond.) You don't feel like saying that? When you feel like talking about it, you'll have to talk to each other about it." No follow up occurs, and the teacher simply tells B's mother about the incident at the end of the day.

When we ask the Manager to leave the Factory, production slows but does not stop altogether as children generally continue to work on assigned arithmetic papers. However, many children laugh and talk loudly. The entire group gasps, "Ohhhh!" and one child comes to the cameraperson to tattle, "He said a bad word." Many times, children threaten to tattle ("I'm gonna' tell.") on classmates for minor infractions. After placing their completed first assignment on the teacher's desk, several children run, dance, and tease each other.

Overall, the emotional tone in this eclectic classroom is relaxed but nevertheless demanding. Children are expected to be quiet during instruction and relatively quiet during activities. Children have some opportunity for self regulation during activities, although the teacher is clearly still the powerholder in the classroom.

Because the teacher maintains continual control, children's interactions with one another are often stifled. Except for the opportunity to play with each other in the pretend center, children have little opportunity to be themselves in the sense of being free to express their feelings and interests. It is the teacher's interests and personality that predominate.

What are the effects of this Manager on children? First, many children seem very unsure about what the teacher wants them to do. This leads to heavy dependence on the teacher's direction. Most children seem to lack confidence. While this atmosphere is less negative than that of Boot Camp, children are almost as tightly regulated by teacher control in the Factory.

Is the eclectic combination of instruction and free activity the best of both worlds? Do children in this classroom learn academics as well as develop their personalities and social competence? Does the teacher's calm but firm style enable children to be autonomously self-controlled?

COMPONENTS OF THE SOCIOMORAL ATMOSPHERE

We state earlier that the sociomoral atmosphere is the entire network of interpersonal relations that make up a child's experience of school. This network can be thought of as comprised of two primary parts: the teacher-child relation, and children's peer relations. While the teacher and child may bring other relations into the classroom sociomoral atmosphere (the family, the teacher-principal relation, etc.), these two components are central, and constitute the primary focus of the book.

The Teacher-Child Relation

The teacher establishes the sociomoral atmosphere by organizing the room for individual or group activities and by relating to children in authoritarian or cooperative ways. The sociomoral atmospheres of our three classrooms may be viewed in terms of differences in the teachers' exercise of power. The Drill Sergeant exerts the most power over children and the Manager comes next. Although the Mentor exerts the least power, she is highly influential as she encourages a reciprocal process of give-and-take in discussions, conflict mediation, and group decisions. The sociomoral atmosphere may also be viewed in terms of differences in child activity and positive affect. On these dimensions, the classes are reversed. The most child activity and the most positive affect occurs in the Community, with the Factory next, and the Boot Camp a distant last.

Peer Relations

When teachers forbid children to interact with one another, as in the Boot Camp, the teacher-child relation comprises almost the total sociomoral atmosphere, except for what interaction children can sneak behind her back. In Boot Camp, children have the experience of shared oppression in their adversarial relation to their teacher. On the other hand, when children have the possibility to engage with one another, as in the Factory and Community, peer relations also contribute to the sociomoral atmosphere. Children's interactions may be harmonious, ranging from silliness to friendly play to sharing secrets and other self-disclosures. Children's interactions may also be tense, ranging from verbal and physical aggression to one-way controlling actions to two-way negotiations aimed at satisfying both parties.

Peer interaction in and of itself does not guarantee a sociomoral atmosphere that will promote children's development. The teacher can influence the quality of children's interactions in a variety of ways, including the provision of activities that engender children's need and desire to interact, and active support of children's cooperation and negotiation. We will discuss throughout this book how a constructivist teacher promotes children's sociomoral development by encouraging peer interaction.

RESEARCH ON SOCIOMORAL ATMOSPHERE AND CHILDREN'S SOCIOMORAL DEVELOPMENT

We attempted to answer some of the questions posed above about each classroom in a study of these three classroom teachers and their children. The 2 days of videotapes for each teacher were transcribed and closely analyzed in order to better understand the sociomoral atmosphere established through teacher-child interactions. The vignettes and sketches given above are based on and summarize the results of careful coding of over 20,000 behaviors for the three teachers.

To explore the effects of these three very different sociomoral atmospheres on children's sociomoral development, children from these classrooms were studied in pairs in two situations. In one, children played a teacher-made board game called Halloween Run in which players roll a die to determine how far to move a marker around a path from Start to a picture of Trick or Treaters at the end. The children were taught the game a few days earlier by a research assistant who played the game with them until it was clear they understood the rules. When the children came with the research assistant a second time they were told, "This time you're going to play the game by yourselves. I have some work to do over here. You just let me know when you're ready to go back to the classroom." In the other situation, pairs of children were given five stickers to divide between them. Based on children's expressed preferences, stickers included only one desired by both children and four disliked by both. The goal in these situations was to see how well children are able to engage and negotiate with each other when no adult controls or influences them.

Detailed, close analysis of transcripts and videotapes of children's behaviors in these two situations shows significant differences in interactions of children from different classrooms. Children from all three groups express their own desires and thus try to control the other. However, children from the Community are more actively engaged with one another. They have more friendly, shared experiences with each other and not only negotiate more but negotiate more successfully. Community children use a greater variety of different strategies and resolve more conflicts than children from the Boot Camp and Factory. Boot Camp children tend to try to resolve conflicts by overwhelming the other physically or emotionally and, in general, relate socially in less complex ways. Moreover, children from the Community use significantly more strategies reflecting consideration for the other's point of view and efforts to achieve mutually satisfactory interaction. Further, in harmonious interactions, children from the Community are also more reciprocal (for example, sharing secrets and recalling past shared experiences) than children from the Boot Camp and Factory (who engage in much more impulsive silliness).

The results of this study suggest that we must seriously consider the possibility that heavily academic, teacher-centered programs may hinder children's development of interpersonal understanding and sociomoral competence. Results also suggest that providing traditional child-centered activities in a generally controlling teacher-centered atmosphere does not compensate for the sociomoral disadvantages of a heavy academic emphasis.

But what about school achievement? Although standardized achievement tests do not adequately assess the achievement of cognitive goals of the constructivist Community, we obtained scores on these tests from the school district and compared the three groups. While children from the Boot Camp had significantly higher scores than both other groups at the end of first grade, by third grade no such differences were found. On some third-grade tests, the children from the Factory scored at significantly lower levels than both Boot Camp and Community children.

It therefore appears that Boot Camp children pay a price for their early academic achievement. The price is especially questionable since its advantage is lost by third grade. (The interested reader will find the details of this study in DeVries, Haney, & Zan [1991] and DeVries, Reese-Learned, & Morgan [1991a].)

We cannot say that all direct instruction classes are as negatively authoritarian as Boot Camp. However, when the teacher focuses on one-way transmission of information to children, he or she also communicates "lessons" about human relations. In this process, the teacher creates the context for children's construction of interpersonal habits, personality, and character.

While the Boot Camp classroom is an extreme case of authoritarian sociomoral experience for children, the experience of children in the eclectic classroom is also predominantly authoritarian. Unfortunately, many adults do not view children as having the same right to respect as adults. They view the adult-child relation as one in which children are supposed to respect adults, and the adults are supposed to wield the power of their authority in order to socialize and teach children. Therefore, disrespectful attitudes toward children permeate our educational system, public and private, and reflect an authoritarian orientation to children in our society. The hidden "lesson" in authoritarian teaching is: Be submissive to those who are more powerful. Piaget (1932/1965) pointed out three unfortunate effects of too much adult control: rebellion, mindless conformity, and calculation (the latter evident when children do what adults say only under surveillance). Are these the types of character we want to perpetuate in our children? From the authoritarian perspective, the answer is yes: Keep children obedient to authority. From the perspective of democracy and equity, the answer is no: Children should be given opportunities to think autonomously. How can we expect to educate children for democracy with totalitarian methods?

THE SOCIOMORAL ATMOSPHERE AS HIDDEN CURRICULUM

Some people feel that the school should not be concerned with social and moral education but should focus on teaching academics or promoting intellectual development. The problem with this view is that schools *do* influence social and moral development, whether they intend to or not. Teachers continually communicate social and moral messages as they moralize to children about rules and behavior and as they provide sanctions for children's behavior. So the school or child-care institution is not and cannot be value-free or value-neutral. For better or for worse, teachers are engaged in social and moral education.

Most often, the sociomoral atmosphere is a hidden curriculum. It is hidden from teachers who are not conscious of the sociomoral atmosphere they provide. It is less hidden from children who are acutely aware of the social pressure of the classroom. When teachers tell children what they are supposed to do and what they are not supposed to do, what children hear is what is good and bad, right and wrong.

Unfortunately, in most schools, the sociomoral atmosphere is mainly coercive and requires children to be submissive and conforming, at the expense of initiative, autonomy, and reflective thinking. Even well-meaning teachers feel that it is their responsibility to be the authority in the classroom, to provide children with behavioral rules and expectations, and to discipline children through the use of rewards and punishments. While most teachers are not as negative as the Drill Sergeant, and many try to combine an authoritarian attitude with affection and child-centered activities, still, children know where the power lies. They feel the effects of coercion.

Some people say that you have to exercise authority over children because they will have to live with it in the larger society. This idea is dangerous for democracy because it contradicts the basic idea of freedom within a system of justice. Conformity to authority is not socialization into a free society. It is more like socialization into a prison atmosphere. Consider some characteristics of most prisons that also characterize most schools. Liberty is suppressed. There is no possibility of demanding rights from authorities. Inmates and children are excluded from power in decision-making. Rewards are manipulated as exchange for compliance with authorities. Punishments are decided bureaucratically, sometimes for minor infractions of petty rules. Let us not force our children to be imprisoned in school.

SO WHAT IS THE CONSTRUCTIVIST SOCIOMORAL ATMOSPHERE?

Having demonstrated that the constructivist Community sociomoral atmosphere is associated with more advanced sociomoral development in children, we explore this atmosphere in more detail in the remainder of this book. We talk about the ways in which constructivist teachers respect children as having a right to their feelings, ideas, and opinions. We talk about how constructivist teachers use their authority selectively and wisely. We talk about how constructivist teachers refrain from using their power unnecessarily in order to give children the opportunity to construct themselves gradually into personalities having self-confidence, respect for self and others, and active, inquiring, creative minds.

In the following chapters, we try to show how the sociomoral atmosphere permeates every activity, every part of the day, and every type of classroom interaction. We begin with a more theoretical discussion of why the respectful sociomoral atmosphere is crucial to implementing constructivist education.

2

What Do We Mean by "Moral Children?"

When we speak of moral children, we are talking about children grappling with issues that are a natural part of their lives. While the content of moral issues in the lives of children differs from that of adults, the basic issues are the same. Children worry about how people (first of all, themselves) are treated long before they can understand the Golden Rule. They worry about aggression, fair use (for example, of dress-up clothes), and equal participation (for example, in clean-up). These are issues of rights and responsibilities just as are adult concerns with crime and violence, equal employment opportunity, and the need for everyone to protect the environment. We are talking about a process, not a product. In this process, children wrestle with questions of what they believe to be good and bad, right and wrong. They form their own opinions, and listen to the opinions of others. They construct their morality out of daily life experiences.

In this chapter, we discuss what we mean by moral children. We begin by stating what we do not mean by moral children, then discuss how children think about moral rules and how they think about others, and give examples of children in constructivist classrooms struggling with moral and social issues.

WHAT WE DO NOT MEAN BY "MORAL CHILDREN"

First, when we speak of moral children, we do not mean children who follow moral rules simply out of obedience to authority. We discuss this at greater length in chapter 3. Here let us simply point out that obedience is likely to be motivated by fear of punishment or desire for rewards rather than by self-constructed principles. Our extensive prison systems attest to the fact that fear of punishment is an inadequate motivator of moral behavior.

We should say that obedience that emerges out of affection and attachment is a different quality of obedience. Instead of being coerced, it results from the adult's appeal to the child's cooperation. Because it engenders a more willing attitude on the part of the child for some time in childhood, such obedience provides a foundation for later moral development. However, if continued beyond the point when the child can begin to understand reasons for rules and demands, this type of obedience can also have unfortunate effects in the long run. That is, the child who continues to obey just to please the adult will not construct his or her own reasons for following moral rules.

Similarly, we also do not mean that moral children simply know what others consider moral. Moral principles are not arbitrary rules like "*I* before *E* except after *C*." Instead, they are rooted in the universal ideal summarized by the Golden Rule, "Do unto others as you would have them do unto you." This ideal underlies more specific principles such as refraining from harming others, respecting the rights of others, and taking responsibility for one's own actions, and it cannot simply be taught directly. Moral children come to understand the spirit of the rule, the moral necessity for treating others as they would wish to be treated.

Second, when we speak of moral children, we do not mean children who simply engage in certain prosocial behaviors such as sharing, helping, and comforting. The problem with defining morality in terms of a list of prosocial behaviors is that this definition fails to consider the motivation for engaging in such behaviors. Teaching children simply to behave in certain ways ignores the cultivation of feelings of necessity for behaving in moral ways. If a child helps another child in order to get the teacher's approval, is this moral? We would say no.

We qualify what we say here by recognizing that children often do engage in prosocial behaviors without moral feelings. Children may imitate the form of moral behaviors without having moral intentions in mind. Such imitation can occur before children are able to take another's point of view and can provide the foundation for decentering and moral feelings. We are not saying such behavior should be discouraged, of course. On the contrary. For example, a child imitating the teacher by patting a crying classmate may find out that the distressed classmate stops crying. The constructivist teacher does not praise the behavior. Instead, he or she may point out that the child made the other feel better. From this experience, the child may decenter somewhat to recognize the other child's feelings. The latter is the constructivist goal. Prosocial behavior without moral intention is not moral. It is merely expedient or obedient. We are concerned with the child's development of moral feelings and intentions, not just behaviors. Therefore, we do not stop short with a limited goal of getting children simply to act in prosocial ways.

Third, when we speak of moral children, we do not mean children who have habits of politeness such as saying please, thank you, and excuse me. Parents and teachers often impose demands on children to say these words without realizing that children view their use as arbitrary convention. Learning automatically to say please, thank you, and excuse me does help the child get along in the social world. However, while these habits of verbal behavior may be motivated by genuine feelings of gratitude or contrition, they do not necessarily reflect moral feelings concerning the ethical treatment of others. Therefore, constructivist teachers do not coerce children into politeness. Instead, they model sincere politeness and make sure children experience politeness expressed to them.

Fourth, when we speak of moral children we are not referring to children who have a list of character traits, such as "honesty," "integrity," and "generosity." Kohlberg and Mayer (1972; see also chapter 1 in DeVries & Kohlberg, 1987/1990) call this the "bag of virtues" approach to morality. They point out numerous problems with this approach. One problem is that of deciding which virtues go in the bag. Who decides? Another problem is that of definition. How does one define virtues such as honesty, integrity, or generosity, except relative to a cultural standard that can be highly variable? As Kohlberg points out, one person's integrity may be another person's stubbornness.

Finally, when we speak of moral children, we are not speaking of religion. While religion is concerned with morality, morality transcends particular religions. It is possible to be moral without being religious, just as it is possible (although some may argue to the contrary) to be religious without being moral. Religion may vary by culture, national origin, race, or family, but certain moral principles remain the same across all religions.

To summarize, when we speak of moral children, we do not mean children who merely exhibit a set of moral traits or behaviors. Nor do we mean children who are merely obedient, polite, or religious.

HOW CHILDREN THINK ABOUT MORAL RULES

An enormous body of research makes the persuasive case that young children think about moral and social issues and relations in ways that differ qualitatively from the ways in which older children and adults think. Research on child morality was stimulated by Piaget's seminal work, *The Moral Judgment of the Child* (1932/1965). Lawrence Kohlberg (1984, 1987; Colby & Kohlberg, 1987) further defined stages of moral judgment, and Robert Selman (1980; Selman & Schultz, 1990) elaborated Piaget's theory of perspective-taking in levels of interpersonal understanding. We briefly describe characteristics of child morality that emerge from this work.

Young children may be described as moral realists because their judgments about right and wrong, good and bad, are based on what is observable or "real" to them. First of all, young children view moral rules (and other rules as well) as arbitrary impositions by adults. Moral rules seem arbitrary when children cannot understand their reasons. This results from the intellectual limitation of the young child who is unable to think beyond the observable surfaces of events. For example, intentions and feelings cannot be directly observed. Reasoning about others' intentions and feelings only occurs when children's general intellectual progress enables them to decenter and take another's perspective. Therefore, when the adult says not to hit or grab, the moral realist experiences this injunction as an arbitrary adult rule. Refraining from hitting and grabbing can thus only be done out of obedience to authority. This attitude of mindless obedience is referred to as heteronomy, in contrast to an attitude of reflective understanding or autonomy. As discussed further in chapter 3, heteronomy is moral and intellectual regulation by others. Autonomy is moral and intellectual self-regulation.

The second characteristic of moral realism is that the letter of the law rather than its spirit should be followed. Because the young child cannot think beyond surface observables, the spirit of many rules is unknowable. The child can only try to follow rules literally. Following a rule not to hit, for example, may not mean to the moral realist that he should also not push someone down or bite.

The third characteristic of moral realism is that acts are judged in terms of observable material consequences rather than in subjective terms such as motivation. For example, the young child whose block structure is destroyed by a playmate's accidental stumble will be just as angry as if the action had been intentional. Concern with material consequences leads to a view of just punishment as "an eye for an eye." Retribution (making the culprit suffer) is viewed as just punishment for misdeeds, and the worse the misdeed, the harsher should be the punishment.

HOW CHILDREN THINK ABOUT OTHERS

The content of moral and social rules deals with our obligations to others. Young children's difficulties in understanding the reasons for these obligations stem from limited ability to take the perspectives of others and to think about others' feelings and intentions. Especially in a situation when self-interest is at stake, it is difficult for the child to think about the other's point of view.

Selman (1980) elaborated Piaget's work on egocentric perspective-taking in the domain of interpersonal understanding. Selman examined the progression from egocentrism to reciprocity to mutuality, or in other words, the development of the ability to take the perspective of the other and coordinate it with one's own. We describe in detail Selman's work on perspective-taking and interpersonal understanding because of its practical value in constructivist education.

Enacted Interpersonal Understanding

Selman and his colleagues developed a model for assessing interpersonal understanding reflected in interpersonal behavior. This model rests on the definition of levels of perspective taking. It offers the advantage of assessing developmental levels of interpersonal understanding expressed at the moment of interaction. It is particularly useful in assessing young children who lack sophisticated verbal skills or who do not respond well to the demands of a reflective interview. It also measures a slightly different dimension of interpersonal understanding than does the interview. That is, Selman's levels of perspective-taking describe how children reason about others, which can be thought of as primarily cognitive. Levels of enacted interpersonal understanding describe what children actually do in social interactions. These involve a combination of cognitive, affective, and situational factors.

Selman conceptualizes developmental levels of interpersonal understanding in two types of experiences. The first is negotiation, in which the developmental goal is identity separate from others. The second is shared experience, where the developmental goal is connection or mutuality with others. These two types of experiences reflect complementary themes in structuring the development of social relations.

Three components of interpersonal understanding are considered in assessing *enacted* interpersonal understanding. First, one infers how the individual cognitively construes the perspective of the self in relation to the perspective of the other, at the moment of interaction. That is, does the behavior imply a consideration of the other's point of view? Second, one infers how the individual perceives and reacts to emotional disequilibrium in interaction. Is affect out-of-control, or is it regulated in the service of successful interactions? Third, one infers the primary purpose of the individual in the interaction. Is it to dominate the other, or is it to cooperate? These three components allow us to assess the level of enacted interpersonal understanding expressed in an interaction.

Social Perspective Coordination

Using data from interviews with children, Selman (1980) conceptualized five levels (0–4) of perspective taking that provide the framework for the two types of interpersonal understanding—negotiation and shared experience (see center column of Figure 2.1). Without going into the technical details, we want to point out that at level 0 (approximately ages 3–6 years), the young child does not recognize that others' inner, subjective experiences (feelings, intentions, and ideas) may be different from his or her own. The child simply does not realize the other has a point of view. Others are viewed as a kind of object. At level 1 (approximately ages 5–9 years), the child decenters and knows that each person has a unique subjective experience, but usually cannot consider more than one perspective at a time. At level 2 (around 7–12 years), the child decenters further to reciprocally consider feelings and thoughts of self and other. At level 3 (generally beginning in adolescence), the child decenters still further to simultaneously coordinate these reciprocal perspectives into a mutual perspective. (We do not discuss level 4 here because it usually emerges only in late adolescence or adulthood, and so does not pertain to young children.)

Figure 2.1. **Selman's Levels of Enacted Interpersonal Understanding**

Negotiation through collaborative strategies oriented toward integrating needs of self and other	Mutual Third-Person Level (3)	Shared experience through collaborative empathic reflective processes
Negotiation through cooperative strategies in a persuasive or deferential orientation	Reciprocal Reflective Level (2)	Shared experience through joint reflection on similar perceptions or experiences
Negotiation through one-way commands/ orders or through automatic obedience strategies	Unilateral One-Way Level (1)	Shared experience through expressive enthusiasm without concern for reciprocity
Negotiation through unreflective physical strategies (impulsive fight or flight)	Egocentric Impulsive Level (0)	Shared experience through unreflective (contagious) imitation

Development ↑

Negotiation Strategies   **Core Developmental Levels in Social Perspective Coordination**   **Shared Experiences**

developmental levels

Selman calls these levels rather than stages because each level remains accessible after the next level is attained. That is, a person capable of level 2 perspective coordination can act egocentrically or unilaterally at times. This is in contrast to the Piagetian stages of operational reasoning where conservers of continuous quantity, for example, do not revert to an earlier mode of thinking that equal quantities (in identical glasses) are no longer equal when one is poured into a glass wider in dimension.

Negotiation Strategies

Negotiation strategies describe interactions that occur when an interpersonal dynamic is in disequilibrium, that is, characterized by some tension. The disequilibrium may be mild, as when one person casually asks another for something, or it may be strong, as when one person forcefully demands that another do something. The separateness of the actors and their goals and purposes is therefore emphasized. The left column of Figure 2.1 summarizes the developmental levels of negotiation strategies described below.

Level 0 strategies are egocentric and impulsive, often physical, and reflect level 0 lack of perspective coordination. Included are means such as flight, hiding, or other types of withdrawal, and exertions of force, such as hitting, grabbing, or yelling. Level 1 strategies are unilateral, and reflect level 1 perspective coordination. These include "will-less" submission or obedience and one-way demands, threats, or bribes. Level 2 strategies are self-reflective and reciprocal, and involve level 2 perspective coordination. These include strategies such as choosing to defer to the wishes of the other, accepting or suggesting a barter, persuading or being open to persuasion, and giving reasons. At level 3, negotiations become mutual and collaborative, and involve level 3 perspective coordination. Level 3 strategies include generating mutually satisfactory alternative strategies and compromising to preserve the relationship over the long-term.

Shared Experiences

Shared experience is characterized by an interpersonal dynamic that is in equilibrium. Since there is no disequilibrium to be resolved, shared experiences are usually relaxed and friendly, and foster connection and intimacy between individuals. The right column of Figure 2.1 summarizes the developmental levels of shared experiences described below.

Shared experiences have in common with negotiation strategies the developmental levels of perspective taking, moving from egocentric and impulsive, to unilateral, to reciprocal, to collaborative. At level 0, shared experiences are characterized by unreflective, contagious imitation. An example might be two children engaging in a burping contest or giggling together uncontrollably. Level 1 shared experiences are characterized by expressive enthusiasm without concern for reciprocity. An example might be children's parallel pretend play, where one child asserts "I'm the mommy" and the other child asserts "I'm Superman." Level 2 shared experiences reflect conscious commonality such as cooperative pretense or two children reflecting on the good time they will have together on a field trip. Level 3 involves collaborative, empathic reflective processes such as an intimate discussion in which two children engage in self-disclosure, and each affirms the other.

Examples of Interpersonal Understanding

In chapter 1, we describe our research showing that children in the Community were more advanced in sociomoral development than children in Boot Camp and Factory classrooms (DeVries, Reese-Learned, & Morgan, 1991a). In our study of those children, sociomoral development was defined in terms of Selman's levels of interpersonal understanding. The results showed that Community children used more level 2 strategies in their active engagement with classmates in a board game and in a sticker-division situation. They even used level 2 strategies during conflict and were therefore more successful in resolving many more of their conflicts than Boot Camp or Factory children. Consider the following examples of child interaction in the board game.

K and C are two boys from the Boot Camp. The overall dynamic of their play is irritable. C is irritated because K makes a consistent counting error.[1] K is irritated because C keeps on criticizing and interfering with his play. C is condescending, critical, and insulting, saying, "That ain't no 5, boy. You can't count," and "Look, lemme count this for you. Boy, can't you count?" C manifests an antagonistic competitive attitude, gleefully gloating, "Boy, I'm whippin' you up." Numerous times, they argue over the counting, but conflicts do not come to a resolution satisfactory to both. C usually prevails by force, and K becomes increasingly frustrated and surly. This interaction is characterized by levels 0 and 1 enacted interpersonal understanding. No level 2 understanding is manifested, and no shared experience occurs.

T and J are two boys from the Community who have the same difference in point of view on counting as K and C in the example above. T makes the logical error consistently. J is transitional, sometimes

---

[1]This error is to count the space occupied as "1." Therefore, when K rolls a 3, he counts the starting space (the ending space on the last count) as "1" rather than going forward one space as the logic of +1 dictates. Many if not most young children make this error in the course of constructing their understanding of number. We call this the "logical error of addition." In fact, children making this error have good one-to-one correspondence and can be considered as having made some advance in their knowledge of number.

making the error but often correcting himself. It is clear that he is aware of the error and is trying to overcome his tendency to make it. To prevent the error, J uses the strategy of saying "Mmmm" for the starting space, then moves one space and says, "One." It is as though he feels he must acknowledge the starting space somehow with a corresponding verbalization, just as the other spaces have a corresponding verbalized number. J frequently notices T's logical error. However, instead of criticizing and insulting T, J tries to teach him his strategy. When T makes the error, J takes T's hand with his marker (in a level 0 grab) and moves it correctly, saying, "Mmm, 1, 2, 3." When T continues to make the error, J says, "Look at my mouth," emphasizing, "Mmmmm, 1, 2, 3." Grabbing T's hand or body impulsively is level 0 negotiation, even though it initiates the helping effort. This is followed, however, by level 1 demands and even some level 2 showing and explaining in attempts to coordinate the two perspectives. T resists at first but then accepts J's obvious effort to be helpful. He learns J's strategy and says "Mmm" on the starting space. This equilibrium is obviously satisfying to both boys as they exchange triumphant smiles. Conflicts are resolved in this pair's engagement with one another. Shared experiences occur in the form of friendly talk about the game and teasingly setting the die on a number without rolling it, then giggling at the inevitable protest and rolling it correctly.

The interaction between another pair of boys from the Community, A and D, is characterized by more shared experiences that embed their conflicts in a predominantly friendly dynamic. Considerable level 2 shared experiences occur in the form of whispering secrets and playful teasing (D puts the die behind his back and says, "I haven't got it" as he shows empty hands, then playfully offers and withdraws the die). Level 2 negotiation includes inquiring into the other's motivation or desires (for example, "Wanta' play it again?" and, in a friendly tone, "You trying to win, ain't you?") In one of the most engaging moments, D complains after rolling a series of low numbers, "I always get 1." A responds to his friend's frustration, offering, "OK, you want me to give you 6?" He then rolls unsuccessfully several times. When he finally rolls 5, he asks, "You like 5?" D refuses, "Nope, I want 6." A then sets the die down, saying, "Here's 6," and D happily moves his marker 6 spaces. In the most serious conflict, D and A disagree about the rule that when one player lands on the Space occupied by the other, the marker there first goes back to start. With both markers on the same space, each says the other has to go back. Having no method for determining who is right, A suggests a level 2 compromise and checks it out with D, "So me and you're gonna stay there, okay?" Neither goes back to Start, and the game continues. These boys have profited from their experience with negotiation in the classroom. When they both want to be first in the game, they settle the argument peacefully by reciting a choosing rhyme similar to "Eenie, Meenie, Miney, Moe." Such negotiation never occurred among the children from Boot Camp or Factory classrooms. A and D clearly enjoy one another's company and are able to work through difficulties by using level 2 negotiation strategies.

Our examples illustrate the ways in which Community children are better able to self-regulate their interactions than Boot Camp children. Similar but less extreme differences were observed between children from Community and Factory classrooms.

OBSERVING MORAL CHILDREN IN THE CLASSROOM

As morality is basically concerned with interpersonal understanding, we find Selman's levels provide a practical tool for assessing children's sociomoral development. We would like to point out that we agree with Selman that most of the enacted interpersonal understanding of children ages 3–6 years (and perhaps beyond) is level 1. In fact, level 1 is appropriate in many life situations, not only for children, but for adults as well. (For example, "Pass the salt, please," while polite, is still a level 1 negotiation strategy.) Nevertheless, with a constructivist experience, young children are capable at times of level 2 interpersonal understanding. Its appearance in young children marks the leading edge of their moral and social development. Even though level 2 may appear only from time to time, it is an occasion for celebrating children's moral progress.

The following example of precocious moral engagement takes place in the Explorers class in the Human Development Laboratory School (HDLS) at the University of Houston. The teacher, Marti Wilson, observed this almost unbelievable incident in the classroom and recorded it in her weekly observations.

S (35 months) and R (35 months) were engaged in cooperative pretend play. Each one had a hat, purse, and doll, and were going to the "store" (across the classroom) for apples and eggs. As they walked across the classroom, another child, T (31 months), decided that he wanted the purse R was carrying. T pulled on the purse so hard that he caused R to fall backwards. When R fell, T grabbed the purse and ran. R cried. S went after T and brought him back to R. Looking at T, she said, "He's having a turn. It's R's purse. He's sad you took the purse. See, he's crying." Then she turned to R and said, "He doesn't understand your crying. Tell him, 'I'm having a turn.'" So R said to T, softly, "It's my purse. It's my turn." T gave the purse back to R. S then told T, "Thanks for listening. Do you want to go to the store, too?" T nodded. "I'll help you find a purse," S offered. She found a purse for T, and the three children continued their pretend play.

S's truly remarkable negotiations illustrate our goal for young children to become involved in the moral life of their classrooms. Undoubtedly, S's competence also reflects her home experience as the daughter of a constructivist teacher. Some of her actions may have been imitations, but their complexity, coherence, and precise adaptation to the other children suggest that her behavior is more than just imitation. In terms of Selman's levels of interpersonal understanding, T's initial behavior is level 0. S seems to enact level 3 as she states R's point of view and feelings to T. She ends with level 2 inquiry into T's desires and offer to help him. We should point out that S was not in a situation in which her self-interest was at stake. It may be easier to mediate another's conflicts at advanced levels than to deal with endangered self-interest in such ways.

We can only surmise what the children learned in this drama. S may have learned that she is an effective mediator, and R that he can stand up for his rights. Perhaps T learned that when he snatches people's purses, he makes them sad.

We want to emphasize that even at young ages, children can grapple with moral issues such as respect for property, injunctions against hurting others, and helping victims of aggression. Our goal for children is that they become involved in the moral issues of their classrooms. We want them to recognize unfairness when they see it, to prefer fairness to unfairness, and to feel compelled to speak out against unfairness.

Let us consider another example of children involved in a moral issue in their first- and second-grade classroom in a constructivist school in Houston called the Sunset-Pearl Elementary School. This involves U, a 6-year-old whose limited peer experience manifested itself earlier in the school year in lots of level 0 hitting and grabbing. The situation in U's classroom is that children are engaged in making simple machines. The conflict involves the use of a plastic section necessary as the support for the revolving part of U's merry-go-round. E has one of the scarce parts U wants. Throughout a 40-minute period, U repeatedly returns to E, using increasingly strong level 1 demands ("Give it to me, please."), passionate assertions ("E, I *need* it!"), and mock barter (offers E a piece E does not want). Several times U puts her hand on E's machine but does not follow through with a level 0 grab. She appeals to the teacher, Linda Carlson, with a level 1 complaint ("She won't give me one."). Later, U complains again ("She still won't give it to me. I asked her three times."). When the teacher intervenes to ask E to use her words and tell U how she feels, E says, "I use my words with her sometimes, and she says no to me." Here we see that the dynamic between the two girls has a history. U cannot appreciate that E's attitude of unwillingness has been established in many previous interactions. Linda asks U if she has heard E and says, "How do you think you girls could work it out? Maybe you need to talk about it some more." U imposes unwanted help on E, putting some pieces in the structure E has created, then appeals to guilt. "E, please give me one. I helped you." Again, U appeals to the teacher. "Linda, I need that thing desperately. I can't get that machine to work without this part. E won't give it to me. She just says, 'Maybe next time you'll get it'" (sarcastic mimicking tone).

Throughout, it seems that U simply believes she should have what she wants and is unable to decenter from her own perspective. The teacher asks, "U, do you understand why she's upset with you?" U honestly does not know and asks curiously, "Why?" Linda tries to help U decenter by saying, "You see, she feels she needs that for her project." U replies, "Well, she's just not considerate. She's got tons more than I do." The teacher points out that T was also working with the same materials and says, "You need to talk with T or E, to try to work out something." When U asks T for the part, T does not seem to hear. Linda asks, "T, U has a problem. Could she explain it to you?" T agrees to let U use the desired part, and U happily completes her project. E and T gather around U to observe her invention. In this incident, we see that she has progressed to level 1 negotiations, though restraint of level 0 urges is observable.

We want to point out that these classroom examples illustrate that level of enacted interpersonal understanding depends more on experience than on age. We saw at least level 2 in a child of about 3 years. We saw a child of 6 years perseverating in level 1 strategies because she could not take another's point of view when it conflicted with her own self-interest.

The teacher familiar with the levels of interpersonal understanding can quickly learn how to recognize negotiation strategies and shared experiences when a child is being impulsive and physical, when a child is being unilateral, when a child is being reciprocal, and when the child is being collaborative.

The teacher familiar with the Selman model can also recognize educational needs based on children's predominant mode of inter-acting. The task of children at level 0 is to learn to be unilateral (level 1). So the teacher mediating a conflict between two level 0 children might suggest that each child tell the other in words what he or she wants the other to do, the logic being that a demand (level 1) is better (higher level) than a grab (level 0). Likewise, a teacher might suggest to a child who demands a toy from another child that the other child also wants to play (pointing out the perspective of the other), and that the child might be more effective by suggesting taking turns or playing together. We discuss further in chapter 4 how constructivist teachers can interact with children to promote their development.

Early in this chapter, we argue that decentering or perspective coordination (cognitive as well as affective) is necessary for con-structing moral views that take into account the perspectives and feelings of others. We now want to point out that the moral child is an intellectually active child. Moral reasoning as well as intellectual reasoning involves cognitive processes such as decentering, consid-eration of causality and means-ends relationships. Moral engage-ment involves intellectual engagement. As we discuss further in chapter 3, the sociomoral atmosphere affects intellectual as well as moral development.

SUMMARY

When we speak of "moral children," we do not mean children who are merely obedient, know moral rules of others, act in prosocial ways, conform to social conventions of politeness, have a list of character traits, or are religious. Instead, we refer to moral children as children grappling with interpersonal issues that are a natural part of their lives. Young children are moral realists. They base their judgments of right and wrong, good and bad, on what is observable, or "real" to them. As inner lives of others are not observable, children focus their moral reasoning on observables such as material consequences and the literal behaviors of rule-following.

The work of Piaget, Kohlberg, and Selman sensitizes us to how children think about moral rules and how they think about others. Selman's levels of interpersonal understanding are particularly helpful to the constructivist teacher. Examples of interactions among children from Boot Camp and from Community classrooms illustrate these levels. Examples of moral engagement in the classroom show how the teacher can observe levels of interpersonal understanding and note progress in perspective coordination and moral engagement.

Understanding the moral life of childhood helps us know what we can reasonably expect from children in terms of morality, both short-term and long-term; it helps us recognize moral development; and it helps us formulate appropriate methods of fostering development.

3

How the Sociomoral Atmosphere Influences the Child's Development

Moral feelings have their origin in interpersonal relationships, according to Piaget (1954/1981), who also stated that "intelligence develops in the individual as a function of social interactions too often disregarded" (1964/1968, pp. 224–225). Interpersonal relations are the context for the child's construction of the self, with its self-consciousness and complex self-knowledge. In fact, the sociomoral atmosphere colors every aspect of a child's development. It is the context in which children construct their ideas and feelings about themselves, the world of people, and the world of objects. Depending on the nature of the overall sociomoral atmosphere of a child's life, he or she learns in what ways the world of people is safe or unsafe, loving or hostile, coercive or cooperative, satisfying or unsatisfying. In the context of interpersonal activities, the child learns to think of his or her self as having certain characteristics in relation to others. Within the social context surrounding objects, the child learns in what ways the world of objects is open or closed to exploration and experimentation, discovery and invention.

Adults determine the nature of the sociomoral atmosphere in which the young child lives, through daily interactions. The child's sociomoral atmosphere is made up, in large part, of the countless adult actions toward and reactions to the child that form the adult-child relationship. Peer relations also contribute to the sociomoral atmosphere, but the adult often establishes the framework of limits and possibilities of peer relations.

Teachers who want to establish a constructivist sociomoral atmosphere in their classrooms must begin by reflecting on the nature of their relationships with children. In this chapter we discuss first how social interaction in general influences children's construction of the self. We then focus on how the teacher-child relationship influences the child's development and talk about the role of peer relationships in the sociomoral atmosphere of school. Finally, we discuss the constructivist teacher's role in peer interaction.

SOCIAL INTERACTION AND CONSTRUCTION OF THE SELF

The young child has not yet constructed the unified personality of a mentally healthy adult who has a certain consistency and coherence in thoughts, feelings, and values. The reader may recall Piaget's classic experiments on intellectual development. He showed that although young children say two balls of clay have the same amount, they believe one has more when it is rolled into a hot-dog or snake shape. Piaget pointed out that young children do not conserve the equality relationship. He extended this notion of conservation to feelings, interests, and values. That is, young children's feelings, interests, and values are labile and tend not to be conserved from one situation to another. The young child only gradually constructs a more stable affective system of feelings and interests that acquires some permanence or conservation.

A central task for the child is to construct a self separate from others. This means coming to view the self as one among others. Consciousness of the self as a social object, according to Mead (1934) and Piaget (1932/1965, 1954/1981), comes about through social interactions. Without going into all the technical details, we can simply say that it requires thinking of the self from the point of view of others.

Consider your own experiences, even as an adult, when you become aware that someone perceives you in a certain way (for example, as generous, intimidating, diplomatic, threatening, inconsequential). These revelations often surprise you and contradict your self-concept. Experiences of realizing how others see us lead to new consciousness of ourselves as social objects and thus to new constructions or elaborations of our self-concepts.

In other words, to realize the attitudes of others toward the self requires decentering to think of the self from their point of view—the object of others' attitudes and actions. Such decentering is necessary for reflection on social relations, in all the complexities of thought and feeling involved in construction of the social world and one's place in it. For example, when A expresses anger toward B, B (say, a 3-year-old boy) may be jolted into self-consciousness through realizing that he or his behavior can be the object of anger. The idea that "I am a person with whom someone else can be angry (or pleased or loving, etc.)" marks an advance in the child's conception of self. The construction of a self proceeds along with corresponding construction of others as having thoughts, feelings, and values, just as the self does.

According to Mead (1934), we become conscious of ourselves in the course of experiencing the reactions of others to our actions. The self is structured through a reciprocal process of making adjustments to the responses of others. The child organizes the perceived attitudes of others toward the self and constructs his or her personality with increasingly stable characteristics. Piaget (1954/1981) talked about the construction of stable schemes of social reaction. He referred to a growing consistency in reaction to others, irrespective of who the others are. If the child actively takes the attitude of the other toward the self in order to understand his or her self, it is reasonable to conclude that the nature of the others' attitudes are crucial to the nature of the child's constructed self.

Elementary feelings of liking and disliking (for self and others) are, for Piaget, the starting point for moral feelings. That is, the child begins to construct a hierarchy of what is valued and what is not. Moral values are both affective and intellectual. They can become organized into permanent values that are regulated by will, the affective aspect of values. According to Piaget, affectivity, morality, and intelligence are developed and transformed in interconnected ways.

THE TEACHER-CHILD RELATIONSHIP

Sarason (1982) notes that "The enormous effort and inventiveness required of a teacher in fostering good relationships both between herself and her children and among her children is sometimes defined as a distraction from her educational role" (p. 165). We agree with Sarason that these relationships must be cultivated in order to promote children's development and even to make the teacher more effective in promoting academics.

In Piaget's research and theory we find the most useful guide to thinking about adult-child relationships. Piaget (1932/1965) described two types of morality corresponding to two types of adult-child relationships, one that promotes children's development and one that retards it.

The first type of morality is a morality of obedience. Piaget called this "heteronomous" morality. The word *heteronomous* comes from roots meaning "following rules made by others." Therefore, the individual who is heteronomously moral follows moral rules given by others out of obedience to an authority who has coercive power. Heteronomous morality is conformity to external rules that are simply accepted and followed without question.

The second type of morality is autonomous. The word *autonomous* comes from roots meaning "self-regulation." By autonomy, Piaget did not mean simple "independence" in doing things for oneself without help. Rather, the individual who is autonomously moral follows moral rules of the self. Such rules are self-constructed, self-regulating principles. These rules have a feeling of personal necessity for the individual. The individual who is autonomously moral follows internal convictions about the necessity of respect for persons in relationships with others.

Surely no educator would support a goal of heteronomous morality in children. We probably all agree that we want children to believe with personal conviction in such basic moral values as respect for persons. Without belief that rises from personal conviction, children will not be likely to follow moral rules. Nevertheless, educators generally manage children in ways that promote heteronomous rather than autonomous morality.

The Coercive or Controlling Relationship

The first type of adult-child relationship is one of coercion or constraint in which the adult prescribes what the child must do by giving ready-made rules and instructions for behavior. In this relation, respect is a one-way affair. That is, the child is expected to respect the adult, and the adult uses authority to socialize and instruct the child. The adult controls the child's behavior. In this sociomoral context, the child's reason for behaving is thus outside his or her own reasoning and system of personal interests and values. Piaget calls this type of relation "heteronomous." In a heteronomous relation, the child follows rules given by others rather than by the self. Heteronomy can range on a continuum from hostile and punitive to sugar-coated control.

In adult-child interactions heteronomy is often appropriate and sometimes unavoidable. That is, for reasons of health and safety, as well as practical and psychological pressures on the adult, parents and teachers must regulate or control children in many ways.

However, consider the situation from the child's perspective in ordinary life with adults. At home, children are forced to submit to a whole set of rules whose reasons are incomprehensible to them. The obligation to eat certain foods at certain times, to go to bed involuntarily, or not to touch certain delicate or important objects, for example, can only be felt by children as coming from outside themselves because the necessity to carry out these obligations cannot be felt from within. At school, too, children do not understand the reasons for most of the rules to which they must submit.

Imagine how it would feel to be continually obliged to do things that do not make sense to you. Such a situation leads to a feeling of coercion by a boss's arbitrary demands. Some might react with defeated feelings and passive acceptance of the other's right to be boss, especially if the boss is affectionate as well as demanding. Some might react with anger, suppressed or expressed, while others might react with the secret rebellion of intelligent calculation, obeying only when under surveillance. Certainly, none of these reactions is good for mental health or future development.

Well-meaning teachers often feel that it is their responsibility to manage every detail of children's behavior. In chapter 1, we saw the Drill Sergeant dictate a right way to sit as well as every correct answer in lessons. The Manager dictates the details of children's actions in academic lessons and art work. In contrast, the Mentor organizes her classroom so that she can leave the details of children's behavior to their own regulation.

Some management of children in classrooms, of course, is unavoidable. However, when children are governed continually by the values, beliefs, and ideas of others, they practice a submission (if not rebellion) that can lead to mindless conformity in both moral and intellectual life. In other words, so long as adults keep children occupied with learning what adults want them to do and with obeying adult rules, they will not be motivated to question, analyze, or examine their own convictions.

In Piaget's view, following the rules of others through a morality of obedience will never lead to the kind of reflection necessary for commitment to internal or autonomous principles of moral judgment. Piaget warned that coercion socializes only the surface of behavior and actually reinforces the child's tendency to rely on regulation by others. By insisting that the child only follow rules, values, and guidelines given ready-made by others, the adult contributes to the development of an individual with a conformist mind, personality, and morality—an individual capable only of following the will of others. Tragically, obedience-based schools simply perpetuate qualities needed for submission.

The child who lives a life dominated by obedience to the rules of others may develop a morality of blind obedience to authority. Such an individual may be easily led by any authority. Or, because of failure to develop a personal feeling about the necessity of moral rules, the obedient child may eventually rebel, openly or privately. Heteronomous morality means that the individual does not regulate his or her behavior by means of personal convictions. Rather, his or her activity may be regulated by impulse or unthinking obedience.

Piaget (1954/1981) drew on psychodynamic theory in discussing the child's construction of self-esteem which begins when the 1-year-old asserts his or her will against adult will. Some people say it is necessary to "break a child's will." However, such heteronomous defeat of a child's will leads to inferiority feelings in the child. Confidence or doubt about the self is a continuing issue for young children who are constructing their personalities. Gradually, the child constructs a system that conserves feelings, interests, and values. These values become permanent and define the self. When the child experiences adults as predominantly controlling, the self that is constructed is an indecisive one that needs or seeks control by others.

Piaget (1954/1981) talked about will as the power of conservation of values, noting that an individual without will is unstable, believing in certain values at certain moments and forgetting them at other moments. According to Piaget, will serves as affective regulator, enabling the individual to achieve stability and coherence in personality and in social relations. Exerting will against a continually heteronomous adult leads to a personality defined by control—giving in to it or struggling against it. Such a relation does not provide the possibility for constructing positive self-esteem or cooperative moral feelings. The patterns of social reaction constructed by the child regulated by too much heteronomy may be defensive. In the context of heteronomous control, the child constructs a doubting self oriented to the control of others. Social reactions can become habitually hostile and/or dependent.

So is obedience bad? Not necessarily. We discuss in chapter 2 the results of obedience based on love. However, strong pressure for obedience for the sake of obedience can lead to unfortunate results in children's development. Emotionally, children may react with a submissive attitude to dominance, feelings of inferiority and acceptance of others' superiority, lack of confidence, and low motivation to think about reasons for rules. Intellectually, the heavily coerced child may react with a passive orientation to the ideas of others, an unquestioning and uncritical attitude, and low motivation to think, instead parroting rote-memory answers. These characteristics reflect low constructive activity that also leads to moral reasoning based on self-interest with little concern for others. In pure obedience, there is no place for the child's autonomous self-regulation. Similarly, an educational experience preoccupied with giving back correct information destroys curiosity and leads to intellectual dullness and knowledge full of misunderstanding. Limited opportunity for personal constructive activity leads to a constricted personality with inadequate social, emotional, intellectual, and moral competence.

External control of children has its limits. Children may conform in behavior, but feelings and beliefs cannot be so easily controlled. As children grow larger physically, the possibility of behavioral control decreases. The only real possibility for influencing children's behavior when they are on their own is to foster their gradual construction of morality, knowledge, intelligence, and personality.

The Cooperative Relationship

Piaget contrasts the heteronomous adult-child relationship with a second type that is characterized by mutual respect and cooperation. The adult returns children's respect by giving them the possibility to regulate their behavior voluntarily. This type of relation Piaget called "autonomous" and "cooperative." He argued that it is only by refraining from exercising unnecessary authority that the adult opens the way for children to develop minds capable of thinking independently and creatively and to develop moral feelings and convictions that take into account the best interests of all parties.

The method by which the autonomous relationship operates is that of cooperation. Cooperating means striving to attain a common goal while coordinating one's own feelings and perspective with a consciousness of another's feelings and perspective. The constructivist teacher considers the child's point of view and encourages the child to consider others' points of view. The motive for cooperation begins in a feeling of mutual affection and trust that becomes elaborated into feelings of sympathy and consciousness of the intentions of self and others.

Cooperation is a social interaction toward a certain goal by individuals who regard themselves as equals and treat each other as such. Obviously, children and adults are not equals. However, when the adult is able to respect the child as a person with a right to exercise his or her will, one can speak about a certain psychological equality in the relationship. Piaget, of course, was not advocating that children have complete freedom because such freedom is inconsistent with moral relations with others.

We also want to assure the reader that cooperating with children does not mean that the teacher dispenses entirely with authority. It is not always possible to cooperate with children. However, when coercion is necessary, it is important *how* the adult approaches children (for example, with a sympathetic attitude and with explanation, in contrast to an attitude of "Because I said so").

Does obedience occur in constructivist classrooms? Yes, it does. Young children are naturally heteronomous and can feel coerced even when a teacher uses cooperative methods. However, the constructivist teacher appeals to children's cooperation rather than to their obedience. The difference between appealing to obedience and to cooperation is that in a cooperative relation, the teacher asks rather than tells, suggests rather than demands, and persuades rather than controls. Children therefore have the possibility for deciding how to respond, and power struggles are avoided. The constructivist teacher encourages children to be self-regulating—that is, to act autonomously.

Does constructivist education encourage children to expect immediate gratification of desires? No. While children do have the satisfaction of pursuing interests, an atmosphere of cooperation requires balancing one's desires with those of others. In a word, respect for both self and others is emphasized.

The general constructivist principle of teaching is that coercion be minimized to the extent possible and practical. What is most desirable is a mixture increasingly in favor of children's regulation of their own behavior. We will discuss in chapter 4 how this idea is translated into specific principles of teaching and into specific interactions with children.

The child who is given opportunities for regulating his or her behavior has the possibility for constructing a confident self that values self and others positively. By respecting the child's will, the cooperative adult can help the child develop self-regulation based on respect for others as well as for self. The child able to exercise his or her will constructs gradually a stable system of moral, social, and intellectual feelings, interests, and values.

Piaget emphasized that the child constructs a hierarchy of social feelings, interests, and values organized as sympathies (liking) and antipathies (disliking). Especially important are feelings of goodwill. Piaget (1954/1981) stated that "moral feelings originate from feelings of goodwill toward individuals who have given pleasure" (p. 47). Such feelings are colored by a sort of gratitude that develops into voluntary feelings of obligation. We may speculate about the opposite situation in which negatively heteronomous adults engender feelings of ill will in children. Do these children fail to develop an attitude of cooperation? Do they, instead, develop negative, uncooperative attitudes?

Respected by adults and benefitting from their attitude of good will, the child progressively organizes feelings, interests, and values into a self oriented to cooperation with others. The possibility for considerable self-regulation opens the way for constructing cooperative patterns of social reaction and a stable personality.

Why is cooperation so desirable? Reduced pressure for obedience combined with encouragement of self-regulation lead to fortunate results for children's development. Emotionally, children feel acceptance and approval, and may respond to cooperation with an attitude of cooperation, feelings of equality and confidence, and active thoughtfulness about reasons for rules. Intellectually, the child may react with an active orientation to ideas of self and others, an attitude of questioning and critical evaluation, and motivation to think about causes, implications, and explanations. These characteristics involve constructive activity that is error-filled and error-informed. With skilled adult guidance and extensive peer interaction, such activity leads to moral reasoning that considers all points of view. An educational experience full of opportunities for exploration and experimentation leads to intellectual sharpness and understanding. Extensive opportunity for personal constructive activity leads to a highly differentiated personality with social, emotional, intellectual, and moral competence.

When we talk about heteronomy and autonomy, coercion and cooperation, we are talking about processes that are simultaneously cognitive and emotional. Adult coercion produces a constriction of children's minds, personalities, and feelings. Adult cooperation produces a liberation of children's possibilities for construction of their intelligence, their personalities, and their moral and social feelings and convictions.

The reader may rightly protest that no child's life is totally coercive or totally cooperative. We agree. We describe here how strong coercion and strong cooperation influence children's development. However, each child presents a unique history of coercive and cooperative experiences. Our stance is optimistic. We are convinced that no child has experienced so much coercion that a cooperative teacher cannot ameliorate, at least to some extent, the effects of heteronomy. Each classroom, too, will provide a mixture of coercive and cooperative experiences. Again, our stance is optimistic. We believe that moral classrooms will promote moral development in children— as well as emotional, social, and intellectual development. We know that no teacher can be perfectly cooperative all the time. However, we hope the ideas presented in this book will help teachers as they assess their relationships with children and develop cooperative ways of teaching.

PEER RELATIONSHIPS

Peer interaction is sometimes vaguely justified as beneficial for socialization, as necessary for children to learn to share and live in a world with others. Unfortunately, education is not usually organized to provide children with the experiences favorable for social competence and moral development.

In classrooms where interactions among children are forbidden, peer relationships play little role in the overall sociomoral atmosphere. Of course, sympathies and antipathies may develop based on children's interactions outside the classroom. However, most classroom life is not designed to promote peer relationships. Children's tendencies to aid each other are usually classified as cheating and may be punished. In the Boot Camp described in chapter 1, the Drill Sergeant often pits children against each other (by row or gender) in competition for praise and avoidance of criticism. The resulting sociomoral atmosphere is stifling, and there is no evidence that anyone wants to be there together.

In classrooms where interactions among children are encouraged, peer relationships play an important role in the sociomoral atmosphere. While some peer interaction is permitted in the Factory classroom described in chapter 1, it plays a minor role in children's classroom experience. The Manager emphasizes the primary importance of academics and draws the line on cooperation by insisting on individual work. Conflicts are squelched, and peer interactions muted. The resulting sociomoral atmosphere is a kind of "nicey-niceness" in which no one is very invested in the experience of being together.

In contrast, the Mentor not only organizes her classroom to optimize its interactive character, but actively engages children with each other. Life in the Community is the main "subject matter," and the Mentor takes advantage of spontaneous incidents to maximize children's opportunities for confronting social, emotional, intellectual, and moral problems with constructive activity. The resulting sociomoral atmosphere is one of vitality and energy invested in the experience of being together.

What benefits are gained from peer interaction? Does this mean the teacher has no role to play?

Benefits of Peer Interaction in a Constructivist Classroom

According to Piaget, peer interactions are crucial to the child's construction of social and moral feelings, values, and social and intellectual competence. As indicated in our discussion of the teacher-child relationship, we do not agree with those who interpret Piaget as saying that it is *only* in relations with peers that autonomous morality and intelligence develops. We build on Piaget's ideas and describe throughout this book how the constructivist teacher can engage with children in cooperative ways.

Peer relations are especially conducive to social, moral, and intellectual development for two reasons. The first is that peer relations are characterized by an equality that can never be achieved in adult-child relations, no matter how hard the adult tries to minimize heteronomy. Peer relations can lead to recognition of the reciprocity implicit in relations of equality. This reciprocity can provide the psychological foundation for decentering and perspective-taking. As autonomy can only occur in a relationship of equality, children are more easily able to think and act autonomously with other children than with most adults. However, as Piaget pointed out, inequalities also exist among children, and autonomy can be violated in child-child interactions.

The second reason peer relations provide a good context for development is that seeing other children as like themselves results in a special feeling of interest that motivates peer contacts. These contacts are social, moral, and intellectual endeavors. In the course of peer interaction, children construct consciousness and differentiation of self and others, schemes of social reaction, and cooperation in thought and action. We discuss these constructions below.

Consciousness and Differentiation of Self and Others

Interest in peers especially motivates the child to widen consciousness from the self and take into account the desires and intentions of others. Interactions with others are much less predictable than interactions with objects and continually confront the child with the differences between self and others. Experiencing unexpected reactions, resistances, and negative reactions on the part of others, the child becomes conscious of the other as separate. This simultaneously results in new appreciation for the self as having unique desires and ideas. Decentering from a narrow focus to consider more and more points of view is at the same time a process with emotional, social, moral, and intellectual ramifications.

Thus, in the course of peer interactions, the child comes more clearly to know self and others. Awareness of differences in intentions is especially important for moral development.

Schemes of Social Interaction

Interest in other children leads to voluntary (autonomous) social efforts. As others respond to these initiatives, experiences of pleasure and displeasure occur. The child gradually constructs more and more consistently organized patterns of social reactions in the course of peer interaction. As the child acts and reacts in more or less stable ways in similar situations with a variety of people, personality becomes more consolidated and can be observed in consistent patterns. Thus, the child may be viewed as "shy," "friendly," "easily upset," "aggressive," and so forth. Behind these behavior patterns lie the child's interpretations and organizations or schemes of social orientation. Thus, peer interaction as well as adult-child interaction provides raw material out of which the child fashions his or her personality.

Cooperation in Thought and Action

Cooperation is a method of social interaction that creates the most productive context for all aspects of children's development. Piaget (1932/1965) argued that it is through cooperation that the child overcomes egocentric limitations and becomes able to take other perspectives into account. Interest in peers motivates children to construct shared meanings, resolve conflicts, and create and abide by rules.

Shared meaning. Shared meaning is obviously basic to human survival, and it clearly has roots in infancy as babies interpret and anticipate the social gestures of caregivers. Communication based on shared meaning begins long before language. Researchers in Paris (Stambak et al., 1983) describe how children less than 2 years of age are capable of an elementary sort of cooperation as they imitate one another, manifest common desires, and carry out each others' ideas with objects (for example, riding empty detergent barrels, imitating an unintentional falling off, vocalizing, and adding various modifications that keep the joyful shared activity going).

The construction of shared meaning among peers is especially observable in pretend play as no external framework is given and children must develop their common framework of meaning. As Verba (1990) points out, children must make reciprocal adjustments to share a theme, assign roles, and manage the action. All this involves proposals, acceptances or rejections, and negotiations. The less a situation reflects socially codified scenes, the more it is necessary for children to express their thoughts and make them precise and clear in order to elaborate the play. The children's mutual comprehension involves compromise between individual wills. As Verba further notes, it constitutes an equilibrium between affirmation of the self and acknowledgement of the other as a partner. She writes, "The link [between partners] is consolidated in moments of agreement and complicity—by prolonged mutual gazes, smiles, and laughs, leading to emotional fusion among the participants" (p. 59; DeVries, translator). A shared meaning system is also necessary for the construction of objective thought. Therefore, children's progress in constructing shared meaning in pretense and other activities constitutes progress in symbolic communicative and intellectual competence.

Conflict resolution. In particular, children's conflicts offer a rich context for cooperation. Of course, not all conflict results in cooperative resolution. However, when peer interactions are characterized by disequilibrium, children are usually motivated to negotiate. Having the desire to keep the other as a partner, the child wants to find ways of continuing play when it is disrupted. Bonica (1990) describes the vicissitudes of communication between two 3-year-old girls in pretend play. Their pretense centers on the feeding of a doll, a general theme proposed by one and accepted by the other. Their efforts to collaborate, however, are full of misunderstandings, rejected proposals, and conflicts, as well as concessions and an overall effort to conserve the theme and the other as a partner. It is this desire to keep the other as a partner that motivates continuing efforts to negotiate a common coherent system of meaning. Cooperation also occurs between children who engage in exploratory play with objects.

Verba (1990) points out that proposals of symbolic meanings to others in pretend play generally occur only among children who have previously shared the same activity or who have the habit of playing together. Thus, it is important to foster friendships among children as contexts in which meanings can be constructed and intelligence and moral feelings elaborated.

Bonica (1990) notes that productive conflict resolution implies an equilibrium between the other's persuasive effectiveness and one's own satisfaction. In addition, productive conflict experiences can result in the construction of a new aspect of the personality (for example, as the child becomes one who can integrate aims of self and other).

Rules. The pleasure found in peer interactions provides the foundation for the child's attachment to the group. Shared experiences lead to the development of feelings of community. These feelings, cultivated by teacher guidance, are the basis for the rules that evolve in a constructivist classroom. This shared system of rules becomes a moral force in children's lives. Children have a feeling of commitment and obligation to the moral code they construct themselves.

In short, peer interaction is a context for progressive adjustment and mutual enrichment among children.

The Constructivist Teacher's Role in Peer Interaction

The constructivist teacher's important role in children's peer interactions involves defining the possibilities, engaging with children at times as a peer, and facilitating interaction when children's self-regulation fails. It is the teacher who influences to a large extent the educational value that derives from children's peer interactions.

Defining the possibilities includes the selection and arrangement of furniture and materials and planning activities that appeal to children's interests. When children gravitate individually to the same activity, the stage is set for interaction.

The value of peer interaction depends not only on children's abilities to engage with one another, but also on the teacher's ability to engage sometimes as a peer. For example, in a board game, the teacher can take the role of a player alongside children. As a player, the teacher must also agree with children on the rules, abide by the rules, and accept their consequences. By giving up authority in this situation, the teacher promotes child autonomy. When children take charge, they bring their best energies to the activity in all its emotional, social, moral, and intellectual aspects. As a player, the teacher can ask direction from children and give them the instructional role. As a loser, the teacher can model an attitude of good sportsmanship,

share feelings of disappointment, and demonstrate methods of coping with defeat.

The value of peer interaction also depends on the ability of the
teacher to intervene when children have difficulties and to help them
maintain a sociomoral atmosphere that is constructive. Conflict can
be a constructive context, but it can also be destructive. Because
children are limited in their abilities to restrain impulses and because
of limited perspective-taking, children left entirely to their own
devices can fail in their efforts to overcome interpersonal difficulties.
Without the guidance of a skilled teacher who promotes cooperation,
children can end up with a sociomoral atmosphere in which might
makes right and in which many unresolved conflicts create a climate
of insecurity, anger, and anxiety. We discuss this further in chapter 5.

Peer interaction in a constructivist classroom, therefore, does
not occur without considerable teacher support and aid.

SUMMARY

The sociomoral atmosphere colors every aspect of the child's development. Adults determine the nature of the child's sociomoral atmosphere through daily interactions of two types. The generally heteronomous or coercive adult orients the child to a morality of
obedience that keeps the child preoccupied with rules and regulations external to the child's own system of rules. The generally cooperative adult encourages the child's self-regulation by means of self-
constructed principles. Peer relations, too, influence the nature of
the child's sociomoral atmosphere when peer interactions are
encouraged by the teacher. Interest in peers leads children to cooperate by constructing shared meanings, resolving conflicts, and creating and abiding by rules. The constructivist teacher promotes peer
interactions by defining the possibilities, engaging with children at
times as a peer, and facilitating interaction when children's self-regulation fails.

4

Establishing a Constructivist Sociomoral Atmosphere

A moral classroom begins with the teacher's attitude of respect for children, for their interests, feelings, values, and ideas. This respect is expressed in the classroom's organization, in activities, and in the teacher's interactions with children.

CLASSROOM ORGANIZATION

The overarching objective of constructivist education is to promote children's development. This objective leads to organizing the classroom for children's needs, peer interaction, and responsibility.

Organizing to Meet Children's Needs

Organizing to meet children's needs includes consideration of physiological, emotional, and intellectual needs.

Physiological Needs

In chapter 1, we describe different attitudes toward children's physical needs for eating, toileting, and resting. It seems obvious that adults should meet children's physical needs. However, we have observed rather callous disregard for these needs on the part of some teachers and schools. Perhaps part of the reason this occurs is that school rules and facilities sometimes make it difficult and inconvenient for teachers to respond to young children's physical needs. Perhaps part of the reason is that schools may not be meeting teachers' needs. Nevertheless, failure to meet children's physical needs creates an abusive situation. The sociomoral atmosphere of the constructivist classroom is characterized by physical comfort.

Emotional Needs

In many schools where children's physical needs are met, emotional needs may be overlooked. We discuss in chapter 3 the unfortunate effects of heteronomy on all aspects of children's development. The Drill Sergeant may be considered an emotionally abusive teacher. The Manager may be considered an emotionally absent teacher. The Mentor is not only emotionally present and available to children, she continually takes children's feelings into account and tries to help them construct a more stable system of feelings and ways of coping with difficult feelings.

Respecting children requires communicating acceptance and affection. It requires providing an environment that encourages and supports children's expressions of feelings, interests, and values. This means accepting the child's right to feel anger and sadness as well as positive feelings.

Children in a moral classroom feel ownership of it. The classroom does not belong just to the teacher. It belongs to the children as well. The moral classroom does not express just the teacher's personality. Walls are full of children's artwork and writing, and their projects are displayed. Of course, the teacher also contributes to the physical environment, but one does not see, for example, the totally teacher-made, elaborate bulletin board displays that so many elementary teachers feel regularly obligated to make. The feeling of classroom ownership is similar to how we feel about our own homes. We feel at home because we have organized it for our safety, security, comfort, pleasure, and convenience. The objects in our home belong to us and we are free to use them for our purposes. So it is in the moral classroom. Children feel safe, secure, and comfortable. They find pleasure and purposes to pursue.

Intellectual Needs

Children have intellectual needs for activities that stimulate their interests and provide content that inspires them to figure out how to do something. Respect for children's intellectual needs leads to recognizing that young children must be physically active and emotionally engaged. Therefore, meeting children's intellectual needs is bound up with meeting their physical and emotional needs. The sociomoral atmosphere is an intellectually engaging atmosphere. The theoretical foundation of activities, discussed later in this chapter, further addresses concerns about meeting children's intellectual needs.

Organizing for Peer Interaction

The child's need to be active includes a need to be interactive. The constructivist teacher promotes peer interaction by organizing the program so interpersonal engagement occurs naturally.

Activity time offers extensive opportunities for peer interaction. Some activities, such as pretend play and group games, especially motivate children to engage with one another and figure out how to cooperate. In physical-knowledge activities, children experiment, observe others' experiments, and exchange ideas. Similarly, art, blockbuilding, and writing can be contexts for peer collaboration. In all these activities, children are free to choose not only their activities but also their playmates.

Organizing for peer interaction at grouptime, the constructivist teacher encourages children to talk with each other, not just with the teacher. Exchanges among children occur at grouptime when children try to help an individual solve a problem, when differences of opinion arise, and when a problem for the group as a whole is addressed.

We caution against over-organizing peer interaction. Teachers sometimes try to promote general community by assigning rotating play or work partners. This approach lessens children's motivation and activity and, in our view, is not respectful of children's feelings. Community cannot be purchased at the price of individuals' initiative and friendships. Such coercion will operate against the establishment of children's feelings of ownership of the classroom. Children should have the freedom to choose their playmates.

In early childhood, children are still constructing their feelings, ideas, and values concerning friendship. Even very young children can develop attachments to other children that have all the characteristics of friendship. Two-year-olds can be observed to have stable preferences for play partners, to watchfully anticipate their arrival, to miss them and feel sad when they are absent, and to express special compassion for them.

We caution against trying to break up special attachments among children. Sometimes teachers are concerned about cliques that form.

We understand and agree with concerns about children feeling left out when excluded from a group's play. However, children's attachments are important to them and mark progress in social development. Stability in preferences reflects conservation of values that is necessary for moral development. Therefore, we suggest that teachers encourage children's special friendships.

If a problem of exclusion and hurt feelings arises, this can be addressed in a variety of ways. It can be a topic for discussion at grouptime as a general hypothetical issue without naming personalities involved. If a child is very upset, the teacher can explore the problem in a private discussion at first. Sometimes it is helpful to suggest that the parents of the excluded child invite a classmate to their home or to share a special occasion. We have seen overnight friendships bloom after such a shared experience. Sometimes it is helpful to coach the excluded child on how to enter into others' play. Sometimes it helps for the excluded child to bring a special game to share with classmates. It is not necessary to mandate that children must play with certain others.

To organize for peer interaction is also to set the stage for inevitable conflicts. Viewing conflict and its resolution as part of the curriculum, constructivist teachers take advantage of incidents of conflict, as discussed in chapter 5. In a conflictual situation, children have the opportunity to realize the other's differing perspective. They are motivated to figure out how to resolve the problem.

Organizing for Child Responsibility

When children feel ownership of the classroom, the stage is set for cultivating feelings of responsibility. The moral classroom is organized so children can take responsibility. Adults often underestimate the amount of responsibility children are willing and eager to accept.

Since children use the materials and furnishings in the classroom, they are able to observe what happens when these are not cared for. When the tops are not replaced on colored markers, they dry up and cannot be used. When the tables are not cleared and wiped, there is no clean space to put lunch. When materials are not put where they belong, children cannot find them. When events such as these occur, the teacher can take advantage of the opportunity for group discussion about how to resolve the problems. We discuss in chapters 6 and 12 various ways in which teachers can share responsibility with children through rotation of daily duties and privileges.

Similarly, feelings of responsibility for the social environment can be cultivated. From the beginning, the constructivist teacher shares with children the responsibility for making rules, as discussed in chapter 7. When children feel ownership of the rules, they are more likely to follow them and remind others to follow them.

When cooperation breaks down, children have the opportunity to understand why they need rules that everyone respects. With teacher guidance, children can discuss their problems and decide what kind of community they want to live in.

It is not always easy to have confidence in children's potential competence. Some educators feel that the overarching objective is for children to learn to follow directions. "Self-regulation," in fact, sometimes is used to refer to compliance with adult demands. This is not the constructivist view. We hope the stories in this book encourage teachers' confidence in children's possibilities for being self-regulating.

ACTIVITIES

Respect for children leads to the definition of constructivist education as active. Specifically, constructivist education:

1. Engages the child's interest
2. Inspires active experimentation with all its necessary groping and error
3. Fosters cooperation between adults and children and among children themselves

We discuss below how interest, experimentation, and cooperation are important for the sociomoral atmosphere.

Engaging Interest

By interest we refer to the child's positive emotional engagement in classroom activities. Such interest is crucial to the constructivist sociomoral atmosphere because it reflects respect for the child's point of view. We address why interest is important in a constructivist classroom and give some examples of how teachers appeal to children's interests.

Why Interest Is Important
Piaget (1954/1981, 1969/1970) referred to interest as the "fuel" of the constructive process. Adults' interests are generally consciously

defined and ordered in priorities. Adults are thus often capable of constructive effort even when their interest is at a low level and they feel the pressure of some kind of coercion. Even for adults, however, the absence of interest can prevent effective effort. When our interest is thoroughly engaged, our efforts are most productive. This condition is even more necessary for young children whose interests are yet relatively undifferentiated. According to Piaget, interest is central to the actions by which the child constructs knowledge, intelligence, and morality. Without interest, the child would never make the constructive effort to make sense out of experience. Without interest in what is new to him or her, the child would never modify reasoning or values. Interest is a kind of regulator that frees up or stops the investment of energy in an object, person, or event. Thus, methods aimed at promoting the constructive process must arouse the child's spontaneous interest that is inherent in constructive activity.

It surprises many people to learn that constructivist education for cognitive development focuses equally on affectivity. This "Piagetian" principle was elaborated well before Piaget by John Dewey (1913/1975), who argued that the aim of education is increase in ability to put forth effort. Dewey cautioned, however, that some kinds of effort are *un*educative. These are efforts in tasks that involve nothing but sheer strain and external motivation for keeping at them. Such tasks he described as not only uneducative, but *mis*educative. They are miseducative because they deaden and stupefy, leading to a confused and dulled state of mind that always results when action is carried out without a sense of personal purpose. They are also miseducative because they lead to dependence on the external pressure of the taskmaster. When the child's interest and motivation lie in avoiding punishment or getting reward from the teacher, it is thus focused outside the task itself. Dewey said we should not look for motives external to activities, but for motives *in* activities. When teachers have to look for artificial ways to motivate children, something is seriously wrong.

Interest in activity is at the heart of constructivist education. Both Dewey and Piaget recommended that we start from the active powers of children. In what ways can young children be mentally active? The general answer to this question is that young children are motivated to be mentally active in the context of physical activity. For Piaget, intelligence originates in infancy in action that is simultaneously mental and physical. Mental development is in large part a matter of gradually freeing mental activity from physical activity. For many years in childhood, however, physical activity continues to be closely associated with and necessary for mental activity.

Examples of Appealing to Children's Interests

Active education does not occur in a classroom where children sit at
desks in isolation from one another, doing paperwork. A constructivist classroom is one in which many different activities go on simultaneously. These activities include those long associated with the
child-development tradition in early education (for example, painting
and other art activities, blocks and other construction activities, and
pretend play). In addition, constructivist teachers add physical-
knowledge activities (DeVries & Kohlberg, 1987/1990; Kamii &
DeVries, 1978/1993) and group games (DeVries & Kohlberg,
1987/1990; Kamii & DeVries, 1980).

At the HDLS at the University of Houston, teachers routinely
consult children about curriculum content. For example, Peige
Fuller asked her Investigator class ($3\frac{1}{2}$–$4\frac{1}{2}$-year-olds) at grouptime what they wanted to know about. The list generated by the
children then provided the content for the rest of the semester.
Here is a partial list of topics: space men, breaking glass, moms
and dads, going to college, apples, washing your hands, dinosaurs,
and flower girls. In an interview (June 1992), Peige explained her
thinking:

> The challenges were to respect children's desires and some-
> how to make constructivist activities from the topics. The
> teacher has in mind, too, some things she wants to get into the
> curriculum, things she wants children to know about in the
> world. Being a facilitator means that you're looking at the
> things they want to know about and trying to figure out how to
> bring activities that will jump from their idea and create
> opportunities for disequilibrium—interpersonal and cogni-
> tive. Constructivist teachers understand that that's where the
> real learning happens.
>
> I learned as a teacher by involving children in their learn-
> ing from the beginning. It takes teachers who respect chil-
> dren's ideas and who know how to raise them to a new plane.
> It's a matter of thinking about what things to pull in—investi-
> gations, places to go, arguments and struggles we could have.
> That's where the excitement of early education is—the excite-
> ment of being with your kids to figure out your curriculum.
> You make the commitment to be the best facilitator of their
> learning that you can be. Then you find out what they want to
> know about. And then you have these really hard planning

meetings where you figure out what all there is in the world that you can bring into the topics.

Taking children's interests seriously led Peige to many unexpected experiences. We recount a few of these in order to illustrate the rewards of following children's interests.

Breaking glass. Peige said, "We were very concerned about this topic when we first heard it. In retrospect, it was the easiest to do." The study of breaking glass was expanded into a unit on safety. Of course, children were not allowed to break glass. Peige explained to them that would be unsafe and that she could not let children be hurt. Instead, children watched as a teacher did this in a safe way (in a box covered with a towel). Peige explained that children just wanted to see what happened when glass broke. She speculated that they learned why adults "freak out" and say to be careful when children handle glass.

Flower girls. This was perhaps the most challenging topic to elaborate into something that not only led to new knowledge but reasoning and understanding. As the Assistant Director was planning her wedding, she was invited to grouptime where she talked about loving relationships, getting married, and starting a family. Children had a chance to think about what it means to form a family, and, of course, they asked if she was going to get babies. She replied, "Yes, someday" and added that children make families even more special. In other grouptimes, the group talked about the many different kinds of families represented in the classroom. Children learned about family names and began to write initials of last names after first names. The dress-up center was appropriately organized. Peige comments:

> For me, the flower girl part was not the major focus, but for the two or three who thought this was important, it was a chance to explore that fantasy. Maybe it was a reality in their lives, a special time they wanted to relive, when they felt sort of grownup and fancy. Feeling fancy is a neat thing to do even if being prissy isn't.

During the exploration of this theme, an argument arose as to whether boys could be flower girls. Peige comments, "We didn't see why someone couldn't have a flower boy if they wanted to, so all the little boys got to wear lace and flowers and all the sparkly stuff, too."

Washing hands. This curriculum suggestion came from a boy who was mystified as to why his parents and teachers told him to wash his hands so often. We are reminded of the story told by the first author's mother about the child who, when asked to wash his hands before cooking, said, "I don't need to. I already had a bath this morning." Peige reflected that although children talked about germs, they had to take their existence on faith. She engaged the help of a mother, a microbiologist, who provided petrie dishes. Peige thought of the occasions when adults tell children to cover their mouths as well as to wash their hands. After children played in sand, Peige took fingernail clippings from them for one dish. After children washed their hands, she took more nail clippings for another dish. At grouptime one dish was passed around for everyone to cough on, without covering their mouths. With another, children covered their mouths and coughed. To get the effect of an uncovered sneeze, one child suggested using a Q-tip to take mucous from her nose. One dish was merely exposed to air. All dishes were labeled and discussed so that children would be clear about what they were doing. The mother took the dishes to a warm and moist place in her lab. When she brought them back 2 days later, dramatic results were visible to the naked eye. One container had become so toxic that it had to be sealed and returned to the lab for disposal! Children remembered what they had done and discussed the findings at grouptime. During activities, they examined the dishes closely. This project made germs observable and more real to children.

Encouraging Experimentation

By experimentation, we refer to the child's actions on physical objects, together with observations of the reactions of the objects to these actions as well as new actions informed by previous observations.

Why Experimentation Is Important

Freedom to experiment with objects is an important part of the constructivist sociomoral atmosphere because it reflects the teacher's general attitude toward the child's interests and ways of knowing. This includes recognition of the importance of children's errors to their construction of knowledge. Up to the age of about 7 years, child thought is dominated by the physical, material, observable aspects of experience. The child's main interest in objects is what happens when he or she acts on them. In infancy and early childhood, especially, children construct knowledge of the physical world by acting on it. In the course of experimenting, according to Piaget, the child constructs not only physical knowledge but also intellectual power—intelligence itself.

The reactions of adults to children's experimentation are crucial to the sociomoral atmosphere. If experimentation is viewed as misbehavior, it may be punished. It is easy to squelch a child's experimental attitude. The challenge for the constructivist teacher is how to foster it.

Examples of Classroom Experimentation

In a constructivist classroom, the teacher actively promotes experimental attitudes among children. In a sink-and-float activity in the kindergarten of the HDLS, for example, Coreen Samuel encourages children's curiosity by providing objects that might arouse feelings of contradiction between children's expectations and observations of objects. She asks questions and makes comments such as "What is going to happen? Is it going to float?" She calls children's attention to individual experiments: "Let's see what happens when ____ tries ____." Experimental children are heard saying, "Let's see what this does." "Let me show you something." "Let's test these." "Try these." They announce their discoveries with pleasure and, frequently, surprise, indicating conscious reflection on a problem. The teacher capitalizes particularly on surprise, as this indicates contradiction between children's expectation and observation. For example, S seems surprised that a medium-sized wooden truck (with metal axles and rubber tires) partially submerges while a larger wooden schoolbus floats. Coreen (T) suggests further experimentation and comparison, and nudges S to think about why these results occur.

S: Watch this. Look, Coreen, it [wooden truck] sank.
T: I wonder, how about a big one?
S: (Puts large wooden school bus in the water; she looks at Coreen with a surprised expression.)
T: Oh my gosh, look at that! I never saw a schoolbus float before.
S: And this one sank (holds up truck).
T: How could this one have sunk? And this [truck] is even smaller.
S: Because it's small.
T: It's smaller, and this one is bigger. Is this (schoolbus) heavier? Let's feel it. Which one do you think is heavier?
S: This [bus].
T: How come this one is floating?

S: (Drops tiny wooden car in water; it floats) How do little bitty things float if they're little?

T: You thought that only big things float?

S: Yeah, but the little car floats.

T: Pretty strange.

S: (Gets cardboard paper towel roll) It's gonna float. Look at it. It's floating like a snake!

T: How about that! Look at this toothpick. What do you think is going to happen?

S: (Drops toothpick in water and sees that it floats)

In this activity, S does not resolve the feeling of contradiction between her expectation based on the idea that only big things float and her observation that small things also float. However, her puzzlement is the foundation for further experimentation, reflection, and eventual resolution of her contradiction.

This example illustrates that children's expectations can surprise us. Thus the teacher, too, continues to construct knowledge about how children reason and modify their reasoning.

Coreen supports children's ideas, even when wrong, and calls others' attention to them. For example, when T hypothesizes that a piece of Styrofoam floats because it has a hole in it, Coreen repeats, "T says if it has a hole in here, it doesn't sink." Then Coreen tries to challenge children's reasoning by observing, "This (plastic strawberry basket) sinks, but it has holes in it." Later, when other children notice that wooden things seem to float, she calls attention to the partially submerged truck with metal axles and rubber wheels, saying, "What's different about this one?" A child says, "'Cause it's carved." He refers to the fact that the truck is made from a single piece of wood. When one group of children concludes that metal sinks and wood floats, Coreen introduces a wooden ruler with a metal edge and asks for predictions.

We would like to point out that Coreen does not avoid including objects having properties of both sinkers and floaters in sink-and-float experiences. While some observations lead to clear conclusions according to classifications by material, others do not. Coreen does not try to protect children from the ambiguities of the real world.

Promoting Cooperation

By cooperation, we refer to operating in relation to another's behaviors, desires, feelings, ideas, and other psychological states. Piaget talked about the cognitive and moral importance of decentering from awareness of a single perspective. Cooperation is not possible unless children decenter to think about the perspective of the other. Cooperation, with its implicit reciprocity, is critical to the sociomoral atmosphere.

Why Cooperation Is Important

Cooperation requires coordination of points of view, a progressive adjustment in understanding the other, accepting initiatives, or reciprocating proposed modifications or counterproposals. The necessity for coordination becomes clear when children act in contradictory ways or openly disagree. The desire to play together arises from children's friendly relations, their socioaffective bonds. The habit of playing together makes possible more complex forms of cooperation. The motivation to cooperate and resolve problems when interactions break down is stronger between friends than nonfriends.

The desire to share one's thoughts with another leads to efforts to understand and make oneself understood. The feeling of understanding another and being understood can create the conditions for the development of friendship. Frequently in children's play, what they are most interested in is not so much the content but the social interaction. Experiences in cooperation provide the foundation and context for developing interpersonal understanding and thinking about issues of fairness and justice.

In the absence of external organization, children who play together must construct agreements on what to do. In pretend play, the meaning of symbols must be shared. In games, children confront the need to agree on rules. In blockbuilding together, children must agree on what to do and who performs various parts of the work. Cooperation is therefore important for intellectual as well as social and moral development.

Examples of Classroom Cooperation

A classroom organized to promote interest and experimentation also invites cooperation. Children who want to use the blocks may decide to work together on a structure. In pretend play, children can develop complex shared symbols as they coordinate their roles and ideas. Cooking the class snack can be organized so two cooks need to agree on what to cook and how to divide the responsibilities.

Some activities such as group games require cooperation. Consider, for example, the case of two 5-year-old friends who play checkers together frequently over the course of a year. The progressive adjustment of points of view is clear as they simultaneously construct rules along with interpersonal understanding. In the beginning, they do not know all the classic rules and unconsciously modify the game. For example, K decides the checkers can move diagonally any number of spaces, as long as the path is clear, like the bishop in chess. J thinks he can jump over two spaces in order to capture an opposing checker. K decides they can move backwards.

In a constructivist classroom, the teacher cooperates with children. He or she invites their ideas on what to learn and facilitates exploration, experimentation, investigation, and invention. The constructivist teacher cooperates with children by consulting them and often acting as a companion, as a player in games, and as a fellow experimenter.

THE TEACHER'S ROLE

As we indicate in chapter 1, the teacher's relations with children are crucial to the sociomoral atmosphere. It is not too much to say that these relations determine the nature of the interpersonal atmosphere. The constructivist teacher attempts to cooperate with children and foster cooperation among children themselves.

Cooperating with Children

When people talk about cooperation between adults and children, they often mean children's compliance with adult demands. This is not what we mean. Rather, we mean the teacher's relations of reciprocity with children. These arise from respect for children as people and respect for the nature of their development. The general principle of teaching is that the teacher minimizes authority as much as practical and possible (see chapter 3 for the rationale). Cooperation is important for the sociomoral atmosphere because it reflects respect for the equality of class members—equality in rights and responsibilities.

We conceptualize the ways constructivist teachers cooperate with children in terms of what teachers try to do. They try (1) to understand children's reasoning, and (2) to facilitate children's construction of knowledge.

Understanding Children's Reasoning

Knowledge of Piaget's research and theory on the preoperational stage of development helps teachers to understand young children's reasoning. We do not attempt a review of that work here but offer a few guidelines and examples that may ease the inexperienced constructivist teacher into a habit of observing and listening to children.

This habit is characterized by taking seriously what children say. For example, when a child says, "The weatherman made it rain today," the teacher recognizes this as a real belief and not just a cute remark. Similarly, the teacher assesses the intuitive nature of an idea expressed by a child on a walk. As the group turns around to return to school, shadows are no longer behind but in front of them. "How come your shadow is in front of you now?" The answer: "The wind blew it." The teacher realizes that the child is not able to think about spatial and causal relations among light, object, and shadow. Similarly, when a child insists that a classmate bumped his block structure on purpose, the teacher recognizes that the child does not and perhaps cannot appreciate that actions may not reflect intentions.

The constructivist teacher does not assume that children think like adults. Rather than making assumptions about what children know and how they reason, the teacher honestly inquires as to what children think and is prepared for surprises.

Facilitating Children's Constructions

Understanding children's reasoning provides the basis for facilitating development. To help children construct knowledge and intelligence, the constructivist teacher engages with children to introduce a new element as food for thought. In a shadows activity, for example, Coreen Samuel observes that B, a kindergarten boy in the HDLS, has figured out that moving back from the screen results in a bigger and bigger shadow. Wondering whether B has taken the light source into account, she asks, "How big can you make it? Make it as big as you can." B responds by moving back and back until he is behind the slide projector serving as light source. "What happened to the elephant shadow? I don't see it any more." B is startled by the unexpected result and waves the elephant in the dark. Seeing no shadow, he moves forward, but out of the path of the light. Waving the elephant from side to side, B accidentally catches the light and glimpses the shadow. This leads him to move into the full path of the light. "There it is!" Coreen again asks, "So how big can you make it?" B again backs up, still unconscious of the light source, and loses the shadow again. "Darn!" He waves the elephant around, places it on top of and beside the projector, and finally recreates the shadow by going back to stand in the place where he saw it last. Over the course of the year, Coreen continues to create situations that challenge B to experiment further with shadows. Making shadows on the ceiling is a particularly exciting situation in which B tests various hypotheses and gradually coordinates the light-object and object-screen relations.

In a group game, the constructivist teacher often takes part as a player alongside children. In this position, he or she can think aloud and thereby help children become more conscious of rules and strategies. For example, in a game of checkers, a student intern in the HDLS says, "If I move that one here, it would be safe, but if I move it here, you'd jump me, so I think I'll move it here so it will be safe." Children thus are challenged to think ahead and reason about possible moves on the part of the opponent.

Many other examples given throughout this book illustrate how the constructivist teacher cooperates with children by taking seriously their particular reasoning and constructions of knowledge.

Fostering Cooperation Among Children

Because so much peer interaction occurs in a constructivist classroom, relations among children comprise an important part of the sociomoral atmosphere. The constructivist goal is for children to construct emotional balance and coping abilities, interpersonal understanding, and social and moral values. All these goals are approached through the teacher's work with children in the interpersonal context of peer interactions.

Promoting Construction of Emotional Balance and Coping Abilities

Construction of emotional balance is a continual effort on the part of young children who are emotionally labile. They have not yet constructed stable personality characteristics and coping competencies. This is in large part due to intellectual limitations in thinking about perspectives and complexities of self-other interactions and relationships. The child who does not differentiate action from intention will be angered at every accidental encroachment on his or her rights. Emotional balance comes about gradually as children learn to withhold judgment and question their own interpretations of others, realizing that they need to find out what others' intentions are. Some adults do not learn to do this very well, jumping instead to conclusions that are really projections of their own attitudes. The constructivist teacher assists children in the process of achieving emotional balance and mental health by facilitating the development of self-knowledge and interpersonal understanding.

The constructivist teacher fosters the development of self-knowledge by helping children reflect on their feelings and reaction tendencies. When children become upset, the teacher can ask children what happened to make them upset. Sympathetically, the teacher can acknowledge children's feelings, letting them know that how they feel is recognized. In the case of an issue with another child, the teacher uses conflict mediation techniques discussed in the following chapter. If the child comes to school upset with a parent, the teacher can listen and perhaps help the child figure out how to talk to the parent about the problem. If the child continues to be upset or is upset about something that cannot be changed, the constructivist teacher tries to help the child let go of and master the difficult feelings by suggesting, "Sometimes you can make yourself feel better. Is there something you can do to make yourself feel better?" When a child seems to be in a destructive spiral of anger or self-pity, it sometimes helps to say, "You can decide to feel bad, or you can decide to feel better." Consider the following interaction between Peige Fuller (T) and a 4-year-old who has been in her class just a few days.

C: (Cries)
T: So, are these tears because something is upsetting you? What makes you sad?
C: I want my mommy.
T: Right. Did something in our classroom happen that made you very sad?
C: (Nods)
T: What happened?
C: I just want my mommy.
T: You just want your mommy? I see that you got your paper towel. Would you like to eat some snack?
C: (Shakes head)
T: No, okay. You know what you could do that would be a big help to us would be for you to have a seat here and help us to clean up some Legos. That would be a very big help. (She holds C in her lap while they pick Legos from the floor and put them in a container.)
(Later, C is still crying.)

T: (Stoops down to C's level, holds his hands in hers, and looks into his eyes.) C, I have to tell you this. You are making a choice to be very, very, very sad. If you would like to stop crying, that would be okay. We would know that you miss your mommy. But if you stop crying, you can make a choice to meet some new friends and play some fun stuff.

C: (Crying) But I miss my mommy.

T: She will pick you up this afternoon, but she can't pick you up now.

The construction of emotional balance and coping abilities is important for the construction of interpersonal understanding.

Promoting Construction of Interpersonal Understanding

Construction of interpersonal understanding is a process of decentering to think about the other's point of view and to figure out how to coordinate it with one's own through negotiation. We discuss in chapter 2 the developmental levels in negotiation strategies as well as shared experiences. As children come to be interested in the psychological states of others and in developing friendships, they construct a repertoire of different types of negotiation strategies and shared experiences of which they are capable. The constructivist teacher facilitates this construction by using advanced strategies, sometimes suggesting them in the context of conflicts, and generally supporting children's efforts to negotiate. For example, the constructivist teacher refers children to other children for help in activities and states children's different points of view in the context of conflict.

Shure and Spivack (1978) provide excellent examples of how to intervene in children's conflicts and how not to intervene. Because these reflect our principles of teaching so well, we reproduce them here. In the following instances, a mother intervenes in conflicts between her son and his playmate. The first example illustrates what *not* to do when the mother observes her child grabbing a toy. The reader may notice that the mother's interventions are mainly level 1 interpersonal understanding, as discussed in chapter 2.

> Mother: Why did you snatch that truck from John?
> Child: 'Cause it's my turn!
> M: Give it back, James.
> C: I don't want to. It's mine.
> M: Why don't you play with your cars?
> C: I want my firetruck!
> M: You should either play together or take turns. Grabbing is not nice.

C: But I want my truck now!

M: Children must learn to share, John will get mad and he won't be your friend.

C: But, Mom, he won't give it to me!

M: You can't go around grabbing things. Would you like it if he did that to you?

C: No.

M: Tell him you're sorry. (p. 32)

After training in Shure's Interpersonal Cognitive Problem Solving skills, another mother interacts in the following way when grabbing is observed. The reader will notice that the mother's interventions this time are level 2 interpersonal understanding.

Mother: What happened? What's the matter?

Child: He's got my racing car. He won't give it back.

M: Why do you have to have it back now?

C: ˈCause he's had a long turn.

Shure comments that the mother learned that her son had shared his toy, a fact that leads the mother to a different view of the problem than if she had immediately demanded that he share.

M: How do you think your friend feels when you grab toys?

C: Mad, but I don't care, it's mine!

M: What did your friend do when you grabbed the toy?

C: He hit me but I want my toy!

M: How did that make you feel?

C: Mad.

M: You're mad and your friend is mad, and he hit you. Can you think of a different way to get your toy back so you both won't be mad and so John won't hit you?

C: I could ask him.

M: And what might happen then?

C: He'll say no.

M: He might say no. What else can you think of doing so your friend will give you back your racing car?

C: I could let him have my MatchBox cars.

M: You thought of two different ways. (pp. 36–37)

These examples illustrate how the adult can promote cooperation among children by facilitating reflection on interpersonal feelings, consequences, and strategies. As children become more competent in interpersonal understanding and action, the sociomoral atmosphere changes accordingly.

Promoting Construction of Moral Values

Construction of moral values is a gradual process of building respect for others. Children do not develop respect for others unless they are respected. The teacher's expression of respect for children goes a long way toward establishing the foundation for construction of self-respect and respect for others. Respect for others rests on intellectual and emotional decentering to consider others' points of view. Through countless situations in which children experience sympathy, community, and clashes with others, the child constructs ideas of reciprocity among persons.

As recommended by Kohlberg (Power, Higgins, & Kohlberg, 1989) in his Just Community approach to adolescent moral education, the constructivist teacher facilitates construction of moral values by upholding fairness, submitting social and moral issues to children for discussion, and capitalizing on the issues that arise in the life of the classroom. Children in constructivist classrooms know that the group is a resource for solving social and moral problems. The group takes on moral authority to which children contribute and to which they feel commitment.

We generally recommend that the teacher not initiate group discussion of problems between two children. However, when many children are concerned about an individual's behavior, group discussion may be fruitful. For example, in our Lab School kindergarten, children come in one day from early morning outside time with a concern about H's behavior on the playground. N enters the classroom, saying, "We need to discuss the problem of H." The teacher, Coreen Samuel, asks if it is for the whole group or if it is something to do at activity time. N is too angry to wait, and other children join in her complaint. N explains, "H was hurting and tearing up my picture, and he threw me down on the hard platform slide." H denies this, saying he didn't remember pushing N down. N accuses, "Yes, you did! You're just lying so you can get out of the problem." Other children support N's story, and A (age 5 years) argues eloquently and passionately about the implications beyond this particular incident. She says:

> I think what we should do about it is let H know how we feel. These problems are really important because if we don't help these problems, they're not going to get any better and kids won't be taught very well and when they grow up, they're prob'ly not gonna' know—If we go on letting people hurt, people will learn to hurt. If we don't stop this, then people will learn to hurt when they grow up. And I don't think that's a very

good idea to leave these problems in front of us and not go ahead and help these problems.

The teacher follows up, "N, A said she saw the same thing with her eyes. She had a suggestion. Maybe you need to tell H how you feel about that. Do you want to talk to H since it's yours and his problem?" N says to H, "H, I don't like that when you push me down and try to tear my paper up." Other children also express concern about getting hurt on the playground. Coreen remarks, "It seems like the playground is not a fun place to be anymore." She asks, "What can those children do when they're having this kind of lack of control?" A again acts as the moral spokesperson:

> We should tell them how we feel. Everybody in the world has feelings. It's like I said, they'll grow up and hurt other people, and I'm not sure we can help it when they're all grown up. That's just the way they've learned and there's no other way they've learned.

Coreen emphasizes decentering, "What we try and tell children to do is to think of other people's feelings. Even the teachers do it. If you're really upset, then we think about what you might be feeling, and we try to help you." J offers, "It's not fun when you're fighting all the time." A once again speaks:

> You know, we're the big class, and we're trying to teach the little kids by our actions. I'm not sure if we're really showing them how a big kid should act—and then they're going to do the same thing when they're in our kindergarten class.

Coreen says, "Let's see what H has to say. Maybe he can help control himself. What can you do to make the playground a better place? It's no fun any more." H replies, "I can not hit." Coreen asks how he is going to work toward not doing that. Then H shows that he heard A's plea, yet assimilated it to Kohlberg's level 1 heteronomous morality motivated by fear of punishment (see chapter 9):

> Well, I think what the same thing A said. Like if you hurt someone and then when you grow up, then you'll learn that hitting is what you should do, and if you hit, then you'll get into trouble.

At this point, the teacher might ask, "Is there any other reason not to hit?" in order to make an opportunity for children to reflect beyond the level of avoiding punishment.

In this example, we see a feeling among the children of moral concern and responsibility that even goes beyond the immediate problem situation to long-term effects on the kindergarten children themselves as well as the younger children whom they influence.

SUMMARY

A constructivist sociomoral classroom atmosphere is based on the teacher's attitude of respect for children's interests, feelings, values, and ideas. The classroom is organized to meet children's physical, emotional, and intellectual needs. It is organized for peer interaction and child responsibility. Activities appeal to children's interests, experimentation, and cooperation. The teacher's role is to cooperate with children by trying to understand their reasoning and facilitating the constructive process. The teacher's role is also to foster cooperation among children by promoting their construction of emotional balance and coping abilities, interpersonal understanding, and moral values.

5

Conflict and Its Resolution

Conflicts are inevitable in an active classroom where free social interaction occurs. In many schools conflict is viewed as undesirable and to be avoided at all costs. We do not agree with this view. Instead, we see conflict and its resolution as essential to a constructivist curriculum. In this chapter, we discuss the role of conflict in development, review research on conflict resolution ability among children from the Boot Camp, Factory, and Community classrooms described in chapter 1, outline the constructivist teacher's general attitude toward conflicts, present principles of teaching with examples, and examine the situation of conflict between teacher and child.

THE ROLE OF CONFLICT IN DEVELOPMENT

It is easy to recognize the practical value of ability to resolve interpersonal conflict. If all adults had this ability, we would have world peace. Practical conflict resolution ability is an important constructivist goal. However, in Piaget's theory, the value of conflict is more complex, and the constructivist rationale also goes beyond the obvious value.

In constructivist theory, conflict takes two forms: intraindividual and interindividual. Piaget viewed both as critical for development, although his main focus was on the first form, intraindividual conflict—conflict within the individual. This conflict is evident, for example, when a child has the idea that the location of his shadow depends on his action. Having seen his shadow when he walked up to

79

one wall, he is surprised not to see it when he walks up to another. The contradiction between expectation and result can lead to a search for spatial and causal relations among object, light, and screen.

Another example of intraindividual conflict occurs during board games involving rolling a die to find out how many spaces to move on a path. As we explained in chapter 2, at a certain point in constructing number, many children apply their knowledge of one-to-one correspondence in a strict manner. They believe it is correct to count the space they are on as "1," rather than moving forward one on the count of "1," as plus-one logic dictates. Many children show obvious conflict when they roll a 1, say "1," and make no forward movement. What usually happens is a sort of stuttering "1—1" as they count the space they are on and then stumble forward one. In the course of such repeated experiences, children may profit from their internal cognitive conflict and restructure their logic. When children make this error, we recommend using a die with only 1s and 2s so they will have more opportunities to experience the conflict between their logic of acknowledging the starting space and their conflicting logic of making progress.

The second form of conflict is interindividual—conflict between individuals. Piaget argued that such conflict can promote both intellectual and moral development. This occurs through decentering from a single perspective to take into account other perspectives and is prompted by confrontation with the desires and ideas of others. Piaget (1928/1976) stated, "Social life is a necessary condition for the development of logic" (p. 80), and argued that when the child has the experience of others who react to the content of what he or she says, the child begins to feel that logical consistency and truth matter. Interpersonal conflict can provide the context in which children become conscious of others as having feelings, ideas, and desires. Increasing consciousness of others and efforts to coordinate self-other perspectives result in higher-level interpersonal understanding (see the discussion of Selman's developmental levels in chapter 2).

Interindividual conflict can lead to intraindividual conflict. For example, a child making the logical error of addition described above may play the game with another child who objects and demonstrates how to proceed correctly. Children often respond with greater openness to correction by children than correction by adults. However, as we see in chapter 2, correction of counting spaces in a board game may not be enough to convince the child who reasons that the occupied space must be acknowledged. In fact, sometimes the child making the logical error tries to correct the child who counts correctly. Interpersonal conflict can lead to motivation for thinking about how to proceed as an issue that elicits different opinions.

Conflict plays a special role in Piaget's constructivist theory. It serves to motivate reorganization of knowledge into more adequate forms. Piaget (1975/1985) stated that conflict is the most influential factor in acquisition of new knowledge structures. Conflicts may thus be viewed as a source of progress in development.

SOCIOMORAL ATMOSPHERE AND CONFLICT RESOLUTION

In the study described in chapters 1 and 2 (DeVries, Haney, & Zan, 1991; DeVries, Reese-Learned, & Morgan, 1991a), we wanted to find out whether children experiencing very different sociomoral classroom atmospheres would differ in sociomoral development. In comparing children from Boot Camp, Factory, and Community classrooms, we found that children from the constructivist Community classroom demonstrated greater interpersonal skill by resolving significantly more of their conflicts than children from Boot Camp and Factory classrooms. Without adult help, Community children resolved 70 percent of their conflicts (54 out of 77), Factory children resolved 33 percent (16 out of 48), and Boot Camp children resolved 40 percent (15 out of 37). Boot Camp children tended to end their conflicts by overwhelming the other physically or emotionally, whereas Factory children tended to ignore their playmates' grievances. Community children tried to work out their differences.

We studied these conflicts further and found that even within conflict periods when interpersonal understanding is most challenged, Community children still used significantly more level 2 negotiation strategies than either of the other groups. In addition, they had many more shared experiences in the course of their conflicts. This means that the tension of their conflicts was moderated by friendly overtures. We think the Community children were more successful because they had learned negotiation attitudes and strategies in their classroom and because they cared more about preserving their relationships.

The Constructivist Teacher's General Attitude Toward Children's Conflicts

As a result of observing and talking with teachers about handling conflict, we distinguish the teacher's general attitude that underlies specific principles of teaching. Thus, the first three principles of teaching underlie the fourteen principles presented in the next section.

1. Be Calm and Control Reactions

It takes practice, but the teacher should learn to appear calm in the face of children's sometimes violently upset states. Even if the teacher does not feel calm, it is important to communicate calmness to children. This means controlling body language, facial expressions, and tone of voice. The teacher should avoid acting on the first impulse or rushing to the rescue, except to prevent physical harm. Children will come to welcome this calm strength as a support for working through their difficulties.

2. Recognize That the Conflict Belongs to the Children

The constructivist teacher does not take on children's problems and impose a solution. He or she believes that it is important for children to take ownership of their conflicts. This attitude leads to the principles of teaching that support and facilitate children's resolution of their own conflicts.

3. Believe in Children's Ability to Solve Their Conflicts

Success in working with children in conflict situations depends on believing that children can solve conflicts. We are continually impressed with the competence of young children who have had the support of a constructivist sociomoral atmosphere, but a teacher will have to construct his or her own confidence out of experiences that reveal children's potentials.

Principles of Teaching in Conflict Situations

The following 14 principles of teaching have been conceptualized in the course of working with many teachers over more than 20 years, but especially in working with teachers in the HDLS during the past 13 years. We give examples that reveal ways in which respect is expressed for children in effective interventions.

1. Take responsibility for children's physical safety.

Clearly, the teacher should prevent physical harm, if possible. When a child is trying to hurt another, the teacher can put his or her arms loosely around the aggressor to prevent the harm. In this situation, the teacher should express how strongly he or she feels. Consider the following examples.

(In Peige's [T] Investigators class, K is crying.)
T: What's up, K?

K: S pushed me down.

T: S pushed you?

K: Yes.

T: Perhaps you should go talk to him about that. Tell him how it makes you feel. Do you feel ready to go talk?

K: (Seems to agree)

T: Let's go get S so you can talk to him about how you feel. S?

S: What?

T: We need you.

S: (Comes over and sits on T's lap)

T: Okay, K.

K: I don't it like when you push me down. That makes me sad.

T: She doesn't like it when you push her down. It makes her sad. Was there a problem that made you upset?

S: (Nods)

T: What happened that made you upset? Were you upset with K?

S: (Shakes head)

T: No, okay. But I have to tell you, S. If you are upset with K, if she does something to make you mad, you can talk to her. You can come and get my help, and I will help you talk to her or I will talk to her, too. But you know what, S? (Turns him to face her.) S, I'm not going to let you hit the children, but I won't let the children hit you, either. So if you're making the choice to do some talking in the classroom, then I can help you with that. When you're making the choice to do some hitting or pushing in the classroom, it's not going to work because I can't let you do that. Were you finished doing the PlaDoh, or do you want to do playdoh some more?

(Peige thus helps S move from the conflict into positive activity.)

In another situation in the Investigators class, R is crying and K stands by. They have been keeping score in a beanbag toss game. Peige (T) sees the incident from across the room. While comforting R, she explores the problem in the following way, in a matter-of-fact, nonjudgmental tone.

T: (Holds R) What's up, K?

K: I wanted to write my letters [score].

T: You wanted to write yours? Well, I have a question. When you started scratching him and pushing him down and all that stuff, did that help to decide who was going to write on your thing?

K: No, but I wanted to write my letter.

T: You wanted to write your letter. When you pushed him and

kicked him, did that let him know that you needed to write your
letter? Did pushing him down help you to write your letter?

K: No.

T: Maybe you could tell him with your words. He's right here. What
do you want to tell him? She has something she needs to tell you.
Okay, he's ready, and we're all ready.

K: I want to do my letters.

T: She wants to write her own letters. What can he write?

K: He can write his letters by himself.

T: You can write your own letters by yourself. But when it's your
time to write your stuff, who do you want to write it?

K: I remember I got 2 in.

T: You got 2 in? She got 2 in and she wanted to write all about it.

R: No.

T: No?

R: She didn't get 2 in.

T: Oh, he says you didn't get 2. How many did she get?

R: She got 1.

T: Oh, K, he says you didn't get 2. You got only 1. So can she write 2?

R: No.

T: How many can she write?

R: She can only write 1.

T: K, he says you can only write 1.

K: (Seems to agree)

T: What do you (R) have to say to K?

R: Nothing.

T: Nothing? Do you want to tell her how you were feeling about
being pushed? Yeah? How did that feel? Or, no, you don't want to
talk about it? No? Are you feeling better? Ready to do some activities? Maybe you guys could get it together and play beanbags
some more now that you know what each other needs.

Here, Peige discovers the root of the problem in a disagreement over
how many points K got. She gives an opportunity but does not press
R to talk about his feelings. She inquires as to whether he feels better
in order to be sure both children feel resolution. Satisfied that resolution has occurred in children's feelings, Peige orients the children
back into cooperative play.

2. Use nonverbal methods to calm children.

In addition to a calm response to children's conflict, it often helps to
stoop or sit and put an arm around each child. If children are too

upset to talk, give them time to pull themselves together before insisting on conversation.

3. Acknowledge/accept/validate all children's feelings and perceptions of the conflict.

Children have a right to feel the way they feel. Even when the teacher believes a child is guilty of violating the rights of another, it is important to respect that child's feelings. From his or her point of view, the actions may be justified. In addition, the adult should not assume understanding of a situation until hearing both sides of the story. "I can see that you both are upset. Can you tell me what happened?" After hearing what children have to say, the adult can acknowledge specific feelings. "You are sad because K took your car, and you are sad because J hit you." The reader will find many examples of this principle in transcripts illustrating other principles of teaching.

4. Help children verbalize feelings and desires to each other and to listen to each other.

It is important not to take sides but to help each child understand the other's point of view, to recognize the other's feelings, and to empathize. The verbal communications of young children are often not very coherent, and children thus often have difficulty understanding each other. In addition, children may not listen well to each other. Children often talk to the teacher instead of to each other. The teacher plays an important role as mediator, helping children to clarify their ideas, repeating them, and helping children exchange ideas and feelings. Consider the following situation in which Peige (T) works with 3-year-olds and tries to help C decenter to become aware of the consequences of pushing and pinching.

(Peige keeps her arm loosely around C as Z talks to her.)
Z: I don't like that when—I feel about that, I feel sad.
T: Oh, C, did you hear that? Look at Z's face. Z, can you tell C again?
Z: I don't like that and I—don't—
T: And how do you feel?
Z: I don't want to be your friend anymore.
T: (To C) You know, when you push, or when you pinch her, she doesn't want to be your friend.
C: (Struggles to get away) I'm going away. (She leaves.)
T: Are you feeling a little better about that, Z?
Z: (Nods)
T: Okay.

In this situation, C seems not to empathize or decenter to think about Z's feelings. However, she may have learned that pushing and pinching will result in a reaction. Z certainly seemed to gain consolation from expressing her feelings and from Peige's validation. Consider also the following argument between two 5-year-olds over use of materials. The teacher (T) is Karen Amos.

(In a boatbuilding activity, N takes a wooden board that is near E.)
E: I need it also. You are going to give it back to me.
N: (Runs away)
E: Hey, Karen, he won't give me that board back.
T: Did you use your words?
E: Yeah.
T: Maybe I'll go with you and you can use your words to him.
E: (To N) I need your wood back.
N: I've been using it.
E: I wanna' put it next to me (grabs wood)—
T: Wait. Can I hold it? (She takes board.)
E: —so I can make my boat.
T: Is this the last piece of wood left?
E: No, there's some more, but I need that.
T: But I wonder if N had this piece of wood and you just wanted it.
E: No, no.
T: Did you have it?
E: I have it.
N: No, I didn't see it in his hand.
E: I had it first.
N: I had it first.
T: You know, I heard N's words saying that he didn't see you holding this.
E: See, I'm putting it next to me because I couldn't hold all of it and put 'em all together.
T: I see. Was it right here, N?
N: Somewhere over here.
E: But it's still mine.
T: E had this next to his boat. He was going to use it. He said he couldn't hold on to all the pieces.
(At this point, another child, J, hands a board to E.)
T: So who should we give this (board in contention) to?
E: N.
T: Okay. Thanks for sharing, J.

Sometimes, children do not empathize. This happened in Peige's Investigators class of 4-year-olds. Z had been impervious to C's distress when Z pinched C. Later, when Z complains that W has hurt her, Peige (T) takes the opportunity to try to get Z to reflect on what her victim felt.

Z: W hurt my leg and I told him, and he kept on putting blocks in, and he was squishing me and hurt me right there. See that?

T: Oh, I see that you're very upset about it.

Z: Right there, that's what he did.

T: You know, Z, it's a problem, because this morning, C was so upset at you for hurting her, but did you help her to feel better?

Z: No.

T: No? Did you, that first time when you pinched her, did you stop hurting her, or did you hurt her some more?

Z: I hurt her some more.

T: See, I'm seeing that you're thinking that hurting is a good idea when you do it. Did you think it was a good idea when W hurt you?

Z: (Shakes her head) No.

T: But, see, I'm seeing that you think hurting is a good idea because you were hurting C. Maybe if you stop showing people that you think hurting is a good idea, then maybe people will know that Z thinks hurting is a bad idea and will think, "I will not hurt Z."

C: And if she hurts her friends, then she's not gonna' have lots of friends.

T: This is very true.

In the following incident, two 3-year-olds disagree over the use of materials. The teacher (T) is Karen Capo.

(H has placed a small ladder across the hole of the beanbag target. M does not want the ladder there.)

T: I'm sorry. I can't hear your words. Can you tell me again?

H: (Inaudible)

T: Oh, then to make it more exciting, you put that there? Is it harder to throw in there, or easier?

H: (Inaudible)

T: Well, M, do you think that would be a fun way to play with it?

M: (Inaudible)

T: Oh, H says it makes it fun for him.

M: It makes it bad.

T: Well, why don't you tell H about that. What would you like to tell him about it?

M: I don't know. (This transcription continues below, to illustrate the following principle of teaching.)

5. Clarify and state the problem.

When the teacher is clear about the problem, he or she should state it so both children understand what the other sees as the problem. Sometimes children are not talking about the same issue. The last conflict above continues:

T: Well, what do you think we should do, because H likes to play with it that way?

M: (Shrugs shoulders, says something inaudible)

T: H, H, you know what? (Sits on floor beside H) I see that we have a problem. You know what the problem is? (H continues to play with ladder and does not seem to be listening.) H, can you hear my words? I see that you would like to play with this (takes ladder). M says that he would *not* like to play with this. So what should you guys do?

H: I want him to play (inaudible).

T: M, can you hear his idea? What is your idea, H?

H: (Inaudible)

T: Did you hear his idea?

M: Um hmm. After we put it away (inaudible).

T: H, can you hear M's idea?

H: Yeah.

T: Let's listen to it. What is your idea, M?

M: I said—

H: (Throws bean bag, seems not to be listening)

T: H, let's listen to M's idea because I heard that he had an idea. (Teacher takes bean bag) H, we'll take just a minute out from playing with the bean bags so that we can hear the other idea. What was that other idea, M?

M: After you put it away, then you could get it out again.

T: Oh, does that sound like a good idea?

H: No, I want to do it like this.

T: H wants to do it right now.

M: Well, he may play for 2 more seconds with that red thing (points to ladder) and then I'll (points to hole and ladder). Well, maybe we could share, I don't know.

T: Maybe you could share? Do you think you could share, H? M said that would work.

H: (Inaudible)

T: Okay! You know what, when you guys give it a try, let me know if you need any help, but I'll bet you can figure it out. (Upon observing a cooperative attitude and, feeling the boys can work it out, she leaves.)

(H and M succeed in playing together, tossing the beanbag at the hole.)

6. Give children the opportunity to suggest solutions.

In the conflict over whether to use the ladder across the beanbag target hole, Karen Capo is careful after stating the problem to ask, "So what should you guys do?" "What is your idea?" Children often suggest solutions that do not seem like solutions to us, but what is important is that children feel satisfied. Karen therefore does not veto any suggestion but simply turns to the other child to find out whether that is agreeable.

7. Propose solutions when children do not have ideas

Children do not always have ideas about solutions. In this situation, the teacher can propose an idea for children's consideration. These suggestions should be proposals, not impositions. Consider the following situation in the pretend center. Peige (T) employs other principles of teaching until she sees that the children are at an impasse. As she notices the children arguing, she approaches.

T: What's up, you guys?

G: This daddy's rocking chair. This daddy's rocking chair. (To M) You don't live here, and you don't live in that chair (tries to pry M out of chair).

T: M, I don't think it's ever going to be solved if you sit there and not talk. You'll probably have to talk to tell him what you think about it.

M: Um, but you got out of the chair and I got in.

G: Well, you're not supposed to live here. We do. We're supposed to live here. You don't live here. This daddy's rocking chair.

M: I'm sorry. I—you got out and I got in.

T: He said you got out and he got in.

G: Well, this was daddy's rocking chair.

T: Well, but did daddy get out?

G: Well, we went to go out to eat, and then we came back to the home.

T: And so—
C: And when—where—when he goes out to eat, I don't come and
    get his things.
T: When you go out to eat, she doesn't come and get your things.
M: Because I don't live here.
C: But we live here.
G: Well, we live here, yeah.
T: They say they live here and you live somewhere else.
K: Because I'm the sister.
G: Yeah, yeah, and I'm your mommy, right?
M: Then what's C doing here? C's not supposed to be here.
T: Maybe he's a brother. Would you like to be a brother?
M: (Nods)
T: He said he would like to be a brother.
C: Okay, and this will be another sister, and then we're gonna' have
    another brother, and that's the last one.
M: (Jumps out of chair to join C as a brother)

In another incident, the same teacher notices that D is trying to grab
the basketball from Y. D is a disturbed child with some autistic-like
behaviors who has great difficulty relating to other children. Peige
says, "You know what, Y? You could have a turn at throwing, and you
could give it to D and D could have a turn at throwing, and then D
could give it to you, and you could have a turn at throwing." To D, she
prompts, "If you would like to have a turn, why don't you ask Y. Say,
'Y, you have a turn. Then I have a turn.'"

8. Uphold the value of mutual agreement, and give children the opportunity to reject proposed solutions.

An important part of the constructivist teacher's role is to insist on
the importance of working out agreements. Sometimes, it is tempting
to accept the first solution offered without making sure the other
child agrees. In the conflict over the ladder in the beanbag toss activity, the teacher asks H for his idea. Then she turns to M, "Did you hear
his idea?" After making sure that H hears M's idea, she asks, "Does
that sound like a good idea?" Consider also the following example in
which two 5-year-olds both want to be first in a game. Here, it
becomes clear that competing in the game rests within a framework
of cooperation. The teacher (T) is Rebecca Krejci.

T: Who should go first?
Y: Me.

C: Me.

T: You both want to go first.

Y: Bubble Gum, Bubble Gum (begins rhyme, pointing alternately to himself and C).

C: I don't like to do "Bubble Gum, Bubble Gum."

Y: Let's take a vote.

C: No, there aren't enough people who want to vote.

The strategies of both children are above the bald insistence on what they want. They focus on the method for deciding. The teacher moderates to keep the discussion going.

T: Okay, so far we've talked about "Bubble Gum, Bubble Gum" or voting, and you don't like either of those. What do you think, C?

C: I think that I'll just pick who goes first.

T: Y, do you like that idea?

Y: No.

T: No?

C: I'll just pick.

Y: No, I said that first. And then you came and speaked when I was speaking. So, I'm just gonna do "Bubble Gum, Bubble Gum."

C: Okay, but that sure does disturb me.

Y's insistence on what he wants brings another impasse, with each child repeating his solution. C grudgingly agrees to go along with Y, but expresses his unhappiness. The problem for the teacher is to respect C's feelings but try to get him to consider the idea of fairness.

T: Do you think "Bubble Gum, Bubble Gum" would be all right with you, C?

C: It's not all right with me, but if he wants to do it (shrugs).

T: Do you think your picking would be fair, C?

Y: No, I don't think C should pick.

With the impasse reasserted, the teacher continues to give the responsibility to the children for coming to agreement, but upholds the value of mutual agreement. By respecting the ideas of both children, she expresses the idea that conflict resolution should consider everyone's feelings.

T: Let's see if y'all can decide on something that you both like.

C: I just wanta' pick somebody. I don't like "Bubble Gum, Bubble Gum."

Y: All right. (He decides to try voting.) Who says to do "Bubble Gum, Bubble Gum?" (He raises his hand.)

C: Nobody. I don't.

Y: (Turns to teacher) Do you wish to do "Bubble Gum?"

T: Well, if I vote, then whatever I say will happen because you both disagree.

C: It's okay with me if you do whatever you want because you're the adult.

The teacher tries to move the children's thinking beyond identifying fairness with whatever the adult authority wants by upholding the idea of the importance of agreement among players.

T: But y'all are playing the game, too. I think y'all should decide, too.

C: Well, I'd just like to pick.

T: Do you have any other ideas, Y?

Y: Well, you need to vote, too.

C: Well, Y, the only thing that doesn't disturb me is "eeney, meeney, miney, moe." You can say that, but not "Bubble Gum, Bubble Gum."

Y: OK. Eeney, Meeney, Miney, Moe.

9. Teach impartial procedures for settling disputes where decision is arbitrary.

As shown in the example above, some of children's disagreements involve privileges that can only be decided arbitrarily. It is helpful to teach children ways of making arbitrary decisions in an impartial way. In the following example, Peige (T) teaches A and N to play a board game. These 4-year-olds know that saying "eenie, meenie, miney, moe" is a method for settling disputes, but they have constructed only part of the form of the procedure.

T: Who goes first?

A: Me!

N: Me!

A: I never get—

N: I want to—

A: You always say that! I never get a turn (folds arms and pouts).

T: (Imitates A) Oh, I don't, either. How shall we decide?

N: Just go "eenie, meenie, miney, moe."

T: Okay.

A: Eenie, meenie, miney, moe (simply recites the rhyme).

N: You're not pointing!
T: You're not pointing!
A: (Starts over) Eenie, meenie, miney, moe. Catch a monkey by the toe. If he hollers, let him go. My mommy told me to pick the very first one and it is me. (As he recites, A points vaguely, then obviously waits to point to himself.)
N: (Looks at the teacher with doubtful expression)
T: Is that okay?
N: Maybe.
T: Maybe. Okay. And then you'll go next and I'll go after you.
N: Yeah.

Peige offers N an opportunity to protest, recognizing that he is not quite satisfied. However, in the interest of moving the game forward, she does not probe his grudging agreement.

We should point out that one can identify developmental levels in the use of rhymes. Initially, children simply view them as a sort of ritual. Then they seem to try to use the procedure to get their own way and use their intelligence to figure out how to make the procedure favor themselves. At a certain point, they "wise up" to others' similar efforts and argue over who will administer the rhyme procedure since whoever says the rhyme gets the privilege! When children no longer view rhyme procedures as an impartial mechanism, the teacher may propose other procedures such as drawing a number, choosing red or black and drawing from a bag of checkers, etc.

10. When both children lose interest in a conflict, do not pursue.

Dora Chen receives a complaint from M, a 4-year-old in the Investigators class. She cannot immediately go with him. When she is able to follow him, she finds the problem has either dissipated or has been solved. "Did you talk to C about it? Is your problem solved or not? Are you all done? Yes? Okay." Making sure the children are both satisfied with their resolution, Dora also lets it drop.

11. Help children recognize their responsibility in a conflict situation.

Frequently, an aggrieved child has contributed in some way to a conflict. It is helpful to children to realize their role in a misunderstanding or altercation. Consider the following example of a conflict in which Karen Amos (T) intervenes. For some reason, the children think it is interesting to put scotch tape over their mouths. M jerks the tape off D's mouth and hurts D, who responds by pinching M.

(M and D are running. They fall over each other, with M grabbing D's shirt.)

T: M, what's wrong?

M: He pinched me.

D: Because you (inaudible), and I had—because he took the tape off [my mouth], and I didn't want to. I didn't take the tape off of you when you put the tape on you.

T: Did he pinch you?

M: Right here.

D: No, no, except he-he-he did that first.

T: He did what first? Put the tape over your mouth?

M: No, he took it off.

T: And so when he took it off your mouth really hard, how did that feel?

D: Not fun because it scratched my face up.

T: It scratched your face, so what did you do after that?

D: Pinch him.

T: Hmmm. Do you know why he pinched you, M?

M: Yeah, I didn't pull it off hard (demonstrates).

D: Nuh uh. That's really hard. That's fast. Fast is hard.

T: How did it feel when you pulled your own tape off?

M: I pulled it off soft.

T: Hmmm.

M: I pulled it off hard.

T: How did it feel?

M: I didn't feel anything.

T: You didn't feel anything? Well, D did, and it really made him angry, and that's why he chose to pinch you. It's not really okay. What should you do instead of pinching?

D: I don't like (inaudible).

T: You don't like what? What did he do you didn't like?

D: I didn't like when he took that tape off hard.

T: So can you tell him that now?

D: I don't like when you took that tape off hard.

M: I don't like it when you pinched me.

T: Can you understand why he did that? I know he probably should have used his words, but do you understand why he did it?

M: (Nods)

T: You didn't use your words. So what should you do, M, the next time if you see that D has tape on his mouth again? What should you say to D?

M: Take the tape off.

T: And what do you think D would probably do? Is it okay now? You
     guys are not angry any more? Is it okay?
(The boys assent, and return to their play.)

12. Offer opportunity for restitution if appropriate.

When one child has violated another, it is important to make restitution possible. If the offending child can do something to make the
other feel better, he or she will be less likely to carry forward feelings of guilt or resentment. Restitution paves the way for reestab-
lishing a friendly relation after the conflict ends and also helps the
perpetrator maintain a positive image—in the eyes of both self and
others. When physical hurt occurs, the teacher should show concern and appeal to empathy, "What do his tears show us about how
he's feeling?" The teacher may ask, "What could you do to make him
feel better?" If the child suggests something, the teacher should ask
the injured child, "Would that make you feel better?" Once the
injured party agrees, the teacher can help the perpetrator carry out
the restitution. In our Lab School, favorite restitutions are to take
the injured child to the kitchen to get some ice and/or a Band-Aid to
put on the hurt. Sometimes, a hug is healing when angry feelings
have dissipated.

In the following example from Peige's Investigators class, children plant flower seeds in small containers. Some children take their
seeds home while others leave them at school in order to watch them
grow. S pulls up C's plant, breaking it off at the roots. C cries, and
Peige (T) takes both children aside to talk with them. What follows is
an edited recounting of a long discussion between S, C, and Peige.

T: All right, S, you pulled her flower out of her flower pot. You didn't
     pull the root up with it, so it will not grow now. What will you do
     about this?
S: I don't know.
T: Hmmm. Do you have a flower?
S: No.
T: No? Why not?
S: My mom must have took it home.
T: Well, since your mom took your flower home, does that mean
     that you can rip up other people's flowers?
S: Yes.
T: Do you think you would like it if C went to your house and ripped
     up your flower?
S: No.

T: So you have your flower. The problem is that you have pulled up
    C's flower. What will you do about this?
C: I want to put this back in so it will grow.
(Peige accepts C's desire to replant the flower as a worthwhile exper-
    iment, but explains that without roots, it probably will not grow.)
S: I want to go clean up.
T: But, S, you have not come up with a solution. You have pulled up
    C's plant, and now she doesn't have a plant. What are you going
    to do about it?
S: I don't know.
T: C, do you have any ideas about what he could do?
C: I don't know.
T: I don't know, either.
C: He's not supposed to do that.
T: He was not supposed to do that.
C: It's gonna' take a long time for another one to grow.
(They talk about how long it takes for plants to grow.)
T: Well, S, I can't think of what you can do, either, to make this bet-
    ter for her. I'm out of ideas.
S: How about more seeds?
T: Put more seeds in there?
S: Yeah.
T: If we have more seeds. We'll have to ask Coreen (kindergarten
    teacher) because she used the seeds. Why don't you guys go ask
    Coreen if there are any more seeds?
(This solution satisfies C, and so the two children leave to get more
    seeds and replant them for C.)

Peige places the responsibility for making restitution squarely on S's
shoulders. She does not blame him but merely states matter-of-factly
that since he pulled up C's plant, he must do something to make it better for C. Her question to S about whether he would like it if C pulled
up his flower served a dual purpose—to help S see the situation from
C's perspective and to illustrate the inadequacy of an "eye-for-an-eye"
solution. Eventually, S thinks of finding another seed and replanting it.
C is happy with the solution, and S is restored to favor in C's eyes.

    We would like to point out that we never ask children to apolo-
gize. This view is a reaction to the prevalence in homes and schools
of such insistence that leads children simply to say the words that
get the adult "off the child's back." Forced apologies are usually
insincere and operate against decentering and the development of
empathy.

13. Help children repair the relationship, but do not force children to be insincere.

Coreen (T) encounters a seriously ruptured relationship between two 5-year-old best friends, R and N, during clean-up. She does not see how the problem began. As we learn later, R accidentally caused a bump on N's head. In this case, other children intervene, as well as the teacher. In this abbreviated account, we see efforts of several children to assist R and N. G, in particular, shares insights based on experiences of her conflicts with a friend.

R: It was a mistake. My hand (inaudible).
N: Shut up!
R: Now you stop that!
S: Are you guys fighting?
T: Yeah, what's—
R: I'm not your friend.
S: You guys, stop fighting.
R: (Walks over to N and hits her)
N: Don't hit!
T: Okay, R, I need you to use your words. You can just choose to not be her friend, but you can't hit her. That's not okay. Would it be okay for teachers to let her hit you when she's angry at you? Sometimes you get angry with your friends, but you can tell them with your words that you are angry.
R: She doesn't want to solve the problem! That's okay with me.
T: She doesn't?
N: Yes, I do.
R: No, she doesn't.
N: I do, but—
R: She does not, either! She does not because she's covering her ears. So that's why I'm not going to talk to her.
T: You're covering your ears?
N: I first did, because I did not want to (inaudible).
T: Oh, maybe that's why she feels like you don't want to listen to her. But if you want to listen to her, you—
N: I want to solve the problem!
R: Well, I'm not solving the problem with *you*!
T: Hmmm.
N: You got to.
R: Well, I'm not solving it.
T: I think R is really upset now, and she's not ready. Do you need some time, R? She's not ready right now. Maybe she could have

some time. Is that okay, N, if she has a few minutes? It's not okay? You want to solve it now?

R: Well, I'm not even solving it, even if you don't give me a little bit of time.

T: Does this mean you're never going to be friends again?

R: (Shakes head)

G: (Strong, skeptical tone) Ah, well, R, I don't know about that. Sometimes friends get into big fights, like me and C get into big fights, but we get over it.

T: Yeah, they do.

G: Don't we, C?

T: And you guys (R and N) get over it, too. You got over it in the past. Maybe you can try what you did last time. What did you do last time?

N: What we did is we stayed away from each other for a while. And then one day, R came up to me and (inaudible).

T: Well, maybe that will work again. Why don't you try that again? She looks like she needs some time. I don't want to force her to talk right now.

N: Sometimes I come up to R and I say sometimes, "Why don't we play?"

T: So it happens both ways?

G: Sometimes N gets mad with R.

R: Look! Why don't you just leave me alone, N!

G: Sometimes N gets mad with R, and then R tries to make N feel better, and now, R got mad with N, just on the case of the bump on the head. And N is trying to make R feel better. So I guess they both really love each other a whole lot, but sometimes friends can get into fights.

T: Yeah.

G: Like me and C are best friends. Sometimes we get into fights, don't we, C?

C: We fight like cats and dogs sometimes.

(Children ask to go outside, and the teacher gives permission. R leaves the room. Coreen and N remain in the room and put blocks away together.)

T: I'm so glad you have patience and are able to wait on R.

R: (Comes back just inside room) N, I'm going outside.

(N follows R outside and joins a game of "Mother, May I?" R watches N, does not join game. She looks unhappy.)

N: You want to be in the game? It's fun. You go 1, 2, 3 (kicks up her legs in imitation of giant steps, causing sand to fly up).

(Both laugh, and N puts her arm around R and steers her toward the game.)

In another situation, two kindergarten boys get into an intense conflict over what occurs in a checkers game. J legitimately jumps one of K's checkers, but K honestly believes J had illegitimately taken two turns in a row. They cannot agree, and their argument deteriorates into upsetting the board and sweeping pieces off the table onto the floor. When the teacher intervenes, J and K cry and scream at each other incoherently. The teacher tries to talk with each one individually, but this does not work as the boys continue to scream at each other while putting their hands over their ears. A bystander, E, comments, "They're not listening to each other." The teacher asks K and J to stay apart until they are ready to talk, and J goes to the bathroom while K sits at a table. Amazingly, K immediately begins watching until J reappears. From across the room, K begins a kind of peek-a-boo with J and imitates J's stiff-legged side-to-side rocking. Upon catching J's attention, K blows on his arm, making a rude sound. When J laughs, K approaches him. Intercepting K, the teacher asks, "What do you think we should do first, talk or clean up?" K replies to the teacher, "Clean up," and to J proposes, "Let's clean up." The teacher asks J if he wants to clean up with K. K and J grin at each other and start picking up checkers from the floor. K continues to blow on his arm, to J's shocked delight.

The relationship is thus repaired by silliness that enables the boys to reestablish a positive interaction. With this story, we simply want to call the reader's attention to the fact that children may have their own ways of repairing a relationship. In this case, they could not resolve the argument itself, but the strength of their friendship and desire to be back on good terms led them to their own solution.

14. Encourage children to resolve their conflicts by themselves.

The long-range goal is for children to be able to resolve their conflicts without teacher intervention. Constructivist teachers therefore refrain from intervening if children are solving or can solve their problems. When children come to complain about another child's actions, Lab School teachers encourage children to deal with the problem themselves. "What could you say to him?" "Can you use your words and tell him you don't like that?" "Can you figure out how to solve that problem?" If children need help, the teacher, of course, responds.

In a constructivist sociomoral atmosphere, children develop an attitude of generally wanting to resolve conflicts and use a wide variety of negotiation strategies. The pleasure and intimacy of shared experiences provide a general context for the ripening of close relationships and the desire to maintain them. Consider the following conflict among three close kindergarten friends, M, D, and N, who are playing a game of Concentration. They take turns turning up two tiles at a time, trying to get a match. N pretends to play the guitar and sings, "I've got to rock-a-my—." M expresses disappointment when D and N fail to get a match, as well as when he fails.

M: (Turns tiles, screams) Look, I got a match! Look, I got a match! (Here, we must tell the reader that M is an exceptionally bouncy and exuberant child whose piercing screams have been the object of class discussions.)

D: M, don't scream.

M: (Looks sad)

D: Doesn't that hurt your ears, N?

M: (Turns his back on the group and puts his head on his folded arms)

N: No.

D: It hurts my ears. N, does it hurt yours just a little bit?

N: Ah, you made him sad, that's all.

D: (To M) I'm sorry, you can be my friend. You were just hurting my ears a little bit.

N: Well, he didn't hurt my ears. I didn't make him cry. You did. But that's all right 'cause I can make him feel better (goes to M and looks into his face).

D: He was just hurting my ears a little bit.

N: M, do you want to play, M?

M: (Turns with a cheerful look) Do you know what, N? Look, I've got a match!

D: And I've got a match! (Shows M)

M: Yeaaa!

N: I've got a hundred match.

M: And I've got a match! (Shows D)

D: And I've got a match! (Shows M)

M: You've got a match!

N: Let's don't play this game.

This is the kind of enacted interpersonal understanding that we hope will result from the constructivist sociomoral atmosphere.

CONFLICT BETWEEN TEACHER AND CHILD

Conflict between teacher and child is not unusual. It occurs when a child becomes angry at a teacher for actions the child sees as unfair or for actions the child simply dislikes. Conflict also occurs when the teacher becomes angry at a child. We discuss these situations below.

When the Child Thinks the Teacher Is Unfair

Perception of unfairness results when the child feels misunderstood. This problem is avoided when the teacher makes concerted efforts to understand children and refrains from judging and blaming children. The principles of teaching discussed above include safeguards against feelings of misunderstanding. Such feelings do not usually develop when the teacher is careful to accept children's feelings and perceptions, clarify and state problems from all points of view, and engage children in focusing on how to solve a problem. When a child does feel misunderstood and angry or hurt, the teacher should acknowledge and accept this feeling, then work to let the child know he or she is concerned about the child's feelings.

Sometimes children do not, and/or cannot understand the adult's actions. This is sometimes the case despite the teacher's best efforts to explain. In these rare situations, the teacher may only be able to communicate regret that the child is upset. It is then important to find a way to reestablish the relationship.

When the Child Dislikes What the Teacher Does

The teacher is sometimes surprised to find that a child is upset with him or her. In such a situation, the comments above also apply. Efforts to explain and reestablish the relationship are important. We remember one occasion in a kindergarten when a child could not accept the group's vote to act out a different story from the one he wanted. He began to cry. In this situation, the teacher had to uphold the majority rule. She acknowledged his disappointment and tried to console him by indicating that they would be able to act out his story on another day. It is important to the children in the majority to empathize with the minority's feelings. In the face of severe disappointment, the teacher may wish to consult the group as to whether they want to plan a compromise. In some cases, however, it is not possible to carry out what the minority wishes. One of the goals is for children to overcome egocentric attitudes and accept majority rule for the sake of maintaining membership in the group.

When the Teacher Becomes Angry with a Child

Most of the time, teachers can manage their feelings and take a professional attitude in relation to children. However, being human, teachers sometimes become angry with children, despite all professional efforts to keep such emotions under control. We know of cases in which teachers have become angry with a child for hurting another. We also know of situations in which a teacher becomes angry at being hit or kicked by a child.

When a teacher becomes so upset with a child that he or she has difficulty staying in control, we must still ask the teacher for the control to take himself or herself out of the role of mediator. The teacher cannot effectively mediate a conflict when he or she is one of the participants. In such a situation, two options are open. One method is for the teacher to explain to the child that he or she is too angry or upset to talk about it immediately and wants to wait until he or she is more in control. Then, the teacher should follow through and find a time to talk with the child about the problem calmly when anger will not be destructive to the child. The second option is to seek another teacher to serve as mediator. Then the teacher can express his or her point of view, listen to the child's view, and try to come to a resolution.

SUMMARY

In this chapter, we examine the role of conflict in development, noting the two forms of conflict in Piaget's theory. Intraindividual conflict (within the individual) is discussed as the particular source of progress in cognitive development. Interindividual conflict (between individuals) can elicit intraindividual conflict and is thus also an important source of cognitive and moral progress. Interindividual conflict is an important context for children's development of negotiation strategies and the interpersonal understanding they reflect. Research suggests the constructivist sociomoral atmosphere is a better context for promoting the development of higher levels of interpersonal understanding than authoritarian atmospheres. The constructivist teacher's general attitude toward children's conflicts must be one of remaining calm and controlling reactions, recognizing that conflicts belong to the children involved, and believing in the children's abilities to solve their own conflicts. Specific strategies for dealing with children's conflicts are spelled out in 14 principles of teaching. Finally, the case of conflict between teacher and child is discussed. When a child becomes angry with the teacher, it is the teacher's task to find a way to reestablish the relationship. On the rare occasions when the teacher becomes angry with a child, he or she must retain enough self-control to remove himself or herself from the situation. If later discussion of the problem is difficult, the teacher must find someone else to take the role of mediator between teacher and child.

6

Grouptime

Of all the classroom activities, grouptime may be the most critical in terms of the sociomoral atmosphere. For many teachers it may also be the most difficult and challenging time of the day. In this chapter we discuss constructivist objectives of grouptime. We outline the role of the teacher in planning and leading grouptime, discuss activities for grouptime, and present recommendations for conducting grouptime. Finally, we tell a story of one class's experience with problem grouptimes.

OBJECTIVES FOR GROUPTIME

Objectives for grouptime fall into two broad categories: sociomoral and cognitive. We discuss these two domains separately, but remind the reader that they are in fact inseparable.

Sociomoral Objectives

The primary objective of grouptime is to promote social and moral reasoning. This aim leads constructivist teachers to build a sense of active community among children, engage children in self-governance, and involve children in thinking about specific social and moral issues.

To build community, teachers use activities that promote a feeling of belonging together. Favorite songs and fingerplays engage children in a repertoire of shared rituals, and contribute to a feeling of group identity. Cohesion can also arise from group identity symbolized in class names. At the HDLS at the University of Houston, for example, classes are called (in order of age) the Explorers, the Experimenters, the Investigators, and the Inventors. These names are especially meaningful to the older children who discuss what it means to be investigators or inventors.

Constructivist teachers engage children gradually in self-governance. In planning group projects and sharing responsibility for taking care of their class, children experience group purposes that transcend the needs and wants of the individual. As children participate in making rules, dealing with class problems, proposing and choosing among options for class activities, and making other decisions, they learn numerous lessons in democracy. They learn that all voices are given the chance to be heard, that no one opinion is given more weight than another, and that they do have power to decide what happens in their class. Children practice mutual respect and cooperation as they work together, listen to each other, exchange opinions, negotiate problems, and vote to make decisions that affect the whole group. We discuss decision-making and voting in chapters 7 and 8.

Constructivist teachers promote moral reasoning through discussion of both real-life and hypothetical social and moral dilemmas. The aim is for children to develop feelings of necessity about what is right and wrong, good and bad, fair and unfair. Social and moral discussions are the topic of chapter 9.

Underlying all these sociomoral activities is the general goal of promoting children's decentration from a single perspective to consider and try to coordinate multiple perspectives. This leads to concerns with fairness and justice in the community in which people care about each other.

Cognitive Objectives

The first cognitive objective for grouptime is to promote the general development of reasoning and intelligence. Decentering to consider and coordinate points of view is an intellectual as well as social and moral endeavor.

Our second cognitive goal of grouptime is to promote knowledge construction in a variety of content domains. Grouptime is an occasion for focusing on an unlimited range of specific cognitive contents. These include logico-mathematical knowledge when children reason about number in varied activities such as attendance, the calendar, addition and subtraction embedded in songs and fingerplays, and votes. Logico-mathematical and physical knowledge are promoted when children are encouraged to think about what will happen in demonstrations of physical knowledge activities such as sinking and floating, or experimentation with parachutes. Children come into contact with printed texts through listening to stories, noticing the written names of classmates, and thinking about how to write and read words in songs, stories, project plans, votes, and so forth. Conventional and logico-mathematical knowledge are involved in thinking about the days of the week, months, holidays, and special themes (such as names and classification of dinosaurs). Cognitive aspects of grouptime, including the definition of the three types of knowledge, are discussed further in chapter 15.

THE ROLE OF THE TEACHER

The teacher's role in grouptime is twofold. First, prior to grouptime, the teacher makes plans. A good grouptime does not occur spontaneously, but requires careful planning. Second, during grouptime, the teacher takes a leadership role somewhat different from the role of the teacher at other times of the day. We discuss these separately.

Planning for Grouptime

Planning for grouptime is important if it is to go smoothly. We have noticed that teachers most successful with grouptime often bring a written agenda that includes an alternative or two in case children do not respond to something introduced. Agendas differ, depending on the type of grouptime. Some grouptimes are storytimes. Some are convened to play group games involving the whole class. Class meetings may be called to deal with special problems or plan projects. We describe a clean-up grouptime in chapter 12.

Generally, the morning opens with a grouptime welcome that includes shared experiences of songs, fingerplays, attendance, identifying the day's Special Helper, marking the calendar, and presenting the day's special activities. Grouptime is a good time to intrigue children with physical knowledge or art activities that can be pursued during activity time. If a demonstration is planned, the teacher should try it out ahead of time to make sure it works. Having everything at hand is essential in order to avoid getting up and disrupting the attention of the group.

Particular plans for grouptime will depend on the needs, abilities, and interests of the group. Some groups may be able to handle choosing what song they want to sing, or what book they want to hear, while the teacher will need to decide for other groups. Likewise, when engaging children in planning or decision making, the teacher must exercise discretion concerning what sorts of decisions children can make and what things are better decided by adults.

The Teacher as Leader

As stated earlier, the role of the teacher during grouptime is somewhat different from other times of the day. During activity time, children generally take the lead in pursuing their play and work. The teacher's role, as we discuss further in chapter 11, is to support, suggest, and facilitate children's purposes. The teacher strives to be equal in power with children. During grouptime, however, the teacher must be a leader. Some constructivist teachers have told us that they felt uncomfortable in the leader's role because it felt heteronomous. They found it difficult to balance these two seemingly contradictory roles. We try to show how these two roles are not contradictory but are in fact complementary.

The specific ways in which the teacher exercises leadership without unnecessary authority are discussed in the next section on conducting grouptime. Let us simply say here that leadership at grouptime is a legitimate role for the constructivist teacher. The teacher should not be timid about leading group. We have seen teachers who were confused about how to balance equality with leadership raise their hands when they wanted to talk or ask permission to say something. These actions confuse children. It is necessary to be clear about who is leading group. If a child is taking the leadership role (we have seen this done very effectively with kindergarten children), then the teacher should act like a member of the group, and follow the customary practices such as hand raising. But if the teacher is leading group, then he or she should lead without feeling apologetic.

Having in mind the general goals and objectives of constructivist education will help the teacher keep the leadership role in perspective. That is, the goal of grouptime is *not* to sing the song, read the story, or do the calendar. These activities are in the service of broader, long-term goals, goals such as the development of self-regulation, cooperation, and perspective-taking. The role of the teacher is to facilitate the children's development by creating an environment that fosters these goals. Especially when faced with grouptimes where children are restless, where no one wants to sing or sit still or listen, keeping these long-term goals in mind will help the teacher know what to do next, whether that is to end grouptime early, to do something totally different, or to engage children in a discussion of what to do when no one wants to participate.

Leadership does not translate into coercive power. Effective leadership relies on appeals to reason, mutual respect, and shared responsibility. Adults recognize that it is much easier to follow a respectful and reasonable leader than a coercive and punitive one. Children are no different from adults in this respect. They will be much more inclined to cooperate with a leader who is reasonable and respectful toward them.

CONDUCTING GROUPTIME

In this section on the "nitty-gritty" of grouptime, we focus on what to do and how to do it. We cover three aspects of grouptime: formal aspects, management, and content. We conclude with some examples of fruitful grouptime activities.

Formal Aspects of Grouptime

Formal aspects include seating arrangements and length of grouptime.

Seating Arrangements

We recommend that grouptime be conducted on the floor in a circle so that children can see each other. Unless it is physically impossible, the teacher should also sit on the floor as part of the circle. This serves as a tangible symbol that the teacher is one of the group. The exception to this would be during storytime, when it is appropriate for the teacher to sit on a chair so that children can see the book.

Some teachers insist that children sit with their legs crossed and their hands folded in their laps. We find this injunction unnecessary and coercive. As long as children are not hurting others, interfering with others' ability to see, or disrupting group with flailing limbs, we believe that it is more respectful to allow children to sit in the position they find most comfortable.

Whether children's places in circle should be determined by the teacher or decided by children depends on children's self-regulation ability. We have seen classes where the teacher needed to determine places because some children could not control themselves when seated next to certain others. One way to do this is to use mats with children's names on them. The teacher can decide where to place the mats in a circle before children come to grouptime. Another approach that can work for older children is to discuss the problem with children privately. The teacher can say something to the effect of, "I know that you and ＿＿ are special friends and like to play together, but when you play at grouptime, it disturbs us, and you miss out on what we are doing. What can we do to solve this problem?" With teacher support and appreciation, the child often decides not to sit beside the friend. The general constructivist goal is for children to be self-regulating, so allowing children to decide where they want to sit is a reasonable long-term goal.

The teacher should be in place before the first child comes to circle, and grouptime can begin when the first child sits down. Favorite songs, fingerplays, and other rituals give the children already at circle something to do while others arrive, and provide an attraction for the stragglers. Some teachers have songs that are only sung to bring children to grouptime so that whenever the teacher begins to sing the song, children know to come to circle.

Length of Grouptime

The length of grouptime is a practical decision that depends on children's interest and ability to focus. We simply encourage teachers to be sensitive to the needs and abilities of the children. Generally, grouptimes will be 5–10 minutes for children under 3 years old, 10–20 minutes for 3–4-year-olds, and 30 minutes for 5-year-olds and older. These times are only approximations. If children are engaged and interested in a topic and are not becoming restless, grouptime can last longer. We have seen 30-minute grouptimes with 3-year-olds, and 45-minute grouptimes with 4-year-olds on occasion, when they were very interested in a topic. If children are interested but restless, the teacher can end grouptime and tell the children that they will resume talking about the topic at the next circle time.

Management Strategies

As it is often difficult for young children to sit quietly, focus on one topic, and listen to each other, the teacher must be ready with both preventive measures that avoid problems and direct strategies that deal with problems when they occur.

Preventive Strategies

Grouptime is fragile in terms of group dynamics, and the teacher's role is to maintain group focus and continuity. The most effective thing the teacher can do to prevent problems is to keep grouptime moving. Pacing is critical to maintaining children's interest and attention. A long gap of silence should be avoided whenever possible because it invites children to fill the void, and the teacher thus loses the lead. Lengthy activities that can only be done by one person at a time should also be avoided. When children are not actively engaged, they become bored and restless, and initiate their own activities.

The teacher should monitor his or her speech patterns, eliminating overworked words or gratuitous phrases that children soon learn to tune out, and that do not give children anything to think about. Included here are phrases such as "I'm waiting for everyone to get quiet" or "We need to get ready to go to activities." Also, the teacher should be on guard for stereotypic phrases such as "Thank you for sharing that," spoken in an offhand manner. It is better to say, "Thank you for telling us about your trip to see your aunt." Responses to children should convey the message that the teacher listened to and was interested in what the child had to say.

The teacher should strive to avoid interruptions that will take him or her away from the group. Parents can be one such interruption. The teacher should let parents know when he or she is available for meetings and should strongly discourage parents from talking to the teacher during grouptime. If there is an assistant in the classroom, the assistant should speak with the parent. Sometimes last-minute communications are necessary, but parents should be instructed to give these instructions to someone else, to write them down, or to call later. Grouptime can fall apart with even a short teacher absence or interruption.

Latecomers can also interrupt the group. One solution to this problem is to have an assistant near the door. The assistant can greet the child and help with his or her things (coat, backpack, lunchbox, etc.), while at the same time calming him or her for the quiet mode of grouptime.

Direct Management

Despite the teacher's best efforts to prevent problems at grouptime, times will arise when more active management strategies are called for. We address what teachers can do when interest in grouptime wanes, when children all talk at once, when children talk only to the teacher, and when disciplinary measures are necessary.

When interest wanes. The teacher should avoid disciplinary remarks and use indirect means to recapture lost interest. Experienced teachers know that if attention wanders, starting a song or fingerplay can regain the group's focus. Generally, minor restlessness of one or two children can be ignored. The teacher can go on with circle as long as most children pay attention. However, if many children are restless, the teacher should take this as a sign that children have lost interest. Losing interest is not a punishable offense! When this happens, the teacher should drop the rest of the plan and wrap up quickly.

When all talk at once. Often, a topic interests children so much that they all want to talk at once. This occurs for a number of reasons. Children's general egocentrism and impulsiveness causes them to be unable to think of something without saying it out loud. Children may feel they have to compete with others for a chance to talk. When more than three or four children have something to say on a topic, the teacher should set up a sequence and assure children that every-one will get a turn to talk. "I'll start with ____ and go around the cir-cle. Everyone will get a chance, so you can put your hand down." By allowing each child a turn (with, of course, the option to "pass"), the teacher avoids problems. Children do not feel compelled to wave their hand in the air while saying, "Call me! Call me!" Children can relax about getting a turn to talk, and so can listen to each other, rather than concentrating on trying to get the teacher's attention.

We urge teachers not to follow the approach of calling on chil-dren who quietly raise their hands. If many children are being quiet and raising their hands, the choice of whom to call on becomes arbi-trary. We have watched many grouptimes where one child sits patiently in circle, hand raised quietly, and never attracts the teacher's attention. It is easy to neglect the quiet, undemanding child. Going around the circle and giving every child a turn to speak prevents this from happening.

When children all talk at once, and the circle becomes noisy, the teacher should avoid shouting over the din. Some strategies that work include sitting quietly and waiting for the noise to subside, holding one's hands over one's ears and looking pained, and whis-pering. The goal is to get back to taking turns. Nagging children to be quiet does not usually work and undermines the teacher's leadership role. In extreme cases, starting a song can bring children back to a common focus.

The ultimate goal in regulating conversation at grouptime is that there be no need to regulate talking. That is, we would like children to be able to talk at grouptime with neither hand-raising nor turn-tak-ing but with the casual give-and-take of polite conversation. However, this is a difficult task even for adults sometimes, and therefore some form of regulation by the teacher may be necessary. Children can be encouraged to solve the problem of people wanting to talk at the same time, and their solutions can be tried.

When children talk only to the teacher. The teacher should encourage children to talk to the entire group, not just to the teacher. This is difficult, because children will always direct their comments to the teacher. It may be necessary to be obvious and say something such as, "Tell this to everybody. Class, R has something she wants to tell us."

When discipline is necessary. Disciplinary comments should be used sparingly. When necessary, however, they should be clear, concise, nonjudgmental, and direct. For example, when a child was making noises at circle, we heard one teacher very matter-of-factly state, "S, please take the 'Ah-ah-ah' noise out of the classroom. When you are finished making that noise, then we would like to have you back in circle." This same teacher, when one child was walking around in the middle of the circle pretending to be a dog, said, "T, do you want to be a dog, and leave circle, or do you want to be a boy, and sit on your mat?" When he chose to sit down in circle, she replied, "Oh, I'm so glad you decided to stay. We like having you in circle."

Sometimes one child will be seriously disruptive. Each child is unique, with different reasons for the disruptive behavior, and we can thus offer no hard and fast rules for working with difficult children (see chapter 16). The teacher must respond to the individual child's entire history, needs, and circumstances. Having said that, the logical consequence of disrupting circle is for the child to leave circle until he or she is ready to come back and participate. If a child must leave circle, the teacher can still show respect for the child by stating, "Can you leave circle by yourself, or do you need help?"

Giving children choices is a good way to show respect while at the same time setting clear limits. This places the responsibility for regulating behavior on the child and gives the child the chance to be self-regulating. For example, when two children cannot refrain from talking to each other, the teacher can give them the choice to leave circle and continue their conversation where it will not disrupt the group or stay in circle and stop talking. Generally, if grouptime activities are interesting, children will choose to stay. The teacher can also give children the choice of sitting next to a friend and being quiet or moving apart.

In the following example from Peige Fuller's class of 3¹/₂-to 4¹/₂-year-olds at the HDLS, the teacher (T) must deal with a child (S) who has a history of behavioral and emotional problems. At this particular grouptime he is bothering another child (C) by touching and crowding him. C has been at the Lab School a short time and is not very assertive. He therefore needs the teacher's support to deal with what he obviously feels is a violation. We want to draw the reader's attention to the nonjudgmental way in which she talks to the problem child.

(At the first grouptime of the morning, C is sitting between S and the teacher. S puts his hand on C's leg, shoulder, and around his neck. C moves S's hand, then scoots closer to the teacher.)

T: (To C) You can tell him, "Don't touch."

(A short time later, S again puts his arm around C. C squirms away and removes S's arm. S touches C's leg.)

T: S, he does not want to be touched. He says no, he doesn't like that (removes S's hand). So, what you will need to do is scoot over so you are not touching him (scoots S away from C). There you go. You may not touch C, because he doesn't like it. Okay? C, if he touches you again and just will not stop, then what you could do is move to another place, okay? And then you will not have that problem. You could move over here (pats the spot on the other side of her).

(S continues to put his hand on C's leg. C scoots closer to the teacher, and S crowds closer to C.)

T: (To C) Would you like to move?

C: (Nods)

T: There's space right here. (C moves) There you go.

(S starts to move his mat over to where C just moved.)

T: S, your space is right here, see. C did not like it when you kept scooting closer and closer and closer and closer. He didn't want that. So since you would not stop, even after he asked you and even after I asked you, he moved. And now he doesn't have that problem anymore.

(Later, the teacher reads a story. S reaches across the teacher, touches C.)

T: (Takes S's hand away, looks directly into S's eyes and speaks matter-of-factly.) S, if you cannot keep your hands off of the children, then you will have to leave circle. You are disturbing circle. So if you touch children, you will have to leave circle.

(The teacher continues with the story. O comes in and sits down next to S. S touches O.)

O: (Whispers to the teacher) Peige, he's bothering me.
T: Then you will have to move.
O: (Moves to another spot)
T: S, there's a problem. You keep touching all the children, and they don't like it so they move away, and now you don't have anybody to sit by.

At no point does the teacher become angry with S. In fact, at one point, recognizing his need for affection, she puts S next to her and cuddles with him, allowing him to touch her leg, arm, face, etc., while she goes on with grouptime. However, she upholds children's rights to decide who touches them and how. She points out to S that the logical consequence of touching children when they do not want to be touched is that he has no one to sit next to him. See chapter 10 for a discussion of the use of logical consequences, and chapter 16 for more on handling the seriously disruptive child.

Content of Grouptime

A number of grouptime activities are not specifically constructivist but are common to all good child development programs. Included in this category are music, literature, daily routines such as attendance and the calendar, celebrations such as birthdays and holidays, special themes, and introducing special activities available during the activity time. Activities that are particularly constructivist include rule making and democratic decision making (see chapter 7), voting (see chapter 8), and social and moral discussions (see chapter 9). In addition, constructivist grouptime includes group problem solving and planning field trips and other activities. We give examples of these activities not discussed elsewhere. In addition, we present an example of a unique way to celebrate birthdays that was invented by a constructivist teacher. Finally, the reader may notice that we do not include Show and Tell, or Share Time, a nearly universal grouptime activity. We discuss this controversial activity and explain why we do not include it in our list of grouptime activities.

Discussion of Individual Problems

In chapter 4 we mention that problems of concern to only one or two children should be handled privately, rather than in the group. We gave an example of the exception, when a problem with one child concerns the entire group. We also hope the group will be considered a resource when a child wants help from classmates on a personal problem. In the following example from a kindergarten class, S brings to the group her problem of always getting to school too late to be Special Helper in the first grouptime. (In this example, T1 stands for the lead teacher, Coreen Samuel, T2 for the assistant teacher, Karen Amos.)

S: I was just wondering if anybody had some ideas of a way that we could see how I could get to school earlier.

N: Um, why don't we send a note to your mom and dad and then they could read it and then they could bring you more earlier.

S: No, no, no, no, no.

T2: Why won't that work?

S: 'Cause I've already talked to my mom about that.

J: Umm, I think, tell your mom to wake you up more earlier.

T1: You know what? I just spoke to S's mom, and she was telling me there was a problem because she wakes up early but sometimes it's hard to get S up.

S: (Nods)

T1: So if it's really hard for her to wake you up in the morning, what can you do, S?

S: Because, because my sister keeps on playing with me in the night.

N: Do you have bunk-beds?

S: No.

T1: You guys, A is really willing to give an idea.

S: A?

A: Shh, shh, quiet down. I have an idea. Do your mom and dad have like an old alarm clock up in the attic, or down? Well, maybe you could like get somebody to, like, buy you an alarm clock, and you could—

S: (Interrupts) No, we already—

A: —you could ask them to put the time on it, and then the alarm clock would ring, and then you could get up earlier.

S: I have an alarm clock already. It's brand new, I got it for Christmas, but my daddy will never set it up.

H: Ask your mom.

S: My mom can't do it because she's growing a new baby.

T1: So she can't set the alarm, huh? Okay, but, S,—

S: It's not plugged in.

T1: Maybe that's something that you can think about, setting the alarm.

S: I can tell my dad to do it 'cause he's never done it. My mom told him to do it, but he hasn't done it since, like, a long time ago.

A: Well, why don't you have a big meeting with your parents, and tell them what you've been missing in school in class.

S: (Talks while holding her nose; cannot be understood.)
T2: Say it again, I can't hear your words like that, S.
Children: (Laugh)
T2: We want to help you, but you seem to be playing, S.
A: If you're not really serious about this, then we'll just cancel it.
T2: We can go on to something else. Do you want us to help you?
A: Then stop being so silly.
T2: Okay. Well, what were your words when you were doing your mouth like this? About having a meeting.
S: Maybe at suppertime I could talk to my parents about it.
T2: That's a good idea.
A: You could write down, like, some rules.
T2: What's your idea, E?
E: When your mother gets her baby out of her stomach, she could, like, set the alarm clock.
S: That would be too much time, because then I can't wake up early enough for my time for the Special Helper. Then I'll have to be last on the Special Helper list.
T1: Well, let's see. C?
C: Well, how I get early is I wake up a little bit early enough, and I get dressed real fast, and then my mom can come to school real fast.

The children continue to give S suggestions about how she can get up and get to school earlier. Throughout the discussion, they are engaged, interested, and concerned about S's problem, and genuinely want to help her. When S acts silly, A even rebukes her mildly, reminding her that this is her problem, and if she wants help in solving it, then she must take it seriously. Discussions such as this contribute to the feeling of community by involving everyone in helping a friend with a problem. The teachers do not pass judgment on children's ideas, even ludicrous ones such as S's idea that her mother cannot set the alarm because she is pregnant, but affirm and elaborate on suggestions.

Grouptime is also, of course, a good time to engage children in generating solutions to problems that affect everyone. In chapter 12 we relate the story of a kindergarten class that had problems with equal participation in clean-up.

Planning a Group Project

Planning group projects, parties, and trips can be fruitful grouptime activities. The teacher will have to decide how much planning children can do and how much must be done by the teacher. In the following example, Peige (T) discusses with her class of 3- and 4-year-olds their proposed field trip to the zoo, to find out whether turkeys can fly (see chapter 8 for the full story of the children's question of whether turkeys can fly). She listens respectfully to the children's ideas and draws out and elaborates their ideas so children participate fully in the planning.

T: Now we had an argument, remember, about whether or not turkeys fly. So we were going to go to the zoo and check out this thing, right? Now, I guess these are the things we'll need to go to the zoo. We'll need to get permission from the moms and dads, and we'll need at least two other moms or dads to go with us.

D: I have one mom.

M: I have one mom.

T: You have one mom? And we'll need some people to drive their cars.

G: I have a mom.

K: My daddy would drive us.

T: He would drive, do you think?

(Children continue to volunteer their moms, dads, and cars.)

C: Peige, I have an idea!

T: Oh, C has an idea. What's your idea, C?

C: If we call all the moms and tell them that we're going to the zoo, and we need 2 more moms, then they'd want to come.

W: But my dad can't come because he's got to go to work.

T: Oh, you guys, listen. W said his dad can't come because he has to go to work. Now, I was thinking, we can't go today because the moms and dads will have to take off work. Maybe we could write a letter to the moms and dads, and then we'll have J (the secretary) xerox it so that each mom and dad can have a copy.

Z: Maybe J could come with us.

T: Oh, maybe J could come with us.

Z: Or maybe A (the Assistant Director).

T: Maybe A could. We could ask them, too. What do you think about writing a note so that the moms and dads will know we want to go to the zoo? And then they could try and take time off work to take us. Do you think that's a good idea?

W: Yeah.

C: Me, too.

G: And we could get lots of moms and dads.

T: We could get lots of moms and dads.

(Peige asks the Special Helper to get paper and a marker.)

C: And we could ride on the train. And we could see some animals and different animals.

T: C was saying we could see different animals. Not just a turkey but different animals too.

G: And they have birds.

T: And other birds.

(Children suggest animals they want to see at the zoo.)

T: (Begins to dictate while she writes) Dear Moms and Dads. What do we want to tell them?

C: We want to go to the zoo.

T: We want to go to the zoo?

D: That we want the moms and dads to come.

T: (Writing) We want to go to the zoo. Do you know how to spell zoo?

Children: Zee-Oh-Oh!

T: Z-O-O. We want to go to the zoo. What do we need from them? What do we need to tell them that we need?

S: Some money.

G: We need some money to go on the train ride.

T: Oh, we need some money to go on the train ride?

K: And, you know, we need tickets.

T: We need tickets to go on the train, so we have to pay money to do that. And we need money to go to the zoo, too. Okay, so we want money to ride the train and money to get into the zoo. Right? Now we also need moms and dads to drive their cars. So how should we ask them to do that? Does anyone have an idea?

C: Please drive your car.

T: Please drive your car. Okay. And we need some moms and dads to come with us. How should we ask them about that?

N: Nicely.

T: Nicely? What's a nice way to ask them?

N: Please.

T: Please what?

C: Please come with us. How's that? Please drive your car. Please come with us.

T: Let's see, we have to decide on a day to go.

Z: Are we going today?

T: Would you like to go—no, we can't go today, because the moms and dads need to be able to get the note.

W: Because they're at work.

T: They're at work. They have to be able to give us the money and come back and all that. How about if we go on next Monday?

Child: Yeah!

Child: No!

C: I have a great idea. We could go on Thursday.

T: On Thursday? Do you think that would be enough time for the moms and dads to get the note and all that?

C: Yes, because on Tuesday they'll put the note up, and then on Wednesday you get the note, and on Thursday you come.

T: I have an idea. Why don't we go on Friday, and then that would give them 2 days to get themselves together.

C: Why?

T: Well, because sometimes it takes a long time for moms and dads to ask for time off and stuff.

D: What do you think about going on Friday?

C: How about Monday?

T: Okay, so we'll go on Friday or the next Monday. We have to take a vote, you guys. Okay, today is Tuesday. The earliest we could go is Friday, but we might get more moms and dads to be able to participate if we go on the next Monday. So the vote is, should we go Friday, or should we go the next Monday?

(They vote, and decide to go on Friday.)

T: Okay, so now our note says "Please come with us and we want to go on Friday."

C: What time?

T: Oh, C said "What time?" Should we go in the morning?

C: Seven o'clock.

T: Uh, we're not in school at seven o'clock. Our circle time starts at nine o'clock. Maybe we could leave at nine-thirty.

Children: Yeah!

T: Okay. We want to go on Friday at nine-thirty. Okay. Oh, do we want to take our lunch and eat it there?

Children: Yeah!

T: Okay, this is what it says. (Reads) Dear Moms and Dads, We want to go to the zoo. We need some money to ride the train and to get into the zoo. Please drive your car. Please come with us. We want to go on Friday at nine-thirty. We want to take a picnic lunch. Okay, now who is this from?

Children: Investigators!

T: So should we write Investigators down here?

Children: Yeah!

T: (Signs) Investigators.

This edited segment of a grouptime illustrates how teachers can involve children in planning a field trip. The teacher listens to the children, solicits their opinions, and respects their decisions, leading the process but not controlling it.

Celebrating Together

Grouptime is a good time for celebrations such as birthdays. We witnessed a particularly endearing birthday ritual, invented by Peige Fuller, in a class of 3½- to 4½-year-olds. Usually, parents bring cake or cupcakes to school on their child's birthday, and there is a party after morning activities. Peige (T) puts the cake in the center of the circle, holds the child in her lap, and tells this story.

T: Once upon a time there was a man and a woman and their names were V and M. And they loved each other very very much so they got married. And before long, V's tummy started to grow bigger and bigger and do you know what she was growing in there?

N: What?

C: A baby.

T: She was growing a baby in there. And one day that baby was born. And they named that tiny little baby M.

K: M!

T: They did. And he was so little, you could hold him in your arm (pantomimes holding a baby) and he had tiny little fingers and tiny little toes and a tiny little nose. And before long he started making noises that sounded like (she makes baby noises). Just like that. Little baby noises. Well, then he grew and grew and when he was 1 year old, do you know what he could do?

Children: What?

T: Walk. He could walk a little bit. Just baby steps. And when he wanted something, he said "Aw Baw" and that meant "I want a ball."

Child: Why?

T: He'd say "Aw awa" and that meant "I want water."

C: Agua!

T: Uh huh, he did. When he was a baby. And before you knew it, he grew and grew and he was 2 years old. And he could do many many things. He could speak more regularly now.

W: He was a big boy.

T: Then he grew and grew some more. He came to school. He made friends, like K and N and C.

S: And like me.

T: And he made friends like D and N and K, and like W and S and M and S and P. And then he was 3. And then one day do you know what happened?

Children: What?

T: One day this boy who used to be a little baby, and who used to be 1 and who used to be 2 and who used to be 3 turned 4 years old.

S: And M!

T: That's right.

(Peige then lights birthday candles, they sing "Happy Birthday," and M blows out the candles.)

Peige told a birthday story for every child, customizing it each time for the particular child, including names of siblings and other relevant information. Sometimes, she showed pictures of the child as a baby or pictures of the mother with her big tummy. The children loved these stories and never grew tired of them.

The Issue of Show and Tell

Many early childhood classrooms assign a day a week for each child to bring a prized object to school and show it to the class or tell the class about something they did recently. While we do not want to convey the message that we think children should not share these personal interests with the group, we would like to point out the problems we have seen with this type of *institutionalized* sharing. First, children often forget when it is their "Share Day," do not bring anything to share, and then become very upset when they get to school and realize their mistake. We have seen children so upset that they had to leave the class with an assistant in order to calm down. Second, sometimes children do not have anything they want to share but feel compelled to share something. They stutter and stammer and feel awkward and inadequate. Third, some children are quite shy and find sharing painful and embarrassing. Sharing for them is simply an occasion to suffer embarrassment and be reminded of their shyness. Finally, some children dominate sharing, going on and on about their trip to the circus or the snake they found in the backyard. It is difficult to get these children to be brief without cutting them off and making them unhappy, and more than one at grouptime can make it much too long, causing children to become restless and cranky.

What can be done about the problems with Show and Tell? We recognize the benefits of having children share things from home. Children feel special, they have an opportunity to be "on stage," and they develop good public speaking skills. First, we suggest letting sharing occur spontaneously. By not institutionalizing it, sharing will probably occur less frequently and involve more meaningful contributions. When only one or two children have something special to share, it can be incorporated easily into grouptime. When more than one or two children want to share, we suggest moving sharing to activity time. If children tell the teacher before grouptime when they have something to share, the teacher can announce this opportunity as part of the description of activities. A sharing table, shelf, or other space can be designated where children can place things they bring from home. The children can stay at the sharing table during the beginning of the activity period and tell children who come to look all about it. They may make signs describing it and can decide whether others are allowed to touch or not. Some children may even prefer to share during activities rather than during grouptime. This system of sharing can eliminate the problems in conducting sharing during grouptime, while not depriving children the opportunity to share things from home.

GROUPTIME LOST, GROUPTIME REGAINED

The following story describes a constructivist kindergarten class experiencing problems with grouptime and the steps taken by the teachers as they tried to deal with their problem.

Once there was a kindergarten class that had two grouptimes every morning. During the first grouptime at 9:00 A.M., they had many things to do. They usually started with a song or two. They figured out who was the Special Helper for that day. The Special Helper counted to see how many people were in the class. Sometimes, the Special Helper had trouble counting, and had to start over, again and again, while the class waited. Then, the children who were scheduled to share that day shared what they brought to class. Sometimes, four or five people shared, and it took a long time. Then the teachers introduced the activities for the morning, and discussed some of them. That, too, took a long time. Sometimes the teacher read a story or a poem. Sometimes, they had problems to solve, and they voted to make decisions. They often did not begin activities until 9:50 A.M.

Many children found it hard to sit still and listen for such a long time. They were restless, and they talked out, forgetting to raise their hands. Sometimes there were conflicts between children at grouptime, and this upset the teachers, who wanted children to listen to each other and respect each other.

After the morning activity time, the class had another grouptime. At second group, they talked about what they did during activities. Sometimes they had stories and songs. If the children scheduled to share did not get a chance at first group, they shared at second group. Soon, second group, too, became very long. Children were restless, and eager to go outside and play. Teachers were frustrated because children seemed not to listen to them or to each other.

Finally, one day, the teachers decided that they had had enough! Children did not like grouptime, they thought, so they would just quit having grouptime. When children came on Monday, teachers told them there was not going to be a grouptime. "Just go straight to activities," they said. "We're not going to have grouptime unless children want it." Children were pleased. They cheered and said they did not like grouptime. For 2 days they did not have grouptime.

On the 3rd day, one child decided that they needed to plan their Halloween party. But how could they plan if they never had grouptime? She went around the class, gathering names of children who wanted a second group, to plan their party. All but four children signed the paper. So all those who wanted to plan stayed inside and had a grouptime.

Slowly, they started having grouptime after activities again. Children had the option of staying for grouptime, or going outside. At first, many children went outside, but soon, they were all staying for group. They liked being together, talking about what they did during activities, singing songs, hearing stories.

After about 3 weeks, they started having first groups again. No one ever said, "Shall we have first group again or not?" It just sort of happened. But when first groups came back, they were different. They did not spend a long time doing attendance and they quit doing sharing. Teachers talked about having short groups and getting to activities quickly. With shorter groups, children were paying attention better, not getting so restless. They still forgot to raise their hands sometimes, but not as much as before. Teachers were not having to spend so much time telling children to be quiet, raise their hands, take turns, listen to their friends. Everyone seemed to enjoy grouptime more.

Doing away with group was fairly dramatic, but the teachers thought it was necessary. They hoped that children would recognize the usefulness of grouptime and would come to miss it. Children did, and when they found their own reasons to participate in grouptime, they suggested having it again. However, the teachers also learned something in this experience. They learned that the important part of grouptime was wanting to be together as a community of people who listen to each other, plan things together, and make group decisions.

SUMMARY

Grouptime aims include promoting intellectual, social, and moral development through activities involving self-regulation, cooperation, and perspective coordination. The teacher takes a more active leadership role during grouptime than during activity time. Special possibilities exist at grouptime for fostering a feeling of community among children. Content of activities include music, literature, celebrations, special themes, routines such as attendance, planning for field trips, and introduction of special activities available during activity time. In addition, grouptime includes rule making, democratic decision making, and discussion of classroom problems and social and moral dilemmas. The teacher must also be concerned with formal planning issues such as seating arrangements and length of grouptime, and with special management strategies that prevent or deal directly with problems. When children seem not to value grouptime, as occurred in one kindergarten, the teacher can discontinue it and help children discover their own needs for grouptime.

7

Rule Making and Decision Making

A unique characteristic of constructivist education is that responsibility for decision making is shared by everyone in the class community. In a constructivist classroom, the teacher turns over to the children much of the power to decide how to run the class. In this chapter, we present the objectives of involving children in decision-making and rule-making processes. We then offer guidelines for conducting rule-making and decision-making discussions, and present examples. Voting, a democratic tool for making group decisions, is discussed separately in chapter 8.

OBJECTIVES

The overarching objective of involving children in decision making and rule making in their classroom is to contribute to an atmosphere of mutual respect in which teachers and children practice self-regulation and cooperation. Inviting children to make rules and decisions is one way the teacher can reduce heteronomy and promote autonomy. Piaget (1932/1965) commented that "Every rule, whether it be imposed on the younger by the older child, or upon the child by the adult, begins by remaining external to the mind before it comes to be really interiorized" (p. 185). We discuss in chapter 3 the importance of the teacher's cooperation with children and reduction of the exercise of unnecessary authority. In a nutshell, this means giving children the possibility to regulate their behavior voluntarily. We also discuss in chapter 3 the importance of creating an environment in which children cooperate with each other. Through group rule making and decision making, the constructivist teacher achieves all these interrelated goals.

Three more specific objectives of involving children in the decision-making process are (1) to promote feelings of necessity about rules and fairness, (2) to promote feelings of ownership of classroom rules, procedures, and decisions, and (3) to promote feelings of shared responsibility for what goes on in the class and how the group gets along together.

Through reflecting on the problems of classroom life together children can be led to realize the necessity for rules. By participating in the determination of what happens in the classroom, children can realize that decisions belong to them. They will have the chance to understand why they have particular rules and why they do things in particular ways. The sense of ownership resulting from sharing in the decision-making process leads children to develop a sense of shared responsibility for what happens in the class, good and bad. This extends even to responsibility for enforcing rules and classroom procedures.

RULE MAKING

Rule making presents a clear opportunity for children to exercise autonomy. Many teachers feel nervous at first about turning the rule-making process over to children. They may believe children cannot make rules. They may fear that children will make unacceptable rules, or worse yet, no rules at all. These fears have not been realized in our experiences of observing young children participate in rule making. Of course, the constructivist teacher does not turn everything over to children, but rather, exercises leadership in guiding the rule-making process and the development of children's attitudes and knowledge about rule making. We suggest some guidelines for conducting rule-making discussions, offer some ideas for how to record and post rules that children make, and discuss involving children in enforcing rules and determining consequences for failure to follow rules.

Guiding Rule-Making Discussions

Teachers who have never involved children in rule making may be tempted to start out with a few of their own rules and simply invite children to add some of their own. We urge teachers to refrain from this course. While we recognize that teachers do feel that certain rules are necessary, we hope to convince the reader that with careful guidance, children will propose these in some form or another, although not in the form the teacher would have given them.

If a teacher believes that a particular rule is important, then he or she must figure out how to present it to the class in such a way that children will also see the necessity for the rule. The teacher should examine the rationales for rules considered necessary. Sometimes teachers impose particular rules without reflecting on whether they are really necessary, or if they are just "the way things have always been done." For example, consider a common elementary school rule, "Walk in a straight, single-file line in the hallways." This usually seems arbitrary and coercive to children. Imagine yourself as a teacher, trying to get children to accept this rule as necessary. What is the justification for the rule? Is it a problem in the school? Do children make noise in the halls and disrupt other classes? If so, it is still possible to avoid arbitrary imposition of a rule. Instead, the teacher can present the problem, "I have noticed that sometimes children make a lot of noise when we walk through the halls, and it bothers the other classes. Other teachers have told me that their children can't hear each other when our class walks past their room. What can we do about this problem?" Children may think of solutions different from walking in a single-file line, such as making the rule that children must be quiet in the halls, or that children should walk through the halls with their hands over their mouths, to keep from talking. This might solve the problem while allowing the children to be self-regulating.

It is important to keep rules in perspective. In the constructivist view, rules are not just a means to the end of smooth classroom organization. While they do serve this function, rules are also an end in themselves. The children's experiences in rule making fulfill developmental goals. On a practical level, we hope to convince the reader that rules made by children are more powerful than rules given ready-made.

We offer here ten guidelines for leading rule-making discussions, with examples to illustrate these.

1. Avoid the word rule at first.

Children may not share the teacher's understanding of the word. They may associate "rules" only with adult prohibitions. To avoid getting from children a list of all the "don'ts" they hear from adults, teachers may introduce rule making with phrases such as "ways to make our classroom safe and happy," "guidelines," "things to remember," or "how we want to be treated." However, if children use the term *rules*, then respect their knowledge by using it too, but expand its use to "rules to make our class a happy place," for example.

2. Conduct rule-making discussions as a response to a particular need or problem.

Generally, it is not a good idea simply to ask children to suggest rules for their class without connecting the need for rules to specific problems. With teacher colleagues we have experimented with rule making at the beginning of the school year. The results of these experiments have been mixed when the teacher simply asks open-ended questions such as "Can you think of any rules we need in our classroom?" This invitation is too broad and usually leads to long litanies of "don'ts" that often do not have any relation to needs in the life of the classroom. For example, we have heard children suggest rules to address problems that had never occurred in the classroom, such as "No throwing blocks at the fish tank" and "No throwing chairs." We have also heard children repeat rules they knew from other contexts, such as "Never talk to strangers." In one instance, we saw children enter into a competition for the most outrageous or elaborate rule. We realized that children were suggesting rules only because the teacher asked them to, not out of any personal need to figure out how to regulate themselves.

It is much better to begin a rule-making discussion with the introduction, "I have noticed that we have been having a problem with (children hurting other children, children taking turns with the blocks, being able to hear each others' words at circle, and so forth). What can we do about this problem? Does anyone have a suggestion about how we can solve this problem?" This focuses the discussion on one topic that all children can share. Young children's attention spans for rule discussions can be fairly short, so discussing rules for one problem at a time allows the teacher to end the discussion when children's attention lags by stating, "We have done a good job of solving this problem. Maybe at another circle we can solve the problem of ____ (if children have mentioned another problem)."

For example, in the constructivist Community described in chapter 1, Mary Wells confronts the problem of a few children mistreating the guinea pig. Other children are upset and complain. Mary makes this the occasion for asking, "Do we need to make rules about how to treat the guinea pig?" The following rules were made by the children.

- Ask Mrs. Wells before you get the guinea pig out.
- Be careful—no hurting the guinea pig.
- Don't squeeze, drop, or throw him. Hold him gently.
- Don't put him on the floor. Hold him.
- Don't pull his hair. Be gentle.
- Don't pull his hand or sit on him.
- Don't let him down in the house. Hold him in a blanket.
- Hold him like a baby.

This example shows particularly how important it is for children to create their own rules. The rules that make sense to children include many that adults would never think of proposing. Children are often better judges than adults of the rules that will be most effective in solving problems.

If a teacher wants children to make rules at the beginning of the year, we suggest focusing the children's attention on areas of potential problems. For example, the teacher can provide leadership by asking, "Can the whole class fit in the block center at the same time? What guidelines do we need so everyone can have a fair turn with blocks?"

3. Emphasize the reasons for rules.

Use words that convey the message that the purpose of rules is to make the classroom a safe, happy place for everyone. Teachers can talk about their responsibility to make sure that all children are safe. Consider the following example, from Angie Quesada's (T) class of kindergarten and first-grade children at the Sunset-Pearl Elementary School in Houston. Some of the children had been in her class the year before and were familiar with the idea of making classroom rules. It is the 3rd day of the school year, at their second grouptime of the morning.

T: Okay, so we've gone into centers, we've had circle time, and sometimes it went really smoothly and we had a good time, and sometimes we had problems. So what might be a good idea, since we started a new school year? Make what?

C: Rules.

T: A list of rules. Why do you think we need some rules? Anybody have any ideas *why* we need some rules?

E: So no one will get hurt when they were playing.

(They decide to start a list entitled "Class Rules.")

We continue with this example below, to illustrate other guidelines for rule making.

When children suggest a rule, ask, "Why do we need that rule?" or "Why is that a good rule?" If they cannot answer, ask, "What would happen if children (do whatever the rule forbids)?" Generally children answer that hitting, kicking, etc., hurts. Include the reason in the statement of the rule. Examples we have seen of children's rules include "Don't hit because hitting hurts," "Don't kick the door because you might hurt the door and you might hurt your foot," and "No throwing sand because it might get in someone's eyes."

It is important to have sufficient discussion so that all children are clear about the necessity for the rule. If the teacher simply writes a rule without discussion of its rationale, children may not feel the necessity for following it.

4. Accept children's ideas, words, and organization.

Even if children's wording is awkward, use it anyway. The grammar matters less than the spirit of the rule. Children will remember and respect the rule more if it is in their own words. In the following example, Peige Fuller (T) is preparing to have a grouptime discussion because her 4-year-old children have been hurting each other. Before the discussion gets rolling, Z calls C a name, and N calls this to the teacher's attention.

N: C is sad.
T: I can see that. Do you know why?
C: Z called me a naughty girl.
T: Are you a naughty girl?
C: (Crying) Noooo!
(Peige suggests that maybe some of the children near C could hug her and make her feel better. They do, and C starts to cheer up a little bit.)
T: Oh, I see a smile! I think she feels loved! Okay, now C, what do you want to be called?
C: My name.
T: Your name. So should we have a rule about calling people by their names?
Children: Yeah!
T: How should we write that? Tell me how to write that.
C: Write "Call them your name."
T: (Writes and repeats) "Call them your name."
C: Don't call them naughty girl or naughty boy.

T: (Writes and repeats) "Don't call them naughty girl or naughty boy." Okay, so that takes care of kids using hurtful words. What about people using hurtful hands and feet?

The suggested rule contains questionable grammar, but the meaning is clear to the children. The wording helps to remind the children of why C wanted to make the rule and why they need that particular rule.

Accept children's organization of rules. Do not attempt to impose an organizational structure on the rules that the children cannot understand. The continued rule discussion in Angie's class (introduced above) provides an example of what happens when children's logic cannot accept sophisticated organization. Children suggest five rules: "No slapping in the face," "No hitting in anybody's eye," "No pinching," "No kicking," and "No fighting." Then E suggests that they simply make the rule "Don't hurt anybody," and erase all the other rules. He explains, "'No hurting anyone' would be the same as writing all of that that's already on there." It is clear that many children in the class do not understand E's class inclusion logic that the category "No hurting" includes all specific types of hurting. Children continue to suggest rules that E thinks are included under his no hurting rule. He objects, "It doesn't make sense to have some things and other rules that mean the same thing. That's just a waste of paper." Angie suggests that they vote about whether or not to erase rules. She starts by having children vote on whether to keep the rule "No slapping in the face," since E claims that the no hurting rule includes slapping. The children vote to cross out the slapping rule, and D exclaims, "We can slap people's face! We don't have a rule!" The more children discuss, the clearer it becomes to Angie that none of the other children understand the inclusive meaning of E's rule. The rest of the children feel a need for each specific rule. Finally, Angie suggests that they vote on whether to keep all the rules, or just E's rule. Despite E's protests, children vote to keep all the rules, including the rule "Don't hurt anyone." The resulting list is thus not a neat logical form, but it makes sense to the children. In such a situation, the teacher can say, "That's a good idea, E, but the other children don't agree today." (This incident contributed to a reevaluation of E's placement, and subsequent change from the K-1 mixed grade class to the 1-2 mixed grade class.)

5. Lead children toward "Do" rules.

Young children, when first invited to generate rules for the classroom, tend to suggest "Don't" rules. The above examples from Angie's class are typical. Children find it much easier to think of rules as prohibitions. The teacher should not reject the "don't" rules. However, children can be led to think of things that they can do. At the end of the example from Peige's class (above), the teacher asks children what they should do about children who use hurtful hands and feet. The discussion continues.

G: That hurts people and it's not nice.
T: That hurts them and they don't like it. So what should we tell children to do?
K: Use their words.
T: Tell them to use their words? (She writes and repeats) "Use their words."
K: And if the words don't work, go get the teacher.
T: (Writes and repeats) "And if the words don't work, go get the teacher." Okay. Is there any other guideline that we need to be able to have friendly people in our class?
D: Friendly hands.
Y: And friendly words.
T: (Writes and repeats) "Friendly hands and friendly words." Is that how everyone wants their friends to treat them? With friendly hands and friendly words? Okay.
W: No hitting.
T: Okay. (Writes and repeats) "No hitting." Investigators, would you like to hear what you wrote? Let's read this so you can hear what it is that we said are the guidelines for having happy people in our class. Okay. (She reads) "Call them your name. Don't call them naughty girl or naughty boy." That will make us happy?
Children: Yeah!
T: Okay. "Use their words. And if the words don't work, go get the teacher." Will that help people?
Children: Yeah!
T: Number 3 says, "Friendly hands and friendly words."
C: Number 4.
T: Four. "No hitting." That should about do it. That's it, only four little guidelines. Four little rules will help us to be very happy people in the Investigators class.

Assisted by Peige, the children create a mixture of do rules and don't rules that expresses how they want to be treated in the classroom.

6. Do not dictate rules to children.

The teacher may lead children toward rules but should not specifically suggest them. As long as decisions are made by others, children will experience these decisions as being imposed from somewhere outside themselves. The teacher can, however, subtly suggest rules to children, without actually stating the rule. In this way, children have the satisfaction of thinking of the rule themselves. For example, if there has been a particular problem in the class, the teacher can say something like, "I have noticed some children not getting along in the block center. I wonder what we could do about that?" We have seen children suggest rules such as limiting the number of children allowed at the center, limiting the number of blocks each child can use, and having children sign up to play there.

7. Cultivate the attitude that rules can be changed.

Sometimes rules need to be changed, for one reason or another. In the following example from Coreen's kindergarten class, an occasion arises in which the teacher (T) thinks perhaps the rule about block structures ought to be changed. The rule, made by children, states that block structures can remain standing for 1 day and then have to be taken down during clean-up time. One child, S, is sad because her block structure was knocked down according to the rule. She wanted it to remain so that her father could see it when he picked her up that afternoon.

T: So should we still keep that rule, S, of the 1 day?
Children: Yeah. No.
S: I think . . . I'd rather . . . mostly I prefer that it would be for 3 days.
T: For 3 days? Okay.
Child: No.
T: Well, if you have another idea then raise your hand and we'll come to you. So S thinks we should have it for 3 days. H wants to say something about that.
H: I want to say something. If she gets 3 when she gets her structure, then we can keep ours for 3 days.
M: If S gets 3 days and we don't, then it won't be fair, so 3 days.
S: You guys are gonna' get 3 days if you want to.
T: So you think 3 days. C, what do you think? Is there any problem with that?
C: Well what I think we should do is we should keep our structures for 5 days, and after 5 days we have to knock it down.
T: But you know what? Five days is kind of like a whole week. You think kids should keep their structures up for a whole week?
C: (Nods yes)
Children: Yeah. No.

T: It seems like you really want to keep your structures up for a
     longer time. Does anyone see any problems with kids having it 3
     and 5 days? That's no problem? N, what do you think, what could
     be a problem if we kept them up that long?

N: If we keep it up 5 days, then that would mean a whole week. And
     then after a whole week the other kids would have to keep their
     structure up for a whole week and if they built a big structure and
     it was blocking the walkway then how would people walk
     through? And how would people walk through the walkway?
     Would they have to bam it down?

T: Okay, yeah, you know, I do see a problem too, N. The other prob-
     lem is that we have how many kids in our room? We have 18 kids.
     The problem is, would everyone be able to have a turn if you guys
     keep it up for 3 days? That's why we made the rule of 1 day.
     Because there were a lot of kids in the room.

(The class votes and decides to allow block structures to remain up
for 5 days.)

T: Okay. It seems like a lot of people want to keep their structures
     up for a long time. And most people don't have any problems
     with that, so we'll try it and see what happens. If it doesn't work,
     then we'll need to come back and try and make a better solution.
     Okay. So it's going to be that kids who make a structure get to
     keep it up for the whole week.

The teacher leaves the situation open-ended by stating that they will
try the solution that the class voted on, but that they can always
come back and try again if it does not work. This helps children learn
that rules are not sacred and immutable; rather, rules exist to serve
specific purposes. When the rules no longer serve the purpose for
which they were designed, or when the situation changes, the rules
can change, too.

8. When children suggest unacceptable rules, respond with persuasion and explanation.

There are bound to be times when children suggest unworkable
rules. In the example from Coreen's class (above), the teacher did not
veto the children's decision to leave block structures up for 5 days,
even though she foresaw problems. Unless the teacher thinks the
rule could lead to consequences that cannot responsibly be permitted, children should be allowed to discover for themselves that a rule
is unworkable. In this way, when they revise the rule, they will do so
with a more differentiated conception of the problem they are

addressing. More complex thinking reflects intellectual as well as sociomoral progress.

Children sometimes suggest rules that the teacher cannot accept. Later in this chapter, we see that Peige tells children why they cannot go on a picnic away from school with only one teacher to supervise. When the teacher must veto a suggestion, it is important to explain why it must be rejected. This can be done respectfully, treating the child as a reasonable human being who will certainly want to withdraw the idea when the reason is explained.

9. Develop a procedure by which everyone can agree to the rules.

Voting, as we discuss in chapter 8, is necessary when children disagree about what a rule should be. Most rule-making discussions, however, result in a rule or list of rules having a consensus in the group. One could conduct a vote to accept the list of rules, but offering the opportunity to vote against the rules may invite a negative attitude that was not present before. It could become awkward if someone votes not to accept. It seems a better idea to have children sign the list, to indicate that everyone agrees to the rules and that they belong to everyone in the class.

The teacher should also sign the list of rules, to underscore the point that the teacher is a member of the group and must live by the same rules as everyone else in the class. We know one teacher who would on occasion intentionally violate a rule in order to give children the opportunity to remind her of the rule. For example, when there was a rule in the class forbidding sitting on the tables, she would casually sit on a table while talking to a child. Inevitably, one child would notice and correct her, whereby she would exclaim, "Oh, I forgot our rule! We can't sit on the tables. We sit on chairs and on the floor."

10. Emphasize that teachers must also follow rules.

Piaget (1932/1965) stressed that adults can contribute to children's moral development by stressing their own obligations to others. Later in this chapter we present an example of group decision making in which the teacher explains that she has to follow guidelines that prevent her from taking the children out of the building for a walk by herself.

We have been impressed with one constructivist teacher who responded positively when children suggested rules for the teacher to follow. This could be especially reassuring to children who have had previous experience with a heteronomous teacher. Examples of rules for teachers might include "Don't yell at children," and "Don't throw away children's art." Teachers can also suggest rules for themselves. The teacher might propose the rule, "The teacher will respect children by letting them choose their activities."

Recording and Posting Rules

Rules made by children should become a familiar part of the classroom culture. One way to achieve this is to ask children, "What could we do if we wanted to remember this suggestion? Would it be a good idea to write down our ideas?" We have found that even children who cannot read recognize and remember written rules when they have been involved in their creation. For this reason, rules should be written down and placed where children can find and refer to them easily. They can be written on a large sheet of paper and posted in the classroom, written on the chalkboard or on a bulletin board. One teacher, Karen Capo, after making rules with her kindergarten class, made a book with each of the children's rules on a single page, and had the children illustrate each rule. Each child signed the title page. Karen then laminated the pages and bound them in such a way that new pages could be added as needed. The rule book remained in the reading center of the classroom for the entire year, and many times she saw children dash to get the book, open it, point to a page, and say, "Look, it says right here that you can't do that. You gotta' follow our rule."

Having the children's rules posted in the classroom also allows the teacher to emphasize that the moral authority of the classroom comes not from the teacher but from the children themselves. About 2 weeks after the rule discussion (above) in Peige's class, she was concerned about an increase in violations, and started morning circle by reading the rules to children again.

T: Before we get started with morning circle, do you remember what these are about? These rules?

H: No.

T: These are rules that you guys told me to write. You told me the words and I wrote your words down. They talk about how we want to be treated in our classroom. Do you remember that? Because some people were doing some hurting of feelings and of bodies and we wrote these words so that people would know how to be friends in class. Do you remember what these are about?

C: The rules about so we can make happy children and some kids are not following them.

T: That is exactly it. Let's read them again so you can remember what they are. (Points to the written rules) This one is, "Call them your name. Don't call them naughty girl or naughty boy."

G:　That's C.

T:　So people want to be called their own name. Okay.

C:　Z didn't call me my name.

T:　"Use their words. And if the words don't work, go get the teacher." If the words don't work, can you pinch and then go tell the teacher?

Children: No!

T:　If your words don't work, can you hit them and then go tell the teacher?

W:　Where's mine?

T:　D, if your words don't work and somebody kicks you, can you kick them back?

D:　No, I don't kick back.

T:　What do you do?

C:　Go tell the teacher.

D:　You know what happened outside today? B threw sand in my mouth.

T:　Really? What did you do?

D:　I telled the teacher.

T:　Did the teacher help you talk to B?

D:　Yes.

T:　That's important. This one says, "Friendly hands and friendly words." So we want to use friendly hands and friendly words. Hey, you know what we could do? We could practice friendly hands.

G:　What is that?

T:　You cross your hands over (demonstrates). Now hold the hand of the person next to you. Now shake. That's the biggest hand-shake. That's friendly hands, huh?

N:　M doesn't have his hands crossed.

T:　That's okay. Now this one says, "No hitting."

W:　I did that.

T:　Do you guys remember those rules?

Children: Yeah!

T:　What do you think? Do you think we can remember them during outside time and during activity time?

Children: Yeah!

Especially with young children, it is important to review the rules frequently, to help children remember them. This need not be an unpleasant task. As we see above, Peige made reading the rules an occasion for a friendly shared experience.

Enforcing Rules

Earlier we stated that one of the objectives of engaging children in rule making is to promote feelings of ownership of classroom rules. These feelings of ownership in turn translate into willingness to enforce rules fairly. Karen Capo's experience with the book of class rules, described above, is one example of this. When children feel the rules are theirs, they turn to the rules when they need them or when others are not following them. Young children can develop the ability to take responsibility for regulating their own behavior.

In the following example, Peige (T) helps children remind each other of the rules at grouptime. A rule in the class states, "No touching when people say 'No.'" Children made this rule in response to the problem of some children touching others in ways that they did not like.

G: (Puts his hand on D's leg)
D: Stop it, G.
G: (Unintelligible)
D: (To the teacher) G touched me.
T: (To D) And what will you do about this?
D: I don't . . . (to G) I don't want . . . No! (To T) You gotta' say "The rule says ____" to G.
T: Oh, you can tell G what the rule says.
D: (To G) The rule says, "No touching."
L: "When they say no."
W: "When they say no."
L: "No touching when people say no."
D: Yeah.
T: "No touching when people say no." Okay.

Peige does not take responsibility for reminding G of the rule, but supports and encourages D to remind G. She remains close by, if needed, but expresses confidence in D's ability to handle the situation.

Children can also be involved in helping to decide consequences for breaking rules, although this can be a little tricky at times. Young children's ideas about justice are often very harsh, and they can show a decided lack of empathy in dealing with rule infractions. For example, in a kindergarten class where there is a problem with children spilling water on the floor around the water table, a child slips on the wet floor and the teacher calls a class meeting about the problem. She explains that a wet floor is dangerous, and asks the children what they think should be done. One child suggests that the children who make a mess at the water table should never be allowed to use the water table ever again. While this is a logical consequence, it is too harsh. The teacher points out, "Never is a long time. I know sometimes I get careless and spill water on the floor accidentally. I wonder if they could play at the water table again if they promise to be careful." Finally, the class decides that if a person makes a mess at the water table, they cannot go there for 3 days.

DECISION MAKING

Children can be involved in many other decisions besides rule making, including decisions about activities, classroom procedures, and special problems. In general, the guidelines for decision making are very similar to those for rule making. The teacher should lead children in decision-making discussions without actually making the decisions for children. We would only add here two other points to remember. First, choose decision-making opportunities carefully. Some issues are too complex for children to deal with, and allowing children to make such decisions can set them up for failure. Second, be willing to go along with children's ideas whenever possible. Remember that the teacher does not have veto power after the fact. The teacher can draw attention to problems with children's ideas, but once given, the power to make decisions is difficult to retract. If you as a teacher know that you cannot live with a particular decision, then do not offer this issue as a decision-making opportunity.

Making Decisions About Classroom Activities

As we discuss in chapter 2, allowing children the opportunity to make choices is very important for children's intellectual and moral development. We believe that children should be allowed to make choices about activities in which they want to engage during at least some part of every day. Children are also capable of many group decisions about activities in their classroom. They can sometimes be involved in the arrangement of the classroom, placement of materials, and choices of activities in the class.

In chapter 4 we describe Peige's experience of asking children what they wanted to learn about and then designing lesson plans around the children's interests. We recognize that curriculum is often mandated in public schools. However, the teacher still has considerable latitude in how to approach specific topics, and children's ideas can still be solicited. When certain topics are mandated, the teacher can still pursue other contents that children suggest. Mandated topics may be worked into children's ideas. Or, the teacher might provide the list and explain that, "These are the things all first-grade children have a chance to learn about." The teacher can ask the children which topic they would like to do first and how they would like to go about it.

Special class projects present a wonderful opportunity for children to make decisions. We have seen children design pretend center restaurants, plan a toy store for Christmas in which they build and "sell" toys to the younger children, and plan parties for parents for which the children prepare all the decorations, food, and entertainment. These projects can be challenging for the teacher who must work behind the scenes to make sure things run relatively smoothly, yet without taking over.

Making Decisions About Classroom Procedures

Children can take responsibility for deciding many classroom procedures, such as how to regulate turns as Special Helper, sharing privileges, and so forth. In discussions about these decisions, the teacher must uphold values of fairness and equality because children may not yet have constructed these principles. (See chapter 8 for a description of two classes' experiences regulating turns being Special Helper, and chapter 12 for the story of how a class decided how to regulate clean-up time in a fair way.) If the teacher presents the need for a particular procedure and what it must accomplish, and invites children to participate in deciding how it will be done, this can result in greater feelings of ownership of class procedures.

In Coreen's (T) kindergarten class, one child (W) objects to the way they regulate talking at circle, with the teacher calling on children whose hands are raised. He thinks there is a better way.

T: I think it's a better idea to raise your hands. I knew that E wanted to talk because she raised her hand. W, you don't want to raise your hand?

N: (Without raising her hand) Then he shouldn't talk anymore.

T: W, what would be a better idea instead of raising hands? What do you think? Does anyone know of any other way we could do it so everyone could talk and we won't talk at the same time?

W: I know.

T: What's another way?

W: Wait until someone else is finished.

T: Well, suppose two people decide to talk after someone is finished?

W: No, you see, the reason I wait until someone is finished is, like when A was talking, and she'd done then I would talk and then C would, and he would wait until I was finished.

T: That's a good idea.

They discuss this issue for quite some time. W is convinced that children can take turns talking without raising hands. He has started to figure out the give-and-take of conversation. The teacher is skeptical that this will work and introduces the problem of what to do if more than one person talks at the same time. W modifies his idea and the group agrees that if only one person has something to say, that person can speak out without raising a hand, but if more than one person speaks out, then they have to raise hands. This system works for the remainder of the year.

Making Decisions About Special Problems

Children can also be called upon to make decisions about problems that arise in the classroom. In the following example, Peige (T) comes to the Investigators (ages $3\frac{1}{2}$ to $4\frac{1}{2}$ years old) with a problem. She explains that construction workers are on the playground, making it too dangerous for children to play there. Notice that Peige does not hesitate to inform children when an unworkable or unacceptable idea is suggested. However, when this is necessary, she explains the reasons clearly, in ways children can understand.

T: There are workers on the playground, and they have dangerous tools and stuff. So we can't be out there. What should we do instead?

S: Just play on the porch (on the playground).

T: But we can't. A (the Assistant Director) said we can't play out there at all.

C: How about up in the booth (the visitors' observation booth)?

T: In the booth? I hear someone up in the booth already. Can you think of something we could do outside that would not be playing on the playground?

W: Maybe we could take care of this.

T: Take care of this? Like, could we go somewhere and do some-
    thing interesting? What do you think?
C: We could go to the cougar's cage (the home of the University
    mascot).
T: We could go to the cougar's cage.
M: We could watch a videotape.
T: We could go to the cougar's cage and watch a videotape?
N: We could watch the water fountains.
T: You mean watch the water fountains on the walk?
N: Yes.
T: Okay, we could do that. We could go to the water fountains and
    the cougar's cage. What else, S?
S: Take a little walk.
C: And watch a video, too.
T: Take a little walk and watch a video, too. Maybe we would have
    time for a video when we got back. What do you think, G?
G: Maybe a bus ride would be good (the University shuttle bus).
T: A bus ride would be good. What do you think, Z?
Z: Maybe we could go find caterpillars.
T: And you think we should find caterpillars while we're out there.
    Okay, what do you think about this? This might use everyone's
    idea. We could take a bus ride, then go to the cougar's cage.
    Then, on the way back from the cougar's cage, we could see the
    fountains. The whole time, we could be looking on the ground to
    see if we see caterpillars.
N: And some acorns.
T: And acorns. Then after that we can go back to school and if we
    have time we could see a videotape.
Children: Yea!
T: What do you think?
G: We're gonna' be hungry.
T: We are going to be hungry when we get back.
G: We could take our lunches on the bus ride.
T: Now that's an idea. What do you think?
C: And we could have them someplace at the water fountains.
T: Now the only problem with that, G, is that if we eat our lunches
    out there, we won't have time for a videotape. So we'll have to
    vote. Picnic or videotape.
H: You know what? I went on a bus and I saw a bus sign, and it said
    "No eating on the bus."
T: If we carry our lunches and we keep them in the sack, could we
    take them with us?

H: No, I don't think so.

T: You don't think we could? But I've been on the bus before, H, and if I keep my lunch in the lunchbag, they don't get mad. But if I eat it, they get mad.

H: You keep it in there?

T: You keep it in there and don't eat it.

H: You keep it in there and they didn't get mad?

T: No, they didn't get mad. It was okay for me to carry it on but if I unwrapped it and ate it, then they said I couldn't do that. They said I had to put it away.

Z: Did you try to open it?

T: I tried one time because I didn't know the rule. And then the guy said, "You can't eat on the bus. Put it away." So I put it away and it was all right. Okay, let's see. Z, do you want to have a picnic or watch a video? Oh (to E, the aide), what time do you have to leave?

E: 11:15.

T: Oh! We have a problem. This is not a possibility. Oh, this is such a serious dilemma.

H: What?

T: We cannot have a picnic this day.

G: Why?

T: Because E (the aide) has to leave and go to her class.

(Note: This discussion is taking place at approximately 10:30. The problem is that the person scheduled to relieve E at 11:15 would not know where to find the class if they took a walk.)

C: Well, we could let her leave right now.

T: But then there's only one teacher, and what if somebody got out of control or had a problem?

C: We would have to wait for A (the Assistant Director) then.

T: Yeah, but see, I would be one teacher all alone with all these children, and do you know what? There are some rules that teachers have to follow. They are called guidelines for childcare. Because we care for children, so we have to have guidelines for caring for children. And those guidelines say that we will have one teacher for every seven or eight children. That means that we have to have two teachers with this group. If we have only one teacher, we are breaking the rules, and I can't do that.

C: We could take A.

T: E is going to see if there is someone else who can go with us.

(E returns with news that there is someone available to go with them on their walk.)

Children: Yea!

T: Okay, great. Well, then let's make a decision. Z, picnic or video? (They vote by polling individuals and decide to go on the picnic.)

Peige wanted to involve the children in deciding what to do since they could not go to the playground. However, she did not think it necessary to put every idea to a vote. Children's ideas were flowing freely, and for the most part, all fit together nicely. In this case, if Peige had put every idea to a vote, they would have spent their entire time deciding and would have had no time left to take their walk. Peige knew this, and so exercised leadership over the discussion, without dominating it.

SUMMARY

Children in constructivist classrooms have a feeling of necessity, ownership, and responsibility in relation to class rules as a result of making the rules themselves. Rule making and decision making are activities in which children practice self-regulation and cooperation. By giving children this power, teachers reduce heteronomy. The teacher's role is to select issues to submit to children, guide rule-making and decision-making discussions, record and post rules, and enforce rules, with the help of children.

Voting

Voting is an integral part of the sociomoral atmosphere of the constructivist classroom. However, like so many constructivist activities, merely voting is not enough to ensure that it is a constructivist activity. Voting can be conducted in ways that defeat constructivist purposes. In this chapter, we discuss the objectives for voting. We then present six guidelines for making the voting experience developmentally beneficial.

OBJECTIVES

The rationale behind voting is threefold. First, voting is a process of self-regulation. When children exercise initiative to make group decisions, they feel in control of what happens in their classroom. They are motivated to formulate and express opinions. Through exchanging points of view, children may be persuaded or make new efforts to persuade others. Children have the opportunity to construct the idea of equality as they see that each person's opinion is valued and given equal weight in the decision-making process.

Second, children come to feel a sense of cooperative group purposes that transcend the needs and wants of the individual. Children can come to terms with the idea of majority rule yet develop sensitivity to minority positions.

Third, children have opportunities during voting to think about writing and number. Through conceptualizing and recording issues and votes, conviction is cultivated about the usefulness of written language. Similarly, as children count votes, decide which is more, and predict how many more votes are needed for a particular decision, they construct number in a personally meaningful context.

GUIDELINES FOR VOTING

Observation of classroom voting and systematic experimentation with voting in the classroom led us to conceptualize several principles of teaching. We present them here, along with examples taken from our observations and research.

1. Choose appropriate issues.

The question is: How does the teacher decide what issues are appropriate to bring to a class vote? First, children must engage in voting out of their own interests and purposes. Otherwise it is just an exercise that children go through to please the teacher.

Second, the issue brought to a vote must be one that affects the entire class. Voting is a group process, where children make decisions that have a bearing on their life together. If an issue belongs to an individual child, or to two children, it is best handled by the parties involved.

In chapter 6 we describe an incident in which the entire class discusses whether or not to change the rule governing how long block structures can remain standing in the block center. While the issue comes to the attention of the group because of the distress of one child, it is clear from the discussion that this is an issue that affects every member of the class. They all enjoy playing in the block center, and they all have opinions that they are eager to share. In the end, the children vote to decide what they want the rule to state, and the teacher supports them in their ability to make group decisions. She assures them that if they have problems, they can always come back and discuss it again.

Third, do not vote unless a difference of opinion is expected. For example, we witnessed one circle time in a kindergarten class in which the teacher suggested playing a favorite game. The children all cheered when the teacher made the suggestion. She then suggested that they vote. A vote was not necessary in this situation as the teacher already had popular support for her idea.

In contrast, in another kindergarten class at circle time, the teacher suggested doing a flannel board story. Some children called out "The Three Bears!" while other children called out "The Gingerbread Boy!" Under these circumstances, a vote was highly appropriate.

While issues brought to a vote should involve a matter of opinion, be careful not to use voting as a means of determining truth. For example, in a 4-year-old class, children had a difference of opinion as to whether turkeys could fly. The teacher, Peige Fuller, related the story to us:

> They were arguing so badly over the question of whether turkeys could fly, I thought they were going to have blows. It was getting out of hand—screaming, "No, they can't!" "Yes, they can!" Someone jumps up and says, "Let's take a vote!" I'm sitting back, because it's their circle and I want to see what happens. So they took a vote, and they voted that turkeys can't fly, which is the best of all outcomes when you carry the story to its conclusion. I raised my hand and asked, "Well, can turkeys fly?" The answer was no. We had voted, and it was a settled question, turkeys can't fly. I said, "We voted and said that turkeys can't fly. But what if they really can?" I asked them whether you can vote about whether something *is* or not. I used "fish swim" to illustrate my point. Can fish swim? Yes. But what if we voted that fish can't swim? Could they still swim? The power of being 4 years old is overpowering sometimes. Some said of course they could still swim. But some of them just weren't sure. "How could we find out?" I asked. Well, we could go see turkeys. Then it was my job to find turkeys. Luckily, they had turkeys at the zoo. We were committed to following this through.

The class took a field trip to the zoo, where they asked the zookeeper if the turkeys could fly. Peige continues:

> We were wrong—turkeys *can* fly! So some things you can vote about, and some things you can't vote about. Some things you have to find out by investigating the world.

As a prelude to hypothesis testing, a vote ("How many people *think* that turkeys can fly?") can be useful. However, we see from this example that the teacher must be careful that children do not get the notion that if more people think turkeys cannot fly, then turkeys cannot fly.

Fourth, avoid issues of individual rights. In the block rule example a problem raised by an individual was an issue in which the entire group had an interest. Sometimes, however, an issue raised by an individual is not appropriate for submission to the group for a decision. In particular, the teacher needs to take care that issues brought to a vote do not favor one child over another or deprive a child of his or her rights.

We present two situations in which children were in danger of having their rights violated by a class vote. Both examples involve children taking turns as Special Helper. The Special Helper has certain duties that the children enjoy, such as calling a 5-minute warning before clean-up time, turning the lights on and off when needed, etc. The privilege moves from child to child according to a list of names posted on the wall. In the first example from a kindergarten class, V announces that, because he is going on vacation and will miss his Special Helper day, he should be Special Helper today, instead of A, who is next on the list. A protests, and the teacher (T) questions V about this.

T: Well, V, maybe you can tell us why you only have 2 days left.
V: Because then I'm gonna go to Aunt Lucy's wedding, and I think it's just gonna be about this many days.
T: Well, does it mean you still won't get a Special Helper Day?
V: No.
T: 'Cause I see your name is really coming up soon.
V: No.
T: Well, you know, A just said she doesn't think it would be fair for her, so I don't know.
V: Let's vote on it.
T: Well, sometimes this is a problem that you guys have to work out alone, but I don't know.
J: But then some people like to play with A and some people (unintelligible)
N: I like A better than V.
T: So that's what would make you vote for A, you think? Well, A, do you want to vote on it, or do you think you should just have your day?
A: I just want to have my day.
V: No, let's vote.
T: Well, what do you guys think? Maybe we should vote on whether we should vote.

The teacher in this example starts out upholding the ideal of fairness, consulting A about whether she wants to give up her day for V. But she begins to get into trouble when she says that she thinks maybe it is a matter for the two children to decide. This problem of keeping track of the order of children's names on the list is too complicated for V, who thinks that he will miss his day. In fact, V is not slated to be Special Helper until he returns from his trip which is only a long weekend. But his understanding of time is not very advanced, and as far as he can tell, he is going to be gone for a long time. This is a problem for the teacher to solve with V, pointing out to him that he will be Special Helper when he returns.

The teacher makes a big mistake when she suggests that the children vote on whether or not to vote. She gives to the entire class the power to remove from A her right to be Special Helper on that particular day. J and N point out the unfairness of the vote when they state that people might vote for A because they like her better than V. One danger in voting is that it can turn into a popularity contest. In the end, they vote twice: on whether to vote and then on who should be Special Helper. Luckily for the teacher, the group votes for A to retain her right to be Special Helper. However, no one feels better. A experiences the stress of almost losing her day, and V feels rejected and misunderstood by the rest of the class.

In a class of 4-year-olds, a similar problem arises. C was next on the list to be Special Helper yesterday, but he was not in school (he only comes to school on Tuesdays and Thursdays), so the Special Helper privilege moved down the list to M. Today, C is at school, and the question is: Who should be Special Helper? Should they move back up the list so that C can get his turn, or does he forfeit his turn? It is early in the school year, and this has never occurred before. The teacher asks the children what they think should happen, who should be Special Helper. Each child suggests himself or herself. The teacher very gently points out to each child that this cannot be, that they have to move systematically down the list. She asks the group whether C should get his turn today, and children call out "No!" Finally, the teacher suggests a vote between allowing C to have his turn, or to miss his turn. After C votes (to have his turn), the next child votes that C should miss his turn, prompting the teacher to reflect on what is happening. She suddenly realizes that the group may vote against C's right. In this difficult situation, the teacher has to retreat from the vote.

> You know, you guys, I'm not even sure that's fair. Now, think about this. I'm the teacher, right? And part of my job is to make sure that everybody gets fair turns, right? I mean, children get fair turns with doing this, helping, and children get fair turns with doing activities, and children get fair turns with snack,

and children get fair turns. Well, if I let you guys vote that C doesn't get a turn, then that's not fair for C, is it? No way! I would not be doing my job. Because one of my jobs is to make sure everybody gets a turn. So, you know what? It doesn't make any sense to vote, because C needs to have a turn. It's my job to make sure that everybody gets a turn. N gets a turn, her name is right here (points to chart) and C gets a turn, his name is here, and T gets a turn, his name is here. (Teacher goes through entire list, pointing out each child's name and position on the list.) Everybody gets a turn. So, you know what? We can't vote (erases board) for C not to have a turn. That would not be a fair thing to do. So, C, you are the Special Helper today. We had to figure all that out. Would you come up here, please?

In this example, the teacher does not have a clearly defined policy of what to do when the Special Helper is absent. She turns to the children to decide something that was better decided by her alone. However, the teacher realizes her error and stops the vote before C can have his right to a Special Helper day taken away. Further, she explains what happened in language the children can understand, in terms of fairness to all children.

This example also illustrates another important point. That is, the teacher should not allow children to vote on anything unless he or she is open to accepting whatever the group decides. The teacher in this segment realizes as soon as she starts the voting process that she cannot live with one outcome, that C would have his Special Helper day taken away from him. Children can often make decisions that seem curious to adults, and certainly it is not always possible to predict how children will vote. Therefore, if the teacher needs a decision to go a certain way, he or she should not suggest a vote.

2. Encourage discussion and define the alternatives.

It is important to conduct a thorough discussion of the pros and cons of the children's alternatives. Ask children to share why they support their choice. If the alternatives are not already defined, ask children to help define them. Be sure that alternatives are stated clearly, preferably by children. The teacher can repeat a child's words, if necessary, to be sure the group understands them. Frequently, it is necessary to help a child articulate an idea so it is clear. If children do not understand what they are voting for, they will not make the connection between the process of voting, and its result and the outcome will seem arbitrary.

During this discussion period, it is important to write the alternatives on a chalkboard or a large sheet of paper, using language appropriate to the age of the children. This helps children be clear on what they are voting for.

Notice in the following excerpt how the teacher, Dora Chen (T), works to clarify exactly what children mean. In this example from a class of $3\frac{1}{2}$- to $4\frac{1}{2}$-year-olds, one child notices a child still eating snack during clean-up time. She believes this to be against the rule and raises the issue at circle. Some children suggest changing the rule.

T: So you think that when one light goes out for 5 more minutes, that's still time to finish up eating? Just like it's time to finish up writing names or finish up pictures and things. But when both lights are out for clean-up, then it's not time to finish up writing names and it's also not time to finish up snack.

A: Or you could, 1 day if you wanted to draw a picture that you didn't finish with, if you could start writing it, and finish it.

T: Can you say that again, A? I didn't really get that.

A: If you don't finish your picture at school, and it goes home, you could bring it back 1 day and draw the part of it.

T: You could finish it the next day?

A: Uh-huh.

G: Or you could finish it at home.

T: That's another good idea, G. Anybody else have an idea about that? C?

C: I do. Well, first, after you, if you draw at that table there, and you do it before it's clean-up time or 5 more minutes, and when it's clean-up, then you clean up, and then when it's outside time, you can stay inside longer to do it.

T: You think that when it's clean-up they should clean up but then when children are going outside after group time, that they could stay longer? And finish it up?

N: Well, if you leave your snack on the snack table, then we'll just think somebody is through and we'll just have to throw it away, and we'll just have to. We clean the snack table every clean-up time.

T: But C was saying that if they don't finish a drawing, or, does this apply to snack too? If they don't finish snack, C, then after clean-up time and after group time, then if they save it, like on the shelf, then they could come and eat it, or take it outside on the bench and eat it, you think?

C: (Nods) Yeah.

T: Okay, so we can vote on whether they could save the snack that they have not finished eating, to eat during outside time, or that they will just have to clean up and throw it out. Is that right?

A: I know.

T: Yes, A?

A: What if the light goes off and someone has not taken a bite of their snack and someone takes it and—

M: Well, they can recognize the bite.

T: Let A finish his thought.

A: And if they, the people that want to eat it, and they didn't get a chance to bite it, and someone throws it away.

T: So if someone already took a bite of a snack, then it has to be thrown away, A, during clean-up time? So you are saying that when it's 5 more minutes,

A: No, clean-up.

T: When it's clean-up time. Well, if they were already eating snack or if they started eating snack, making snack at 5 more minutes, and the light goes off, they will have to throw it out?

A: And if they eat all their snack at clean-up, they can't do that.

T: Okay, so when the light goes out for clean-up time, they cannot eat their snack. They will have to throw it out, clean it up just like any other activity. Okay, that's A's idea. And C's idea was to give them a chance to come back and eat it after group, after clean-up. Right? Okay, B, you have something else to add about snack?

B: I thought maybe we might, we could bring it outside if they're not finished and they could eat it while some people are playing.

T: Okay, outside? So that B and C are saying that if someone has started to make snack at 5 more minutes and if during clean-up time they are not finished eating, then they could save it on a paper towel and maybe put it on that table there and save it until after clean-up and after group, and when everyone's outside and they could eat it outside? Give them a chance to finish eating that snack after group time?

B: (Nods)

T: Okay, then let's take a vote about that. (Stands up, writes on board) "No chance to finish eating snack during"—when it's time to clean up? How about if I say "when the light goes out?" Does that make it clearer?

Children: No.

T: (Reading) "No chance to finish snack when the light goes out."
Well, how about if I say "Throw away snack during clean-up
time?" Does that make it clearer?

Children: No.

T: (Erases board) Let's try this again. I'm not saying it right today.
Let's see. How about "Children must clean up snack during clean-
up time?"

A: No. No.

T: How shall I say it, A?

A: Say, if you . . . I don't know either.

M: I do, I do.

T: Yes, M?

M: Um, if the children take a bite of their snack and take a few bites,
at 5 more minutes, and then the light goes out, you could just put
it on the shelf, not up there, but over there, and then —

A: That's the happy part.

T: That's the happy part, A says. J (student intern)?

J: How about "No more eating at clean-up time?"

Children: Yeah, yeah.

T: That's great. (Writing) "No more eating during clean-up." That
means, this side here also means that you have to throw it away.
That means that you will not get to eat it, even afterwards, okay?
(Writing) "Throw out snack." And this side here, we will vote on
C and B's idea about getting a chance to finish it as part of outside, during outside time, after group. Okay? So we will have
(writing) "Get chance to finish snack after clean-up and group
time." Okay. Let's start with. . . . Think about which way you
are going to vote for it, okay?

The teacher goes on to conduct the vote, and the children decide the
rule will be that they must throw snack away during clean-up time.
We want to draw attention to the extensive discussion that takes
place. Children have strong opinions about this topic, and they struggle to make themselves understood by both the teacher and each
other. We also want to draw attention to the careful way in which the
teacher makes sure that she captures on the chalkboard the exact
rules the children suggest. She writes, erases, checks with children,
and rewrites, until she writes what the children want the rule to state.

While helping children understand alternatives to be voted on,
teachers should be alert to the fact that children often see no logical
problem in voting for two mutually exclusive possibilities. For example, if the field trip choices are "zoo" and "farm," children may enthu-

siastically raise hands for both. This is why we recommend voting with polling procedures (discussed below). When children are asked, "Do you want to go to the zoo or the farm?" the mutually exclusive nature of the choice is clearer to the child.

We have observed two types of errors in teachers' definitions of voting issues. One is failure to present alternatives, and the other is confusion of the nomination process with voting.

Teachers inexperienced but committed to the idea of voting frequently fail to present alternatives, and instead ask children to vote on a single activity. For example, we watched a kindergarten teacher ask, "Who wants to sing 'Down by the Bay'? Raise your hand." Without an alternative, children who raised their hands were not really making a choice but were simply responding to the teacher's enthusiasm. If children had not agreed to the teacher's suggestion, a vacuum might have been created, and the teacher would have been trapped in a cycle of rejected suggestions. Voting should be employed to decide between two (or more) positive alternatives, such as "Sing a song" or "Hear a story."

We have also observed situations in which children thought they were nominating alternatives but teachers interpreted the nominations as votes. For example, in a kindergarten class in which a turtle had recently been added to the collection of animals, the teacher suggested at circle that they might want to name their turtle. She went around the circle, asking each child in turn his or her idea for a name and writing down every suggestion. Then, she looked at the list, noticed that two names had each been suggested twice, and declared that since those two names had gotten the most "votes," they would choose between those two names. The rest of the children's ideas for names were erased. This was very distressing for children whose ideas were discarded.

Similarly, in a kindergarten class, the children plan a picnic for Valentine's Day. The previous day, children made suggestions at circle about what foods they would like for their picnic. At this circle, the teacher has children vote on what foods to have. However, the teacher decides arbitrarily to limit the vote to the items that got the most "votes" (meaning nominations) yesterday. She looks at the list and sees four items that could be considered desserts: ice cream, popsicles, bubble gum, and hot chocolate with marshmallows. Ice cream and popsicles had received the most nominations, so she asks, "Who would like to have ice cream?" She does not specify that the vote is between ice cream and popsicles, and she ignores the suggestions for bubble gum and hot chocolate with marshmallows. She then looks for proteins on the list, and asks "Who wants heart-shaped sandwiches?" without presenting another choice. When she gets to the beverage, she asks "Who wants lemonade?" failing to mention the nominations of coke and milk.

In this teacher's defense, she wanted the children to make the decisions for the picnic, and she also wanted to ensure a balanced meal. However, she could have done some organizing without being coercive or subtracting from the children's involvement, and could have had a much easier and more fruitful class discussion. Our suggestion is that she might have categorized, or enlisted the children's help in categorizing the list of food ideas by food group (protein, fruit, dessert, beverage, etc). Then the class could have voted on the choices within each category. In this way, children would have been involved in the process, while the teacher's concern for a well-balanced meal would have been satisfied.

3. Use voting procedures understandable to children.

When preparing to conduct a vote, it is crucial to make sure that children understand the method of voting. If the children cannot follow the vote, the outcome will appear to be arbitrary, undermining the whole purpose. The particular method of voting used in any class will vary, depending on the age and developmental level of the children. Voting methods we review here include raising hands, polling children, casting ballots, and counting bodies in a line. We also discuss how to deal with tie votes and lobbying.

Counting raised hands. Probably the most familiar method of voting, counting raised hands has serious problems when used with young children. We cannot recommend it for a variety of reasons. Often, very young children (4 years old and under, and some inexperienced 5-year-olds) are so excited to raise their hands that as soon as the teacher says, "Raise your hands if—," hands shoot into the air. The fact that they have not heard what it is they are voting for does not bother them in the least.

Children often raise their hands halfway, or wave them around, or raise and lower them, making it difficult for the teacher to count. Sometimes children tease the teacher, saying, "I was just scratching my head." By the time the teacher has counted all the votes on the first option, some children may have forgotten that they voted, and vote again, for the second option. The teacher ends up having to exhort the children to keep their hands up, not to vote twice, and so on. Often everyone ends up confused about what happened.

As mentioned previously, children who vote more than once may not understand the mutual exclusiveness of the alternatives. Children old enough to understand that one should only vote once still believe that it is unfair for someone to vote twice because that way, it is as though that child's vote is worth twice as much. They have not yet grasped that if you vote twice, and there are only two choices, your two votes cancel each other out. Therefore, the best way to deal with the problem of voting twice is simply to use methods where it cannot happen.

When the teacher counts hands from a distance, children often are not sure whether their hands have been counted. The teacher may look at children as he or she counts them, or point, or may even name them (B-that's 1; F-that's 2; C-that's 3; etc.), but it is still possible that children do not realize that they were counted. Young children need something concrete to assure them that their vote has been included. Also, if the children are too young to understand numbers as representing quantities, simply announcing, "Five people want X and seven people want Y, so we will do Y," is not a good idea. When children do not know what 5 and 7 mean, this announcement may leave many children bewildered about what just happened.

Having said all that, if the situation arises where hand raising is the only method of voting available, there are ways to make it work better. Ask a child to do the counting. Emphasize the mutual exclusivity of the choices. If the vote is between X and Y, state "If you want X *and not* Y, raise your hand." Then, "If you want Y *and not* X, raise your hand." We cannot guarantee that this will help, but it might.

It is important to ask for votes on all options. Do not subtract the number of votes cast for X from the total number of children, and determine the number of votes for Y. Most young children cannot follow this arithmetic. Children will think that since they did not vote, their vote was not counted.

Polling children. We consider polling to be one of the best ways to conduct a vote with young children. Although there are many variations, all polling methods basically involve asking individual children to state in some fashion how they vote.

One way to do this is to go around the circle or the class systematically, asking each child individually how he or she votes. When children state out loud "I vote for X," they become more conscious of points of view, their own and others'. They also feel more of a sense of ownership of class decisions. The vote is a concrete symbol of the child's participation in the group. Even the shyest child can whisper to the teacher what he or she wants and in that way can share in group decisions.

Allow for abstentions. Sometimes children do not care which way the vote goes, and they should not be forced to make a choice. Young children easily learn that if they do not want to vote, they can say "Pass."

The danger of unreflective voting was constructed by one first-grader who passed when asked who she wanted to be President of the United States. Questioned about why she "passed," she answered, "If you don't know who the best person is, you could accidentally help the wrong person."

Polling requires making a written representation of each vote. Adults usually do this with slash marks, but we recommend this representation only for older children experienced with voting. Young children understand polling best when their votes are represented by their names or initials. When the teacher writes a list of voters under a written option, children can see their vote and know that it has been counted for the alternative they chose.

We have also used name cards when polling, with great success. The teacher can hold up a card with a child's name written on it, ask that child how he or she votes, and then place the name card in that choice's pile or line.

Regardless of how the votes are recorded, place the votes in physical one-to-one correspondence, either vertically or horizontally. This is very helpful to children who do not yet have a solid understanding of number. They can look at the lines or rows and see which one has more, without counting. The teacher can point out the length of the two lists, asking "Which one looks like it received the most votes?" The counting will make more sense when combined with the strong visual cue.

Involve the children in counting the votes. As stated earlier, voting is an excellent number experience. When children are truly interested in the outcome of the vote, then they will be interested in understanding the number aspect. As they become better able to reason about number, they will begin to predict outcomes. For example, if there are 15 children in the class and the vote is 8 to 4, some children might say, "It doesn't matter now, 8 is the most. That one has 8, so it wins." We would not suggest that the teacher call off the vote at that point because the children who had not yet voted might feel as though they did not count. The teacher could stop briefly to ask "How do you know? Why do you think that X will have the most? Let's

see if that works out." The teacher thus capitalizes on the spontaneous math experiences that arise in voting.

Casting ballots. One of the problems with the polling method is that
it is conducted publicly. Especially with children over about 5 years
old, peer pressure can become a problem. Sometimes children's
attempts at persuasion can turn into bullying or a popularity contest.
When this is a problem, some form of casting ballots can be used.
This can be done with neutral ballots (pieces of paper, checkers, etc.)
and containers for each choice. Or it can be done with a neutral container and different ballots for the choices (such as pieces of paper
that children write their choices on). It can be conducted in the open
or in secret, depending on the needs of the group. Everything that we
said above about counting votes when polling children holds true
here as well. No matter how you do it, make sure that you count the
votes in a way that the children can follow and that is meaningful to
them.

Counting children's bodies. In this type of voting, children vote with
their bodies, by standing, sitting, or otherwise moving their bodies to
the place designated for the voting option desired. This is a good
method to use if the class is outside and the teacher does not have
access to paper and pencil. However, we have not had good results
using this method with children 4 years old and younger. Often, while
the teacher can see both lines in their entirety, the children cannot.
Even after drawing attention to the one-to-one correspondence by
having children opposite each other hold hands, and seeing how
many people are left in one line, children are still not sure why one
line has more. However, with children who understand the importance and implication of correspondence, this method can work.

Another problem we have seen with this method of voting is that
when children are settled in a circle, having them get up to vote
invites chaos and confusion. This method should probably only be
used when children are already on their feet.

Dealing with tie votes. Tie votes provide great opportunities to
engage children in social problem solving. "What should we do? Six
children want X and six children want Y. What is the fair thing to do?"
Some children suggest that the fair solution to a tie vote is to do both
things, even with two mutually exclusive choices. Other children suggest voting again, and this sometimes, although not always, results in a
different vote. In one of our experiments, 4-year-olds voting on which

of two books they wanted to have read to them had a tie vote. The only solution that the children could think of was to read four pages from each book. So the adult read four pages from one book, put it down, and read four pages from the other book. The children were very surprised as they witnessed the inadequacy of their solution.

Another solution to a tie vote is to have children line up facing each other in one-to-one correspondence in two rows (according to which option they voted for). For a certain length of time (say, 1 minute) give each child in the row voting for X the opportunity to try and persuade the child opposite him or her to change votes. Then give the other row the same opportunity. After this time of intense political persuasion, take another vote. (This solution may be more appropriate for older children.)

Dealing with lobbying. As mentioned earlier, sometimes children can become vigorous in their lobbying efforts (for example, threatening loss of friendship unless a child votes a particular way). Mild lobbying can be a good thing, giving children experience in negotiating with others. It certainly shows that children understand the process and respect its power. The teacher's role is to make sure that the lobbying does not become destructive. In cases where children's lobbying appears to be getting out-of-hand, the teacher can step in with gentle reminders that "K can vote for what she wants, and you can vote for what you want. That's why we vote, so everyone can have a say."

Sometimes, children will cheer when votes are cast for what they want and boo when they are not. This can upset the children who are not voting with those cheering, and the best way to deal with this is to point out how the others feel when children cheer. Ask one of the children in the minority to tell those cheering how it feels. Remind them of other times when the children doing the cheering were on the minority side, and try to get the children to take the perspective of the minority.

Participate as a Voter

We advocate having teachers take part in the vote. This helps to demonstrate that the teacher is fully a member of the community and that the teacher's opinion is worth neither more nor less than any other person's opinion. Having brought an issue to a vote, it is imperative that the teacher does not have veto power in the class voting process. The teacher's vote is one vote among many. The teacher can try to persuade, but in the end, he or she must accept the wishes of the majority, just as the children must. In the vote on how many days to leave block structures up (refer to chapter 7), the teacher believed that 5 days was too long. However, she could see that no harm would be done by allowing children to experience the result of their decision. If 5 days was too long, that would become apparent to the children at some point, and then they could change the rule.

One teacher told us that she often votes last, or near last, and votes with the minority whenever possible. She explained that her purpose was to demonstrate being disappointed with the outcome of the vote but dealing with the disappointment. In this way, she offered a model for being in the minority and fostered sensitivity to minority viewpoints.

By voting last or near last, the teacher can subtly manipulate votes. If a tie vote is coming up, the teacher can either cast the tie breaker, if in the teacher's opinion the tie needs to be broken, or the teacher can create a tie, if the children are ready to discuss what to do in the case of a tie.

Teachers can also demonstrate how to handle differences in opinion by voting opposite each other. If there are two adults in the class, one adult can make a point of respectfully disagreeing with the other adult by casting an opposite vote. The children see that disagreements do not mean that people are not friends, just that they hold different opinions.

4. Foster acceptance of majority rule and respect for minority views.

After the vote has been conducted, the teacher should interpret the outcome of the vote for the class with an attitude of accepting the ideal of majority rule. State something to the effect that "This vote means that more people want X than want Y, so we will do X." Use the language of fairness, pointing out that "Since more people voted for X, the fair thing to do is X." Avoid the language of winning and losing. We recognize that this may be difficult because children use these terms spontaneously. We have often heard children erupt into a spontaneous chant "We won! We won!" This is an opportunity to remind children gently of their friends who wanted the other choice and how those friends feel right now.

The teacher should show sensitivity to the minority viewpoint. In the Investigators class after a vote over which book to read, E raised her hand and was close to tears, saying, "My book always loses." The teacher, Peige Fuller, recounts that she struggled over what to do with the minority opinion. Children had strong opinions. "This book won." Peige decided to act as E's advocate. "Yes, but E is sad. She says her book never wins." Some children just wanted to move on to reading the book. Peige recounts, "What we finally came to was a compromise solution where the book that won got read first and the book that didn't win got read second—at second circle or whenever it worked out. That was a powerful lesson in fairness. What does it mean to be just and to take everyone into consideration?"

If the vote is to choose between doing one of two things, the teacher can suggest that maybe another day, the class can do the other choice. The teacher can uphold the worth of all the choices by stating matter-of-factly, "We had two really good suggestions, and we voted, and decided that we would choose this one." In cases where a vote addresses a problem, the teacher can state that the solution voted on will be tried, and if after a certain length of time that solution does not work, they can come back together and try to find another solution. This leaves open the possibility of trying the other choice, the one that received fewer votes.

SUMMARY

The educational objective of voting is principally to promote children's self-regulation by giving them real power to make decisions about what happens in their class. Voting also gives children the possibility of coming to terms with majority rule and developing sensitivity to feelings of minorities. In addition, children can construct their knowledge about written language and number in a personally meaningful context. The constructivist teacher chooses issues to be voted on that are of concern to the group as a whole on which a difference of opinion is expected. Discussion is encouraged and alternatives are defined. Voting procedures that are understandable to children include polling and casting ballots, and do not include counting raised hands. Tie votes challenge children to solve the problem of what to do. Instances of lobbying reflect active negotiation and appreciation of the voting process. However, if extreme, the teacher may raise the issue of how the minority feels when many people are cheering the defeat of its view. Constructivist teachers participate as voters and provide models of disagreement among adults and sometimes use their votes to create a tie and to illustrate minority acquiescence to the majority.

9

Social and Moral
Discussions

In previous chapters we discuss ways in which teachers can establish a constructivist sociomoral atmosphere through fostering community and an attitude of cooperation, turning over to children the power to make decisions, vote, and resolve conflicts. Teachers can also include in their lesson plans activities specifically aimed toward promoting sociomoral development. Focused concern on how to resolve social and moral dilemmas is an important aspect of the sociomoral atmosphere. In this chapter we discuss how teachers use discussions to promote children's reflections about social and moral issues.

First, we explain what we mean by "social" and "moral" discussions, and why we use the term *sociomoral*. We provide a brief theoretical foundation for understanding moral judgment, then go on to discuss two different types of social and moral discussions and offer advice on where and how to find materials for these. We present six guidelines for conducting social and moral discussions in the classroom. Finally, we describe research on conducting moral dilemma discussions in classrooms at the University of Houston HDLS.

WHAT IS "SOCIAL," "MORAL," AND "SOCIOMORAL"?

The reader may wonder about the distinction between "social" and "moral" as well as the meaning of "sociomoral." Some moral development researchers (Nucci, 1981; Smetana, 1983; Turiel, 1983) make a distinction between matters of morality and matters of social convention. Using pure prototypes, such as pushing a child off a swing as an example of a moral issue, and calling teachers by their first names as an example of a social convention, they demonstrate that even very young children make distinctions between social and moral issues and reason differently in the two domains. However, we have found that frequently the issues arising in the lives of young children are not so clearly social or moral.

Some issues that arise in classrooms for young children can be categorized as clearly moral. For example, issues concerned with hurting others are moral because they deal with the basic human right to physical safety. Likewise, destruction or theft of property are considered moral issues in our Western culture.

While all moral issues are social in nature, an issue may be social without being moral. In chapter 6, we describe an incident in which a child brought a social problem to the group for solution. She sought from other children ideas about how to get to school on time so she would not always miss her turn to be Special Helper. This problem contained no moral implications, but was strictly social.

Sometimes, agreement over whether issues are social or moral may be lacking. For example, whether to say "please" in making a request or "thank you" upon receipt of a gift or favor is considered by some to be a matter of social conventions about what are regarded as good manners in a particular culture. However, others may consider polite manners to reflect respect for others and therefore to be an issue of morality. One might also argue that moral politeness exists only when an individual's attitude is truly respectful of the feelings of others.

Many issues cannot be clearly categorized as social or moral because they contain elements of both. Some issues that appear on the surface to be matters of social convention may have underlying moral implications. For example, the rule that children eat snack only at the snack table is a social convention. There seems to be no moral reason why children should have to eat snack there, as opposed to anywhere else. However, the underlying moral implication of eating snack at the snack table is that if children eat snack elsewhere in the room, the class will become littered with snack remnants, making clean-up difficult, attracting insects, and in general having a negative effect on the quality of life for everyone in the classroom. Similarly, the issue of the number of children allowed in the block center, a matter of practical social convention, can become moral. For example, in a K-1 classroom at the Sunset-Pearl Elementary School, the rule was that four children could be in the block center. When a fourth child entered the center and found only four blocks available for use, what was a matter of simple practicality became a moral issue concerning the rights of all children to participate equally in the block center.

One problem encountered in disentangling the social and moral components of an issue revolves around distinguishing between the means and the ends of a situation. For example, the issue of classroom turn taking is moral in the sense that justice demands that equal rights be respected. Equality is a moral end. The debate over the means by which to regulate turn taking, however, is strictly social.

Another problem with trying to disentangle the social and the moral is that young children do not always distinguish between the two. For example, children often experience not getting what they want as unfair and, therefore, as a moral issue. Conversely, to the young child, telling an untruth may simply represent an intelligent way to avoid punishment rather than a moral issue.

We often find it difficult in practice to maintain a clear distinction between the social and the moral. Situations may vary in the degree to which they are more or less social than moral. Therefore we use the term "sociomoral" to refer to phenomena that are both social and moral.

MORAL JUDGMENT THEORY

Our work in sociomoral development has been informed primarily by three theorists—Jean Piaget, Lawrence Kohlberg, and Robert Selman. We discuss Piaget and Selman at length in chapter 2. Here we review briefly Kohlberg's work on developmental stages of moral reasoning.

Using Piaget's work as a springboard, Kohlberg did extensive research on moral reasoning in children and adults. With moral dilemma interviews, he probed to uncover how people reason about moral issues and identified six stages in the development of moral reasoning. These stages appear to be hierarchical and sequential, and the first five have since been verified in numerous studies (See Colby & Kohlberg, 1987; Kohlberg, 1984, for reviews). We present here an outline of the first four of these stages that pertain to children.

Stages 1 and 2 are both very individualistic and are referred to as Preconventional morality. In Stage 1, right is defined in terms of that which avoids punishment or is in obedience to a higher authority such as parents and other adults. Actions are judged in physical rather than psychological terms. That is, the child's concern is with material damage to persons or things rather than with intentions. Interests of others are not considered. In fact, there is no recognition that the interests of others differ from one's own.

At Stage 2 (often called the stage of instrumental purpose and exchange), right is defined as that which is in one's own self-interest. As everyone is recognized as having self-interests, what is right is viewed as simply relative. This is the stage in which we see an "eye for an eye" morality, and where children are concerned with strict equality—for example, measuring to make sure each one gets the same amount of cake. Children at this stage begin to cooperate with each other in order to get what they want, a sort of "You scratch my back, I'll scratch yours" mentality.

Stages 3 and 4 are more social in nature, and are referred to as conventional morality. Stage 3 is the stage of mutual relationships, and what is right is defined in terms of the immediate social system (family, class, circle of close friends, etc.) The child begins to act in terms of the expectations of people important to the child. Children in this stage are concerned about being a "good girl" or "good boy" and will act to gain approval. The Golden Rule is understood in a concrete way, as putting oneself specifically in someone else's shoes.

At Stage 4, the larger social system begins to enter the picture, and right is defined in terms of societal norms, laws, duties, and expectations. There is the recognition that everyone must submit to a system of shared laws, for the common good.

To summarize, in moving through Kohlberg's stages, the child's social perspective becomes increasingly larger. The child moves from the position of looking out simply for the self, to considering one other person, then to considering a slightly larger group, such as the family or class, and then to an even larger group, such as the society as a whole. At the higher Stages 5 and 6, what Kohlberg calls Post-conventional morality, the perspective becomes even larger and considers humanity in general. Each succeeding stage also involves a transformation in how children think about what is right.

Kohlberg and numerous other researchers have demonstrated in research with older children that over time, dilemma discussions can foster stage-wise development (reviewed in Power, Higgins, & Kohlberg, 1989). When children are exposed to reasoning one stage above their current stage of development, they tend to prefer the higher level reasoning to their own. When dilemma discussions occur in a classroom context emphasizing community, individual moral growth occurs as well as growth in the moral culture of the community.

MORAL DILEMMAS

Most moral discussions focus on dilemmas. Let us define what we mean by dilemmas, discuss the different types of dilemmas, and suggest sources of appropriate dilemmas for discussions with young children.

Definition of Moral Dilemma

A moral dilemma is a situation in which competing claims, rights, or points of view can be identified. For example, the classic moral dilemma used in Kohlberg's (1984) research is known as the Heinz dilemma. A poor man named Heinz has a wife who is dying of a rare form of cancer. A druggist in the town has discovered a drug that will save her life; however, he wants $2000 for the drug. Heinz does not have that much money. Should he steal the drug? Here the competing rights are Heinz's wife's right to life, and the druggist's right to property.

There is no clear right or wrong solution to a dilemma. Kohlberg examined the reasoning behind people's answers to the questions about what the actors in the dilemmas should do. He states that people can advocate the same action for very different reasons that represent different stages of reasoning. For example, a child might say that Heinz should steal the drug because if his wife dies, then he will not have anyone to cook for him—Stage 2 reasoning—or because if his wife dies, their children will be very sad and they will be upset with him—Stage 3 reasoning. In contrast, persons can advocate different actions using the same stage reasoning. For example, a child at Stage 1 might say that Heinz should not steal the drug because he might get caught and get sent to prison, or that Heinz should steal the drug, because if he doesn't, his wife's father might come over and beat him up. In assessing level of moral judgment, the emphasis is on the ways people reason, not on the specific actions they advocate.

Types of Dilemmas

A dilemma for discussion can take one of two forms—hypothetical or real-life dilemmas from the children's own experience. It is our opinion that discussions focusing on both types can be useful, for each has its strengths and weaknesses with respect to the purpose of promoting children's development of sociomoral judgment.

Hypothetical dilemmas are not as emotionally laden as real life dilemmas, since children are not personally involved in the issue. There is some emotional distance between the children and the story. No one stands before the class angry, or hurt, or bleeding. Impersonal issues can often be discussed more rationally, and it is safer to express opinions when no one will react personally or suffer a real consequence. Children can engage in "What if__?" thinking and can discuss what is right or wrong without the risk of hurting someone's feelings by failing to take a particular side in the issue.

On the other hand, real-life dilemmas offer certain advantages for discussion as well. Since they occur spontaneously, the situations are intimately familiar to children. The actors involved are themselves and fellow classmates, and the situations usually bear directly on the life of the classroom so children feel genuine concern about what happens. They also offer the advantage of having consequences children can recognize and evaluate fairly easily.

Sources of Good Dilemmas for Discussion

Children's literature is one source of hypothetical social and moral dilemmas. However, we are discovering good moral dilemmas in children's literature only very slowly. Children's stories often have moral lessons but not moral dilemmas. By this we mean that there are lessons, right answers, embedded in the stories. For example, the moral of the story of the boy who cried wolf is that you should not trick people because then they will not believe you when you tell the truth. It is a good moral and may be a good story to read to children, but it is not a dilemma.

Everyday life in the classroom is another source of dilemmas. Children are the first ones to complain "That's not fair!" when something happens in the class that violates their sense of justice. Teachers can listen to these complaints and sometimes find good topics for discussion. For example, if children leave the caps off markers and the markers dry up and are ruined, what should happen? Is it fair to deprive all the children of markers because some children are careless? If the class gets new markers, should the children responsible for ruining the old markers be allowed to use them? Children can grapple with these moral issues and the answers are important to them. They tend to feel strongly about these kinds of issues. Later in this chapter we discuss stories that we have written in response to the need for moral dilemmas that are drawn from children's everyday lives, but can be discussed as hypothetical.

OBJECTIVES OF SOCIOMORAL DISCUSSIONS

Our long-term goal in conducting sociomoral discussions is that these experiences will contribute to children's progress with regard to the stages of perspective taking and moral reasoning. Specifically, we want children to think about interpersonal issues in more differentiated ways, becoming better able to think beyond their own perspective to see and consider multiple perspectives in issues.

However, before children can begin to make stage-wise progress in reasoning about social and moral dilemmas, they have to recognize the dilemmas. This is more difficult than one might think. Because of their limited perspective-taking ability, young children tend to focus on only one side of the issue and fail to recognize the two perspectives that define the dilemma. Therefore, our goals are perhaps a little more modest than those of others who have worked with older children. Our first goal in using moral dilemmas with young children is to get the children to recognize that there are opposing points of view in the situation. Having accomplished this goal, we then try to help children to think about resolving moral issues in ways fair to everyone involved, to generate and evaluate possible solutions in terms of all participants.

GUIDELINES FOR CONDUCTING HYPOTHETICAL
SOCIOMORAL DISCUSSIONS

Conducting sociomoral discussions is a delicate matter. We present six concrete guidelines.

1. Choose an issue about which you can reasonably expect to find a difference of opinion.
Disagreement among children is necessary for a dilemma discussion to be successful. In one sense, this is the test of a dilemma—whether

or not there is a conflict of rights in the story. For example, in the story of the boy who cried wolf, if asked the question, "Was it okay for the boy to trick the townspeople like that?" probably no child would say yes. However, take, for example, the story of the three little pigs. Even though the pigs are the good guys and the wolf is the bad guy, some children might be expected to sympathize with the wolf. If asked, "Was it okay for the wolf to blow down the pigs' houses to eat them?" some children might state that the wolf was hungry and he needs to eat, too. The children's book *The True Story of the Three Little Pigs* (Scieszka, 1989) presents this familiar story from the wolf's perspective. This book can be a good basis for a moral discussion.

2. Read dilemma stories many times to children.

One of our hypotheses is that it takes many hearings of a story to enable children to think about the perspectives of all the different characters and all the subtle nuances of the dilemmas. The children may not notice the dilemma the first, second, or even the fifteenth time they hear the story. Be patient.

One children's book that we have seen used in moral discussions is *Heckedy Peg* (Wood, 1987). In this story, a witch has stolen a mother's children, with the intent of eating them. The mother goes to the witch's house to try to get her children and, in the process, tricks the witch. Peige Fuller states that she had read this book to one group of Investigators at least a hundred times. They loved it and knew it by heart. Peige did not expect the book to be the subject of a moral discussion. Then one day, when they get to the part where the mother tricks the witch, a child says, "She's lying!" Peige (T) decides to follow up on this comment. The dilemma in this story becomes the mother's obligation to tell the truth versus her obligation to save her children.

T: (Reading) "Let me in!" the mother called. "I want my children back." "You can't come in," said Heckedy Peg. "Your shoes are dirty." "Then I'll take them off," the mother said. And so she did. "Let me in!" the mother called. "I want my children back." "You can't come in," said Heckedy Peg. "Your socks are dirty." "Then I'll take them off," the mother said. And so she did. "Let me in!" the mother called. "I want my children back." "You still can't come in," said Heckedy Peg. "Your feet are dirty." "Then I'll cut them off," the mother said. And she went away.
E: She's not. She's lying to her.
T: "She went away as if to do so. But instead—"
J: (Unintelligible) her feet. She's lying.
C: She's tricking the witch.

T: "—the mother hid her legs behind her and crawled back to the
     witch's door." I had a question. C says the mother is just tricking
     the witch, and J and E say the mother is lying.
L: I know! She's tricking the witch.
E: Huh-uh!
T: Well, E, I have a question. Do you think that what the mother is
     saying is okay?

We return to this example below and show how the discussion continues. Here let us point out simply that Peige listens to her children
and picks up on the disagreement over whether or not the mother
was lying. However, we have tried the same story with some children
who could not even understand the question. It went right over their
heads because they did not understand the concept of a lie. The lesson is to listen to your children closely and be prepared to discuss
moral issues that children discover in familiar stories.

3. Help children to recognize all points of view in a story.

A familiar theme in children's stories is that of a small or weak creature tricking a larger or more dangerous creature in order to save his
or someone else's life. Stories that take this form can often be effective in helping children to examine multiple perspectives. The book
Doctor DeSoto (Steig, 1982) follows this theme. A fox has a toothache,
and goes to the only dentist in town, a mouse named Dr. DeSoto. Dr.
DeSoto has a policy of not treating cats and other dangerous animals,
but Dr. DeSoto's wife is moved by pity for the fox, who is in tremen-
dous pain, and they decide to treat the fox. It becomes clear that the
fox plans to eat the mice after they fix his tooth, so Dr. DeSoto and his
wife come up with a plan to trick the fox so he will not be able to eat
them. They paint his teeth with a "secret formula" that they tell him
will prevent him from ever having toothaches again. But the secret
formula is really glue, and they glue the fox's teeth together tem-
porarily, making it impossible for him to eat them. Children generally
think it is great that the mice out-fox the fox. After reading the story,
the teacher asks a group of kindergarten children, "Was it okay for
Dr. DeSoto to trick the fox like that?" Most children say yes, that the
mice did not want to be eaten, etc. However, some children take the
perspective of the fox. They worry that, with his mouth glued shut,
the fox will starve. One child is concerned that the fox will still get
toothaches because the glue is not really the secret formula. The children are able to look at this story from the fox's point of view and
think about his rights as well as the mice's rights.

In the class of 4-year-olds, the responses to the same question are unanimous. All the children think it is okay, and they cheer at that part of the story. However, one child surprises us by her reasoning. While most children state that it is okay because the mice do not want to be eaten, this child states that it is okay because if the fox eats Dr. DeSoto, then there would be no one to fix teeth in the town. She takes the perspective of the larger community. This appears to be Stage 4 in Kohlberg's stages, remarkably high level reasoning for a 4-year-old. Remember to ask children for their reasons.

4. Ask open-ended questions.

If you ask children whether something is fair, or right, or okay to do, follow it up. Ask questions such as, "Why do you think that was a fair thing to do? What do you think ____ should do? What would happen if ____ does that? How will the other people in the story feel?" Probe to get at children's reasoning. Do not assume that you know what children think. Get them to explain their reasoning if they can. Sometimes they cannot, but when they do, it usually spurs further discussion.

The discussion about *Heckedy Peg*, begun above, continues as Peige probes children's reasoning about why they think it is okay or not okay for the mother to trick the witch.

E: Uh-uh, it's—she's lying.
T: Is it okay to lie in this case?
E: Huh-uh.
Children: No!
T: No? Why? Can you tell me why it's not okay?
E: Because it's bad.
J: It's bad, and she will look at her and say, "You have feet." and she'll say "Yes I do." That's a lie, right?
T: That's a lie? Well, C, what do you think about it? Do you think it's okay for the mother to tell the witch she does not have feet?
C: (Unintelligible) she does.
L: She's tricking her.
T: The mother does have feet. But she told Heckedy Peg she cut them off. Is that okay for the mother to say?
L: Yeah.
T: Yeah? Why is it okay?
C: 'Cause it's not (unintelligible) anything.
T: Because it's not (unintelligible) anything? Why do you think it's okay that the mother told Heckedy Peg that she cut her feet off?
N: I think she was lying because—because she just told Heckedy

Peg that she was hiding her feet behind her.

T: She was sly, huh?

H: She's just lying.

T: She was lying? Was it okay for her to lie, or was it not okay for her to lie?

H: Yes, it was okay.

T: Why?

H: If you're just, if you're not (unintelligible), then it's not okay, but if you're just tricking people so they wouldn't do something like that, then you can, it's okay.

T: I see.

E: Huh-uh! You're wrong! You know nothing!

T: A, I see that your hand is raised.

E: I know better! You can't come to my house!

A: I think that she's just trying to trick the witch. I think that she's just trying to get her children back.

T: She's just trying to get her children back? So it's okay to lie in that case?

A: Yeah.

H: That's what I meant.

Children: Yeah.

E: Huh-uh.

A: Only if it's very important.

T: (To H) That's what you meant?

H: Yes, that's what I meant. I meant what she said.

T: Okay, E has a disagreement. (To E) Tell us what you think. Do you think A and H are right, it's okay to lie to save your children?

E: Huh-uh, it's not.

T: It's not?

E: It's bad.

T: Is it ever okay to lie?

E: No!

J: No.

T: Never?

Children: Yes.

T: Yes? Well, we have a difference of opinion.

C: You could call someone to help.

T: Yes, you could call someone to help. Let's see what the mother does (continues reading).

Peige's questions are worded so as to encourage children to elaborate the reasons why they believe as they do.

5. Help children clarify their reasoning by repeating their ideas back to them.

Sometimes children's words are disjointed, garbled, or otherwise difficult to interpret. A good habit to get into (and this holds true not just for moral discussions, but for all discussions with children) is to repeat back to children what you think they said, with a questioning inflection in your voice. This will often prompt them to elaborate what they have said, offering reasons or corrections.

Repeating children's ideas in a clear way helps other children understand and inspires them to formulate their opinions. The teacher should strive to foster open discussion *among children* of the moral issues being presented, not simply discussion between a child and the teacher. Becoming aware of classmates' differing opinions can be a mechanism for reassessment and growth. Within a group discussion, the role of the teacher is to keep the focus of the conversation on issues of fairness and equality.

6. Accept all opinions and positions.

It is important, but enormously difficult, for the teacher not to place value judgments on children's reasons. Doing this sends the message that there are right answers to these questions and that the teacher knows the right answers. In the discussion about *Heckedy Peg* quoted above, Peige does not pass judgment on the children's reasons why lying is or is not okay. She questions, probes, repeats, and follows up, but she refrains from approving or disapproving children's ideas.

Try to resist the urge to get the class to come to a consensus about a hypothetical issue. Keep in mind that the goal of the discussions is to foster children's awareness of different points of view, not to convince them of a particular moral rule. Consensus is neither necessary nor particularly desirable. The teacher can, however, restate the opposing positions at the end of the discussion. This serves to wrap up the discussion, and to emphasize the point that people's opinions can differ. For example, at the end of a discussion about *Doctor DeSoto*, the teacher can state something to the effect that, "So some people think that it was okay for Dr. DeSoto to trick the fox because he did not want to be eaten. But some people think it was not okay because the fox's teeth were glued together and he couldn't eat and he might starve." Do not worry about leaving the issue unresolved.

These principles of teaching also apply to real-life moral discussions and hypothetical dilemmas drawn from real-life experiences, discussed below.

REAL-LIFE MORAL DISCUSSIONS

An active social environment inevitably provides real-life dilemmas. These are situations in which the rights of one child conflict with the rights of another child or of the group. Conflicts involving access to toys, supplies, and space to play can become moral issues. We encourage teachers to take advantage of these situations as opportunities to focus children's attention on rights, fairness, and consideration of others. The important point to remember in these situations is to uphold the value of fairness to all persons concerned. It is the teacher's task to remind children about fairness and to make sure that children feel as though they are being treated fairly.

In an incident in the kindergarten class at the Lab School the assistant teacher, Karen Amos, introduces consideration for the feelings of wrongdoers. Children had been leaving the caps off markers, causing them to dry up. Karen brought her own personal markers to school, on the understanding that if the children could demonstrate care for the markers, then they could ask the Associate Director to buy them some new ones. However, one child suggests a new rule: If children leave the caps off the markers, they will not be allowed to use them. A moral discussion ensues. The discussion is moral in the sense that it pits justice against mercy. The child who suggests the rule that children who misuse markers cannot use them takes the side of justice, and Karen argues for mercy in assuming the role of advocate for those who forget the rules and misuse the markers. At first, children suggest that those who misuse the markers should never get to use them. Karen gets the children to specify a length of time, and they suggest 3 days. Karen truly believes that 3 days is too long to deprive children of markers. She suggests that perhaps they should simply remind children of the rule to replace the caps, and she goes on to defend children who forget to replace caps by stating, "I know sometimes I forget, too." Popular opinion is against her, however. They vote and decide that the rule will state that children who misuse the markers will not be allowed to use them for 3 days.

Often, what appears on the surface to be a moral dilemma is actually a conflict between children, although the distinction between the two may be fuzzy at times. (See chapter 5 for a discussion of conflict resolution.) Usually in a conflict between children, one child's rights have been violated by another and the victim protests. But in a moral dilemma, the conflict is not so much between children as between rights. For example, one year in the kindergarten class at the Lab School, children had 1 day each week assigned to them as their sharing day when they could bring items from home to show to the entire class. One child, showing his item to his classmates while walking around the circle, selectively allowed some children to touch it but not others. Children protested, "That's not fair!" The question was who has the right to decide whether children can touch someone's possession. Some children thought that it should be an all-or-nothing proposition. Either everyone can touch, or else no one can touch. Other children thought that the owner of the object had every right to decide who can touch. Issues such as this are difficult to solve, and there are no easy answers.

As we state above, the teacher's task in moral discussions is to uphold fairness, equality, and reciprocity. One problem with moral discussions that arise in real-life is that it is not always clear what is fair, and yet solutions are needed. As in the situation about touching sharing items, a decision is called for regarding how the class will handle the problem. Submitting moral issues to a vote is generally not appropriate. However, if there is no clear moral precedent, often the best thing the teacher can do is to conduct a thorough discussion and then have the class vote to decide how to handle the situation. The important point is to discuss the issue thoroughly because it is in the discussion that children will challenge each other's reasoning and perhaps come to a new understanding of the moral issue.

HYPOTHETICAL DILEMMAS DRAWN FROM REAL-LIFE EXPERIENCES

Another problem with conducting moral discussions about real-life events is that they are unpredictable. One never knows when an issue will arise or what it will be about. This problem led us to write and illustrate our own dilemma stories, drawn from actual experiences with young children. Unlike the dilemmas used in Kohlberg's research, which are too far removed from the experience of young children, the situations in these stories are ones that young children can be expected to be familiar with. With these stories, teachers can conduct moral discussions without having to wait for problems to arise in the classroom and without worrying about children's rights actually being violated.

One story is called "When Friends Refuse to Share." In this story, the rule in the classroom is that four children can play at the block center. Three children are there, building an elaborate zoo, with cages for the animals and a fence around the whole thing. Another child comes to the block center, sees that there is room for him, and starts to build a tall building. However, only four blocks are not being used in the zoo, so he asks the three children for some of their blocks. They refuse, saying that they worked a long time on their zoo, and now they want to play with it. The dilemma is between the right of the child to play with the blocks, and the rights of the children who were there first to use as many blocks as they need for their zoo.

When discussing this story with the kindergartners, the children at first were sympathetic primarily to the child who wanted more blocks and suggested various ways of sharing or finding more blocks. So we introduced the question of whether it would be fair to expect the three children to tear down their zoo. Some children switched loyalties and defended the children building the zoo. In general, children took one side in the story and could not coordinate the competing claims. One child suggested a compromise, that the children make shorter houses and a shorter fence for the zoo, thus freeing up some blocks for the one child. The difficulty children have in seeing more than one perspective in this story makes clear why children have such difficulties in real-life conflicts.

Our goals in this dilemma were, first, that children would be led to think about the problem from both perspectives. We wanted the children to see that both parties had a valid argument, and that sometimes problems cannot be solved simply by finding out which side is right. Second, we wanted children to think about how the children in the story might feel about what was happening. Often, young children can think of only a small repertoire of feelings (we refer to this as "mad, sad, glad" because this seems to be the extent of their thinking about feelings). We want children to think in more differentiated ways about feelings. We have tried to introduce words such as *disappointed*, *frustrated*, and *afraid*, to describe children's feelings. Finally, we hoped that children would begin to explore different ways to solve the problem, whether taking turns, sharing, or some other solution, and how these proposed solutions would cause the children in the story to feel.

Another story, entitled "When a Friend Steals," tells about a young boy, Jack, who comes to school hungry every day because he does not get up in the morning early enough to eat breakfast. His solution is to take items of food from his classmates' lunches while they are outside playing. Eventually, the teacher discovers him stealing food, and they have a class discussion. Children tell Jack that they do not like having their food taken. The teacher in the story asks children if they can think of any solutions to Jack's problem.

In discussions with Lab School children about this story, children suggest numerous solutions to the problem of what Jack can do about being hungry in the morning. They suggest things that Jack can do, such as getting up earlier, getting an alarm clock or a rooster to wake him up, and packing a breakfast to eat in the car on the way to school. They also suggest things that the entire class can do, such as writing a note to his parents asking them to pack him a breakfast to eat at school and bringing extra food for Jack to eat in the morning. This leads to a moral question. Should Jack be punished for taking the children's food, or should the children try to help Jack? In the kindergarten class we find a difference of opinion. One child is very clear that Jack should be punished because, "He takes stuff out of people's lunches." The injunction not to steal is powerful, and, in his view, punishment is the expected consequence—no justification necessary. Another child, however, disagrees. He thinks that the children should help Jack. When asked why, he explains, "Because then he'll stop doing it. If they punish him, then he might take two things out of people's lunches." We were amazed that a 5-year-old could understand that punishment is ineffective and that cooperative methods are preferred. This reflects the kind of reasoning we hope to promote in children.

SUMMARY

Moral discussions are one way in which teachers can promote moral reasoning in young children and contribute to their moral development. The constructivist teacher plans specifically for grouptime discussions of social and moral dilemmas as one way of promoting perspective taking and moral reasoning. Teachers can use moral dilemmas taken from children's literature, from everyday life in the classroom, or they can use hypothetical stories drawn form everyday life. The important points to keep in mind are that there are no right and wrong answers to a moral dilemma, everyone's ideas are valuable, and the goal is not to come to a consensus, but to promote reasoning. Guidelines for conducting social and moral discussions focus on helping children recognize opposing points of view and think about how to resolve issues in ways fair to everyone involved.

10

Cooperative Alternatives
to Discipline

"Discipline" usually refers to methods of controlling and punishing children in order to socialize them. A dictionary (Morris, 1973) definition of the verb *discipline* lists two usages, including (1) "to train by instruction and control; teach to obey or accept authority," and (2) "to punish or penalize." As these usages imply that adults do something *to* children, we therefore say that we do not "discipline" children. Rather, we work *with* children as they gradually construct their own convictions about relations with others. Construction, not instruction, is our goal for children. Moreover, we do not "train" children in obedient self-control. As discussed in chapter 3, autonomous self-regulation is our goal rather than obedience to authority.

This does not mean, of course, that children in constructivist classrooms are allowed to "run wild." Certainly, teachers must develop strategies for managing a classroom of children and coping with inevitable breakdowns in cooperation. Constructivist teachers are not passive. On the contrary! Constructivist teachers are highly active in their efforts to facilitate children's self-regulation. Their activity, however, does not take unilateral forms of training, drilling, or punishing. Rather, it takes cooperative forms, to enable children to construct convictions and follow their own social and moral rules that are independent of adult coercion. Children's self-constructed social and moral rules are rooted in their everyday personal experiences. These personal experiences with peers and adults lead them to construct cause-effect relations between their actions and the reactions of others.

What we mean by "discipline" through cooperation is that the teacher co-operates in terms of the child's point of view. (The hyphen in "co-operates" is intended to emphasize the operation in terms of the child's perspective.) That is, the teacher establishes an atmosphere in which children feel that the teacher cares for them, enjoys being with them, and respects them by taking their feelings, interests, and ideas into account. When children experience the teacher's cooperation with them, they are likely to be willing to cooperate with the teacher and with each other.

In this chapter, we take up the question of the role of personal experience in social and moral development. Piaget's distinction between two types of sanctions is presented, with examples. Finally, we suggest guidelines for implementing constructivist alternatives to discipline.

THE ROLE OF PERSONAL EXPERIENCE IN SOCIAL AND MORAL DEVELOPMENT

The challenge of socializing children is to figure out how to help them control impulses, think beyond the here and now, and become able to reflect on consequences of their actions. This involves decentering to consider views and feelings of others. The alternatives to discipline that we discuss in this chapter are organic in their integration of children's personal social and moral concerns in daily living in the classroom.

In his research on children's moral judgment, Piaget (1932/1965) pointed out that children can often reason at a higher level when they focus on their own experiences instead of hypothetical situations. In personal experiences, children are more likely to realize that their own intentions are relevant to judgments of their actions. It seems likely, then, that it is through personal experiences that children may first begin to consider the motivations behind actions. By so doing, they begin to move beyond a view of others as objects to a view of others as having ideas and feelings. In constructivist education, we therefore advocate an emphasis on children's personal experiences for fostering social and moral development. These personal experiences occur in a natural context where children choose and pursue their interests.

TWO TYPES OF SANCTIONS

In discussing how adults deal with children's misdeeds, Piaget (1932/1965) distinguished between expiatory and reciprocity sanctions, described below.

Expiatory or Punitive Sanctions

Piaget described expiatory sanctions as reacting to transgressions with coercion and painful punishment. Expiatory sanctions are arbitrary in the sense that "there is no relation between the content of the guilty act and the nature of its punishment. . . . All that matters is that a due proportion should be kept between the suffering inflicted and the gravity of the misdeed" (p. 205). Expiatory sanctions are intended to make the child suffer.

Expiatory or punitive sanctions, being arbitrary, convey revenge or vindictiveness. Some people think that making the child suffer is a preventive measure. Piaget (1932/1965) found, however, that older children view such punishments as ineffective and as simply making "the offender insensitive and coldly calculating" (p. 225). The attitude is "Daddy will punish me, but he won't do anything afterwards!" (p. 225). Piaget further commented, "How often, indeed, one sees children stoically bearing their punishment because they have decided beforehand to endure it rather than give in" (p. 225). One of us (BZ) was told the story of a teenager who had been forbidden by her parents to get her ears pierced. One weekend when her parents were out of town, she had a friend pierce her ears. When her parents returned and saw her ears, they were furious. Her punishment was to do the family ironing for 6 months (and this before permanent press!). Some 25 years later, she still insists that it was worth the punishment.

Expiatory punishments include spanking, making the child stand in a corner, and making the child write "I will not __" 100 times. Humiliating children and chastising them in an emotionally overwhelming way are also expiatory. Any punishment designed to make the child suffer falls in this category.

Piaget found that young children believe that punishment is necessary and just, and the sterner, the better. They believe that the punishment invoked should be related quantitatively to the misdeed. Older children, in contrast, do not assess the value of a punishment in terms of its severity. Instead, they believe that punishment for the purpose of making a wrongdoer suffer does not make sense. They believe that sanctions by reciprocity are more fair and more effective. Constructivist teachers agree with these children. We do not punish children. Instead, constructivist teachers invoke sanctions having the characteristic of reciprocity.

Reciprocity Sanctions

While expiatory sanctions are properly termed *punishments*, this is not the case for sanctions by reciprocity. Unfortunately, the English translator of Piaget's *The Moral Judgment of the Child* (1932/1965) translated *sanctions* as *punishments*. Rather than viewing reciprocity sanctions as punishments, we recommend thinking of these as consequences. In contrast to expiatory sanctions, sanctions by reciprocity emphasize the social bond broken by a child's misdeed. All misdeeds occur in a social context and involve social relationships that are disrupted in some way as a result of the misdeed. When materials are misused or broken, others who enjoy the use of the materials are deprived of that use and may be angry or sad. When someone lies, others may feel that they no longer can trust the one who told the lie. A rift occurs in the social bond that requires repair. When this is the case, the teacher only needs to call attention to the consequence of the break in social relations. Piaget points out that "Censure no longer needs to be emphasized by means of painful punishment: it acts with full force in so far as the measures taken by way of reciprocity make the transgressor realize the significance of his misdeeds" (p. 206).

For a sanction to be effective, the child must value the social bond and wish it to be restored. Thus, the close personal relationships between constructivist teachers and children provide an important foundation for the effective use of reciprocity sanctions. Similarly, children's relations with one another are also crucial to the effectiveness of reciprocity sanctions.

Sanctions by reciprocity have in common the communication of a break in a social bond such as disappointment, anger, or loss of trust. That is, mutual good will in a relationship has been interrupted. In a sanction by reciprocity, the person wronged responds to offense or injury by withdrawing trust or goodwill. The person wronged clearly signals that mutuality is disrupted and that the wrongdoer can no longer enjoy the pleasures and advantages of the former relationship. To reestablish the former mutuality, the wrongdoer must act to compensate the bad feeling and restore the relationship.

Piaget (1932/1965) discussed six types of reciprocity sanctions that provide a useful way of thinking about how to respond to classroom transgressions. Each is described below, with examples. The reader should keep in mind that any of these sanctions by reciprocity may be implemented in a punitive way that short-circuits the reciprocity and turns it into punishment. In addition, children may still interpret reciprocity sanctions as expiatory. Therefore, great care must be taken in invoking these sanctions. Sometimes, however, despite a teacher's best efforts, a child may experience a reciprocity sanction as unfair.

Sanctions by reciprocity include natural and logical consequences. Logical consequences include restitution, depriving the transgressor of the thing misused, exclusion, doing to the child what he has done, and censure.

Natural Consequences

Natural consequences result directly from actions. These take on a social meaning when the transgressor knows that the social group also suffers the consequences. If pages are torn from a book, the natural consequence is that no one can read it. If carelessness results in damaged or lost game pieces, the game is less enjoyable to use. If you talk and don't listen to the introduction of activities at grouptime, you won't know what you can do. If you leave the tops off the colored markers, they dry up and no one can use them. In chapter 12, we describe how a teacher let children experience the natural consequence of not cleaning up their toys and materials. The room was a mess when they came in the next day! No one enjoyed this, and most children began to take clean-up more seriously, reminding each other and helping each other.

Restitution

Restitution means paying for, repairing, or replacing a broken or stolen object in order to restore the situation prior to the misdeed. H, for example, a kindergarten child, brought a new dinosaur to the class to replace the one whose tail he had bitten off. K, who tore E's picture, repaired it and gave it to her. Actions taken to repair a broken relationship are also restitutions. Apologies, when freely offered in a spirit of contrition, can be a form of restitution. While constructivist teachers never require apologies (see chapter 5), they rejoice when they witness sincere requests for forgiveness as a sign that children recognize how their own actions affect others' feelings toward them. In chapter 5, we suggest how restitutions are sometimes appropriate in conflicts.

Depriving the Transgressor of the Thing Misused

Depriving the child of objects and opportunities when these are abused can help the child construct attitudes of responsibility. Examples of this type of consequence include asking a child to find another activity when he or she misuses materials. In the Inventors kindergarten class, Coreen asked whether children who do not clean up should be allowed to use the materials. A (a 5-year-old) responded, "No, 'cause I'm not sure if I can trust the kids tomorrow to clean up their activities. It's like when E took away the ____ and went away with it, and I wasn't sure I could trust her with it any more."

In another incident in the Investigators class, when K and G run around in a dangerous way on the carpet, Peige withdraws the opportunity to play on the carpet.

> K and G, sit down, please. Running in the classroom makes people fall down. I need for you to be safe. It is my job as the teacher to help you be safe. If you run again inside, then you will need to sit very quietly in a chair and read a book and that is all. I must know that you are safe, and if you are not being safe, then I must do something to make you safe, and that's the only thing I can think of. Okay, you have some choices to make for 5 more minutes (remaining in the activity period). You may not be on this rug because I have seen today that you two are out of control on this rug. There's painting, there's construction, there's finger painting, there are puzzles to work, and there are books to read.

As Piaget points out, the young child may interpret these consequences as punitive. With explanation and emotional support, however, the child will gradually come to understand the logic of the reciprocity involved in this consequence.

Exclusion

Exclusion from the group is a logical consequence of violating the rights of others. Children frequently exclude others from playing when they violate rights. For example, 3-year-old Z responds to R's pinching by telling her that she doesn't want to be her friend. If a child behaves aggressively on the playground, the teacher may require him or her to play alone for awhile. Exclusion is involved in the example described in chapter 6 when S would not keep his hands off C during grouptime. When S continued his unwelcome touching,

Peige enabled C to move, and when O sat next to S and was similarly bothered, she, too, moved. Peige emphasized the exclusion consequence to S when she said, "You keep touching all the children, and they don't like it, so they move away, and now you don't have anybody to sit by."

This consequence is often difficult to invoke without making it a punishment. "Time out" is a widely used punishment that is not a reciprocity sanction. We object to "Time out" because it is unilateral and arbitrary. We discuss approaches to this consequence in the section below on principles of teaching.

Doing to the Child What the Child Has Done

This sanction is rarely appropriate for adults to use with children. However, we have seen a situation in which a teacher appropriately reminded children that they refused to help her, and that makes her reluctant to help them. Among children, this sanction is sometimes used in a punitive way. Situations may arise in which a child refuses to cooperate, yet later wants the same cooperation from someone else. A child who hurts another may not recognize the reciprocity when another hurts him or her. In chapter 5, we describe how Z was remorseless when she hurt C, but complained when W hurt her. Peige reminded her that she had done to C what W did to her.

Censure

Piaget (1932/1965) pointed out that censure alone (the other's simple opinion that one has let the other down or has, in some way, disrupted the relationship) is a reciprocity sanction when it makes "the transgressor realize how he has broken the bond of solidarity" (p. 209). The first author remembers vividly that day at about age 4 or 5 years when her mother responded to a wrongdoing by pulling her close and, with a note of sadness, telling her how disappointed she was in her. The remorse was far stronger in reaction to this consequence than to spanking.

We must caution strongly that to be a sanction by reciprocity, censure cannot be presented as coming from authority. It must be based on disruption in a relationship.

Piaget (1932/1965) noted that reciprocity sanctions do contain an element of suffering. But he pointed out that the suffering is not inflicted for the purpose of suffering, but "is simply an inevitable result of the breach of the bond of solidarity" (p. 206). The purpose of the consequence is to communicate that the wrongdoer has disrupted an interpersonal relationship.

GUIDELINES FOR IMPLEMENTING CONSTRUCTIVIST
ALTERNATIVES TO DISCIPLINE

To reduce the possibility that children will experience consequences as arbitrary and punitive, we suggest implementing the following constructivist teaching principles.

1. Avoid expiatory sanctions/punishments.

It is not unusual for an adult to feel that a child should be made to suffer for a misdeed. This may be vengeance based on anger, or it may derive from the common idea that if the child suffers, he or she will not do the misdeed again. Suffering *may* lead the child not to do the act again, or it may lead the child to resent or even hate the perpetrator of the suffering. It may lead the child to feel inwardly that he or she is bad and thereby negate self-esteem. Or it may lead the child to be more calculating next time so the adult does not find out. From the point of view of the child's psychological development, punishments are risky and most likely counterproductive if the adult wants to promote the child's moral development.

It is clear that any consequence, even the reciprocity consequences, can become expiatory if implemented with a punitive tone and attitude. To avoid turning reciprocity consequences into punishments, be matter-of-fact and supportive of the child.

2. Encourage children's ownership of logical consequences.

Logical consequences can often be discussed with children as a group. The teacher can help children become conscious of a problem, make sure that children agree and truly believe that a problem exists, and ask children for opinions about what to do about the problem, with an emphasis on preventing future occurrences. Once the group has agreed on a logical consequence, children are more likely to understand the logic of the consequence. Constructivist teachers point out that even when children are warned of consequences, they sometimes still seem surprised to confront them. Children may not be able at times to think of consequences until these are experienced.

3. When children suggest a consequence that is too severe, ask the wrongdoer to say how he or she feels, and support this feeling.

When consulting young children about consequences, the teacher must be prepared for expiatory (punitive) suggestions. For example, in one class, the Special Helper was using a spray bottle of water to aid his cleaning. When D, an adult from a nearby office, walked past, the child deliberately sprayed water on her. At second grouptime, the children discussed the event and voted that he should be deprived of his Special Helper privileges for the rest of the day, and that these should be taken over by a teacher. The mistake here was in letting this issue be dealt with by the group. It should have been dealt with as an individual matter between D and the child. As mediator, the teacher could have led the child toward an understanding of D's point of view. The class's action, in contrast, only led the child to resent the punishment.

In Peige's Experimenters classroom (3-year-olds), urine was found on the bathroom floor over several days. Peige did not know who was responsible but suspected that more than one child was involved. She figured that they were not being malicious but thought it was funny. She brought the problem to the group for discussion. They talked about the health aspect, the unpleasant smell, the problem of trying not to step in it, etc. The children generated an elaborate set of rules that were posted in the bathroom. The rules included "Put pee-pee in the potty," "Wash your hands after you pee," etc. Also posted was the consequence the children created for breaking the rule. This was "You can never use the potty at school again." Peige did not question the severity of this consequence because she knew that it made sense to the children and that they would not change their view until confronted with implementing it. A week later, children found K urinating on the floor. A class meeting was called to discuss what to do. K was terribly distressed, and Peige asked the Assistant Teacher to hold him and be his advocate. She herself could not do this because her responsibility was to be the moral voice of the class. When the children insisted that K could never use the potty again at school, he began to fall apart. Peige asked him if he did not like that idea. He was able to say, "But what if I need to go potty and I can't wait 'til I go home? I'll wet myself." Peige was then able to elaborate his point and represent this view to the class. She pointed out that that would make a mess and be sad for K. Peige invited K to talk about whether he was really through peeing on the floor. The group did not withdraw its consequence but decided that K could have one more chance, to his relief.

4. Verbalize the cause-effect relation when natural consequences occur.

Children do not always make the cause-effect connection when natural consequences occur. Peige (T) brought such a consequence to children's awareness when she showed them a broken classroom decoration at grouptime.

T: Before we get started on the story, we have a little problem. Do you remember we had talked about how careful we needed to be if we had delicate decorations in our class? (Holds up broken decoration)
Children: Yes.
T: And we decided we liked this one?
Children: Yes.
T: Well, this delicate decoration has been ruined and will have to be thrown away because people didn't take care of it. (A matter-of-fact, nonjudgmental tone of voice avoids the possibility that children will hear it as a criticism.)

5. Selectively allow natural consequences to occur.

Teachers sometimes rescue children from natural consequences and lose an opportunity for children to construct the relation between action and consequence. For example, the teacher may separate children in a conflict without letting them experience the other's reactions. Or, the teacher may constantly put the caps back on markers. We understand the concern for waste but believe that the lesson on consequences is well worth a wasted marker.

Two kindergarten boys during a cookie-making activity were careless and did not pay close attention to the recipe. They put in one *cup* of baking powder instead of one *teaspoon*. The teacher observed their error and could have prevented it. However, she felt that the only way the boys would become more serious and careful about cooking was to experience the result of their carelessness. At snacktime when everyone tried the cookies, children were disappointed and said they tasted "yucky." The teacher was able to review the recipe with them and help them realize their error. The next time they made cookies, they were more serious and careful.

In the instance involving running in the classroom, mentioned above, Peige decides to intervene before a natural consequence occurs. Her responsibility for the safety of her children is too important to risk injury as a natural consequence of K and G's out-of-control behavior. Instead, she talks to K and G and invokes a logical consequence, depriving the children of the thing misused (in this case, the opportunity to play on the carpet).

6. Offer opportunities for restitution.

Restitution helps a child regain dignity and self-respect after a misdeed as well as repair the rift in the social bond between the misdoer and the victim. In the following example, Peige (T) matter-of-factly handles the situation when G slaps K's hand and causes him to drop his wet clay object on the teacher's sweater. After attending to the hitting issue, she says:

T: Do you know what happened? You knocked his thing down which might have broken it, and it got it all over my sweater. I didn't like that when you got it all over my sweater. So, could you please do something to get this off of my sweater?
G: Yeah.
T: Okay, what can you do?
G: Wipe it off.
T: Okay, thank you very much.
G: Can you get that game off the shelf for me?
T: Remember, G, you're getting something to wipe off my sweater 'cause it's really yucky.
G: (Gets paper towel and wipes sweater) It comes off easy.
T: Thank you.

Restitution can take the form of making a hurt child feel better. Once a conflict discussion turns in the direction of recognition of the other's pain, the teacher can open the way for restitution. We caution that if restitution is done as a result of coercion, it turns into punishment.

7. When exclusion is invoked, open the way to reinstatement.

The exclusion consequence should never be invoked by the teacher without indicating how or when the child may be reinstated as a participant in the group. It is best if the control of the exclusion can be given to the child. When W complains to Peige that D keeps on hitting him with his head, Peige makes several efforts to mediate a conflict resolution, but this does not seem to lead to a reduction in hitting. Peige then approaches D in the following way. "If you are going to hurt children, you cannot be with them, so you will either need to stop hurting or, if you keep hurting, you will need to get away from the children. Which one will it be?"

At grouptime, young children sometimes talk or play and disturb others. In chapter 6, we discuss how to approach children in respectful ways, to give them opportunities for regulating their behavior voluntarily. If a child seriously disrupts, the teacher may have to ask him or her to leave. One strategy that sometimes works well is to give children the opportunity to take themselves out of circle, to sit quietly at a table and return when they feel ready. The teacher thus cooperates with the child by recognizing that he or she may not want to be in circle and by offering a nonpunitive way in which to withdraw that protects autonomy. While this is different from the arbitrary and punitive use of "Time out," it can still be experienced by the child as punitive.

We should also say that there are times when a child refuses to leave voluntarily and a teacher must make the child leave, in order to protect the rights of children who want to enjoy circle. In order to reduce the coercion as much as possible, the teacher should explain why the child has to leave. If no assistant is available at the time, the teacher should find a later time in which to talk with the child. This conversation should be relaxed and sympathetic but firm about the logic of the consequence. By trying to learn the child's perspective, the teacher may be able to lead the child to understand something of the perspective of others in the group.

8. When children exclude others, help the excluded child find a way to reenter play and improve peer relations.

It would be disrespectful of children's feelings to insist that they play with a child they have excluded. In chapter 5, we tell the story of the child excluded from pretend play. When the teacher asks if he can be a brother, they happily agree. Often the teacher can help the excluded child find a role that will be valued by other children. Sometimes, the problem is less easy to solve if it reflects a longstanding experience of the children with each other. For example, an aggressive child may be excluded "because you have hurting hands." Or an overly competitive child may be excluded as children complain, "You cheat all the time, and you don't listen to our words!" In these cases, the teacher will have to work to help the child decenter and cooperate so that his or her behavior will be more acceptable to the peer group.

9. Avoid indefinite consequences.

A consequence should be clear and definite so the child knows what to do to avoid it in the future and what to do to reinstate him- or herself when it is invoked. In the following example, the teacher leaves the consequence so vague that children are left in doubt as to what they can do to reinstate themselves. When children scatter the Construx all over the floor, despite the teacher's effort to get children to keep them on the table, the teacher invokes the logical consequence of withdrawing the children's possibility of using of these materials. After collecting all the Construx, three children, H, S, and C leave the class to take the Construx back to the kindergarten class from which they were borrowed. The children play in the hallway, and H falls and hurts himself. The teacher has a conversation like the following with each child.

T: S, you really like doing special stuff and going to other people's classes. Do you like to do that?
S: (Nods)
T: But when you do it, do you know what happens? You make the choice to fool around instead of just going and doing it. So, S, that shows me that you cannot be safe if you do these things, and if you cannot be safe, then you can't do them. So that will be something that you cannot do for a while until you show us that you know how to be in control and just go to that class and just come back.

The teacher gives the children no indication of how long this privilege will be revoked, or what the children might do to regain the teacher's trust.

In contrast, after a 4-year-old is excluded from field trips, Peige adjusts the lesson plans in order to help the child reinstate himself. R was a problem whenever the Investigators went on a field trip, running away from the group and violating other rules. As a class they discussed field trip rules and decided that any child who could not listen to the teacher's words and follow the rules on field trips would not be allowed to go on the next field trip. Sure enough, this happened to R on a trip to visit the campus newspaper. However, Peige knew that a big field trip to the zoo was coming up, and she did not want R to miss it. So she planned two small field trips before the zoo trip. On the first, R was not allowed to go on a walk across campus to play on some favorite trees. Peige emphasized that this was the consequence on which the group had agreed. Before the second campus trip, Peige talked with R about his behavior, explaining that if he did not follow the rules, he would not be allowed to go on the zoo trip. She asked him if he could demonstrate to her that he could be trusted on field trips now. He said that he could. Peige gave him the opportunity to regain her trust on the second small trip so that he would not experience the disappointment of missing the big trip.

SUMMARY

Constructivist teachers do not "discipline" children in the sense of controlling and punishing them. Rather, the constructivist alternatives to such discipline focus on strategies to foster children's construction of convictions about relating to others in cooperative ways. Piaget's distinction between expiatory and reciprocity sanctions provides the basis for planning general responses to misdeeds. More specifically, the criterion of reciprocity leads constructivist teachers to six types of sanctions (discussed by Piaget) that emphasize the social bonds broken by children's misdeeds. To reduce the possibility that children will experience consequences as arbitrary and punitive, constructivist teachers follow nine guidelines that protect children's autonomy and lead to development.

11

Activity Time

Although we devote a great deal of this book to grouptime activities, children in constructivist classrooms spend a significant portion of each day in individual or small group activities. For 1 to 1-and-1/2 hours each morning and afternoon, they choose and freely engage in activities such as group games, physical-knowledge activities, pretend play, literacy activities, blockbuilding, and art.

This period of the day is sometimes referred to in early education as "free play." In the best classrooms, what is "free" about free play is children's freedom of choice among a variety of activities. In the worst classrooms, what is "free" is the teacher's freedom from teaching responsibility. A teacher new to the HDLS understood free play in this second way and commented that free play does not occur in our classrooms. She saw free play as a time when the teacher reads or gets caught up on records or housekeeping chores while the children play by themselves. In this sense, our activity time is not free play. Although activity time in a constructivist classroom may look a lot like free play to the untrained observer, a trained observer will note the constructivist teacher's very active role.

Children are especially socially interactive during activity time. The challenge for the teacher is to take advantage of this opportunity to cultivate a sociomoral atmosphere of mutual respect and cooperation in which children are intellectually active and interactive. Following a presentation of the objectives and rationale of activity time, we illustrate how constructivist teachers respond to this challenge by discussing three categories of knowledge reflected in activities, planning, and implementing activity time.

OBJECTIVES AND RATIONALE

The general objective of activity time is that children will be intellectually, socially, and morally active, and more and more self-regulating. In chapter 4, we discuss the rationale for the constructivist
sociomoral atmosphere that is at the same time an intellectual atmosphere. It is both at the same time because the teacher's attitude
sends specific messages to children about whether they should be
intellectually and morally active. For example, constructivist teachers ask children in a physical-knowledge activity to reflect on why
some objects sink and some float, encourage children to consider
contradictory opinions, and support the search for truth through acting on objects and discussing results. The constructivist teacher also
asks children to reflect on how to take turns with the sink/float activity, helps them become conscious that many want this privilege at
the same time, and suggests that they try to figure out a way to agree
and satisfy everyone.

When constructivist teachers refuse to be all knowing or all powerful, they open the way for children to struggle with issues and not
rely on adults for truths and values. Teachers who take a "boss" attitude lead children to look to adults to define both truth and moral
values. When ready-made truths and values are "pasted on" the
child's egocentric understanding, these are empty verbalisms that do
not transform the child's reasoning. In contrast, adult cooperation
liberates the child's mind to construct its own beliefs about truth and
value. Instead of telling the child what is true and right, the cooperative teacher invites the child to discuss these matters. This invitation
communicates that truths and values are open to reflection and
mutual searching.

One way to state our fundamental objective for children during
activity time is to refer to Eleanor Duckworth's chapter, "The Having
of Wonderful Ideas" in her book by the same title (1987). We want
children to be so engaged in pursuing their interests and purposes
that they will be inspired to have wonderful ideas. This is the essence
of the process of constructing moral values and intellectual truths.

THREE CATEGORIES OF KNOWLEDGE REFLECTED IN ACTIVITIES

Piaget's (1964, 1969/1970) distinction among three kinds of knowledge is useful to teachers in thinking about activity time. These are

physical knowledge, logico-mathematical knowledge, and conventional arbitrary knowledge. Briefly, we describe these and discuss how they help constructivist teachers in activity time.

Physical Knowledge

Physical knowledge is based on experiences of acting on objects and observing their reactions. This may be action simply to find out what will happen, with no preconceived ideas. For example, a child may drop an object in water to find out whether it sinks or floats. A second type of action is to find out if the object will react as one predicts. An example is the child who expects an object to sink before dropping it in the water. The source of physical knowledge is therefore partly in observing properties of the object. The child cannot construct physical knowledge without getting information from the object's reactions to actions on it. However, physical knowledge cannot be elaborated without logical reasoning: Knowledge about floating requires observation of various kinds of objects and inferences drawn from these observations as in the examples below of the rollers activity.

Logico-Mathematical Knowledge

Logico-mathematical knowledge is the result of reflective mental actions on objects that introduce characteristics that objects do *not* have into the individual's ideas about those objects. For example, number is not a property of any group of objects. Rather, it is a system of relationships created by the knower. That is, the "twoness" of a book and a cup does not exist in either object but in the mind of the knower who gives the objects this numerical characteristic. The knower would not have to see the two objects as "two," but could simply see them as a book and a cup. The source of logico-mathematical knowledge is therefore the knower's own constructive processes.

Logico-mathematical knowledge is particularly important because intelligence can be described as a framework of potential logico-mathematical relationships. In early education, constructivist teachers recognize that the young child is still dependent on contexts involving physical action for construction of logico-mathematical relationships that constitute both knowledge and developing reasoning. Let us take an example.

In a rollers activity, children try to make catapults using cylinders and boards. One child, R, manages successfully to make sponges and paper balls fly into the air. He places a board on a wooden roller, puts an object on the end of the board resting on the floor, and jumps on the board's elevated end. R's reasoning includes several logico-mathematical relationships. One is the relationship between the raised end of the catapult and the action of jumping on it. Another is the relationship between the end of the board where the object is placed and the opposite end on which R jumps. As R works his catapult, we notice a remarkable lapse in his coordination of these relationships. At one moment, R places his sponge not on the lower end but on the raised end of the board. He even goes to the lower end and flexes his knees in preparation to jump. At this moment, he realizes that he has made a mistake, and he corrects it by moving the sponge to the lower end of the board and jumping on the higher end to make the sponge fly up. This example shows that R's logico-mathematical relationships are unstable. They are not yet consolidated into a well coordinated network of relationships. We speculate that R momentarily thinks that if he wants to send the sponge *up* in the air, he must place it on the "up" end of the board. He thinks about the relationships noted above one at a time instead of thinking about them as a coordinated system. In a coordinated network, it would be impossible to make the error described because the raised end could not at the same time be the jumping end and the end occupied by the sponge.

This example provides an illustration of the way in which a system of logico-mathematical relationships becomes gradually coordinated and consolidated in the course of physical experience with objects and of how physical experience is organized by logical reasoning. Young children still think most actively in terms of specific, physical, observable content.

Conventional Arbitrary Knowledge

The third kind of knowledge, conventional arbitrary knowledge, is arbitrary truth agreed upon by convention (such as that December 25 is Christmas Day) and rules agreed upon by coordination of points of view (such as the rule that cars stop when a traffic light is red). The source of arbitrary conventional knowledge is other people, through various means of communication.

Using Piaget's Three Kinds of Knowledge

Having made these distinctions, Piaget quickly points out that it is difficult to conceive of pure physical or conventional knowledge. Virtually all knowledge involves logico-mathematical construction. In regard to physical knowledge, for example, the child who pushes a ball may notice that this object reacts differently than a cube or other object. The difference does not exist in either object. It is created by the knower. The child putting objects in water may notice similarities and differences, such as that wooden things float and metal things sink. In regard to arbitrary conventional knowledge, the child who knows the color blue knows it in a system of similarities and differences with other colors. A child who knows that Houston is in Texas has constructed a relation of spatial and logical inclusion. These are logico-mathematical relations constructed by the child. The first author is reminded of a 5-year-old seated next to her on an airplane. As the plane left Houston, he asked, "Is Houston by Texas?" indicating the lack of spatial inclusion and/or lack of the conventional knowledge that Houston is the name of a town in Texas, the name of a state.

How are these distinctions useful to planning? First, they are useful because the constructivist teacher realizes that young children construct logico-mathematical knowledge particularly in the course of physical-knowledge activities. This leads the teacher to plan activities in which children can act on objects and reason about the relationships embedded in thinking about their reactions.

Second, the constructivist teacher uses the distinction among three kinds of knowledge to think about what kind of knowledge is involved in curriculum topics. For example, a study of dinosaurs involves a lot of knowledge that is arbitrary conventional in nature, such as the names of dinosaurs and the class names carnivore, herbivore, and omnivore. Children can construct knowledge of herbivores, carnivores, and omnivores only if the teacher explains the meaning of these words. While the names are arbitrary conventions, the classification of dinosaurs is logico-mathematical. That is, children have the possibility to understand the mutually exclusive nature of the subcategories herbivore, carnivore, and omnivore and their hierarchical relation to the superordinate category "dinosaurs." In contrast, in sinking/floating activities children are motivated to construct logico-mathematical relations in order to understand why objects react as they do. While the teacher would not hesitate to inform children of the definition of herbivore, he or she would not tell children about the principle of specific gravity. The three kinds of knowledge therefore help the teacher make decisions about how to engage with children in activities. We discuss this further in the section below on fostering reasoning. Readers wishing to read more about the distinctions among the three kinds of knowledge, in addition to referring to the references to Piaget's writing, may see DeVries and Kohlberg (1987/1990) and Kamii and DeVries (1978/ 1993).

PLANNING FOR ACTIVITY TIME

It takes special competence on the part of the teacher to manage a productive activity time that meets sociomoral and intellectual objectives. The first challenge is to get a "five-ring circus" of activities going simultaneously. This calls for careful planning. The teacher plans the variety of activities so that teacher assistance and intervention are not required beyond teacher availability. For example, sinking and floating and parachute making would not be planned for the same day because each of these requires teacher intervention to promote children's reasoning.

Constructivist education is not a "cookbook curriculum." Therefore, we talk about a general approach and offer examples of planning, to aid teachers in creating their own curriculum that will be tailor-made for their children. One of the secrets of a successful activity time is planning to appeal to children's interests, purposes, reasoning, and cooperation. We discuss these below, following a presentation of the general categories of activities.

General Categories of Activities

Teachers in the HDLS write lesson plans that, in addition to group-time activities, include each day a physical-knowledge activity (see Kamii & DeVries, 1978/1993), a special group game (see Kamii & DeVries, 1980), an art activity, special literacy activities, and a theme for the pretend center. Developmental rationales are written in order to clarify activity goals and to guide their implementation. These include a number of activities long associated with what we refer to as the child-development approach in early education. Other activities unique to constructivist education are group games and physical-knowledge activities.

Rationales for general categories of activities were written by the first author and teachers in the University of Houston Lab School. They are posted in the hallway on a parent bulletin board so teachers do not need to repeat these in weekly lesson plans (see Appendix). Examples of rationales for specific activities are given below in the section on planning for children's reasoning.

Appeal to Children's Interests

We discuss in chapter 4 the importance of interest as the affective fuel of activity that leads to intellectual and sociomoral progress. How does the constructivist teacher select activities that will interest children? It is not always possible to be sure ahead of time. Constructivist teachers take an experimental attitude. However, you can begin with the general categories of activities listed above as appealing to children.

Careful observation of children's spontaneous activities can be a source of new ideas for activities that appeal to children's interests. Children's direct suggestions are excellent resources for activities. We describe in chapter 4 how one constructivist teacher consulted children about what they wanted to know. Lab School teachers routinely do this now and find that it is an important way to communicate to children that they can find out what they want to know in school. Children bring a special energy to activities derived from their own expressed interests.

Appeal to Children's Purposes

Interest is the springboard for purpose. General interest in materials gives the teacher the opportunity to challenge children to pursue a specific purpose. We feel strongly that we must help children find *their* purposes in activities. This principle, however, does not mean that the teacher should never suggest purposes.

When we say that activities must appeal to children's purposes, we mean that children must find in the activities something that they are motivated to do out of their own interest, not because they are being asked to do them by the teacher. For example, if a teacher sets out a boat-making activity, the goal is to make the activity so fascinating that children will want to figure out how to make a boat and test it to see if it will float.

In contrast to these activities, consider an activity once described to us in which the teacher's goal was for the children to learn their colors. One week, the theme was "blue." Everything the children did related to the color blue. They made blue PlaDoh, made and drank blue Kool-Aid for snack, painted with blue paint, etc. The problem with this type of approach is that "blue" in itself does not appeal to children's active purposes. Rather, the children's purposes were to act on the playdoh, mix and enjoy the Kool-Aid, and create paintings. Recognizing and naming the color blue is not a difficult task for a young child and is best taught as a secondary objective in activities such as art in which children have something to figure out how to do. If the teacher's objective is limited to teaching when to use the color name *blue,* more worthy objectives may be lost and the teacher may not think of engaging children in more challenging activity.

Appeal to Children's Reasoning

After appealing to children's interests and purposes, reasoning is close behind. The constructivist teacher plans in terms of possible interesting purposes that will engage reasoning. For example, Marti Wilson, the Explorers' (18 to 30 months) teacher at the HDLS, wrote about her plan one week in the following way:

> In Art, children will explore different media to figure out how they work. We will be experimenting with chalk, pastels, crayons, and markers. The children will be figuring out the best way to hold these to produce marks on their paper. If the tool is held in a different way, will they still be able to produce the marks? Does the amount of pressure used affect the marks produced? Through these experiences with the different media, the children may begin to construct some cause-effect relationships, such as "When I move my hand a lot, I get many big marks, but when I move my hand a little bit, I get fewer small marks." I do not expect the children to verbalize these relationships, but I do believe they will be able to observe these differences. I will verbalize what I see children doing, to help them become conscious of their actions (for example, "I see that you are pushing harder").

Stephanie Clark, the Investigators' (3½ to 4½ years) teacher, wrote the following.

> Physical knowledge activities will focus on sprinklers. Monday, I will put containers without holes in the water table. Tuesday, I will ask the children if they have any ideas about making sprinklers out of these containers. We will use a variety of tools to make these changes. Where do I need to make the holes? How many holes do we need? Can we use these sprinklers for something useful like watering plants? Thursday, I will put out a variety of tin cans perforated to facilitate

the flow of water. Which can will pour the most water? I expect the children to guess the largest can (with only one small hole). Then I will show the children the perforations (some just around the edge of one can, some in a straight line across the middle of one, and many all over the bottom of a small can).

Peige Fuller, when she was the Investigators' teacher, wrote as follows:

We will play Sardines outside. This game is sort of like Hide and Seek in reverse. One person hides, and everyone else sets out to find him/her. When children find the hider, they join him/her in the hiding place, until eventually everyone is jammed into the hiding place. Children experience disequilibrium when they see that they cannot choose the same kind of spots they do for regular Hide and Seek because the places are not big enough.

It is clear in these plans that teachers take into account children's levels of reasoning and thinking about what children might be challenged to think about.

One key to planning activities that promote children's active reasoning is to choose materials that are open-ended and can be engaged at more than one developmental level. Children at a variety of levels can thus find something challenging to do. For example, in activities involving shadows, very young children will just begin to see the correspondence between the shapes of objects and their shadows. Somewhat older children will find it challenging to figure out how to back away from a screen on which their shadow falls without losing their shadow (by staying in the path of the light). Children who can do this may still find it difficult to figure out how to make a shadow on the ceiling. Still others who have figured out the spatial relations among light, object, and shadow, will puzzle over changing densities in shadows, whether merged shadows are still there, and the nature of light. In any one class, teachers may have children at several levels, and the same activity can appeal to all of them.

In planning, it is important not to underestimate or overestimate what will challenge children's reasoning. The goal of teaching "blue," for example, is too easy for children. While the blue activities offer challenges, the teacher did not plan for any learning beyond the color name. Had she thought of the educational advantages for painting and mixing PlaDoh and Kool-Aid, the color name objective would have shifted to a secondary emphasis. Without planning for children's reasoning, it is unlikely that the teacher will intervene in ways to promote reasoning.

In contrast to activities that are too easy, many preschool programs set goals that are much too advanced for children. For example, it is both unrealistic and not particularly useful to teach 5-year-olds to count to 100. Even if they master the rote memorization, it has no effect on their ability to understand number as a system of relationships or solve a numerical problem.

Appeal to Children's Cooperation

In chapter 4, we discuss why it is important to appeal to children's cooperation. Planning for cooperation involves thinking about what kind of cooperation may be possible or necessary in activities. This can range from simple preparations such as deliberately setting out only one stapler for four children to share at the art table to devising physical-knowledge activities that require two children to work together, such as building and talking to each other over paper-cup-and-string telephones. Cooking is a particularly good activity for promoting cooperation if it is set up as a team effort in which children have to negotiate who gets to read out the ingredients needed, gather them from the pantry, read the recipe, measure ingredients, stir them, and so on.

We do not mean to imply that all activities should be cooperative or that children should not work or play alone. Children sometimes want and need to be alone, and their wishes should be respected. Constructivist teachers do, however, stay on the lookout for ways to facilitate cooperation between children during activity time.

IMPLEMENTING ACTIVITY TIME

The implementation of activity time is a different kind of challenge in comparison with grouptime. In grouptime activities, the teacher is clearly the leader. During activity time, however, the teacher's leadership is more subtle as children are encouraged to take the lead. We discuss below five general principles of teaching related to implementing activity time.

Pique Children's Interests

Activity time begins, in a sense, at the end of grouptime when the teacher introduces the special activities that will be available that day. We can think of three general ways in which to pique children's interests.

Suggest Possible Purposes

We discuss above the importance of considering the possible purposes children may pursue in an activity. Sometimes, especially with materials unfamiliar to children, the teacher wants to open an activity to any and all purposes. For example, in the rollers activity, Maureen Ellis introduces the activity by saying, "See whatever you can think of to do with these things." When materials are familiar or when the teacher wants to promote a particular purpose, this can be suggested to children. For example, in shadows activities, we noticed that children were thinking about the shadow, the object, and the light, but not about what happens in the space between these. We therefore worked with Coreen Samuel to develop situations that would inspire children to think about what happens between the light and the object and between the object and the shadow. In one activity, we hung a two-dimensional cut-out of a house from the ceiling. Coreen cut out a door and windows, leaving shutter flaps so these openings could also be closed. She made a figure of "Uncle Wiggily" (inspired by the book *Uncle Wiggily's Happy Days* by H. R. Garis, 1947) and glued him behind the shutters of one window. Two scenes were prepared on movable dividers to represent the Forest and the River. These dividers were placed behind each other between the house and the wall. The wall had a permanent rainbow painted on it. Finally, a slide projector was positioned behind the house with a paper cone over the lens to focus the light in a circular spot on the back of the house. The purpose suggested to the children was, "Can you figure out how to make Uncle Wiggily's shadow appear in the Forest, then in the River, and finally, in Rainbow Land?" Children were intrigued by these materials and eagerly took up the purpose as their own, figuring out how to open the shutters in the house to make Uncle Wiggily appear in the Forest, and moving the barriers one at a time to make him appear on the River and Rainbow.

Suggest Possible Techniques

When introducing activities, it is sometimes helpful to show children some examples of what they might want to try to do in an activity. For example, to introduce paper sculptures, Dora Chen showed an example of strips of paper forming inverted U-shaped loops pasted at each end on a flat piece of construction paper. Some strips were fringed, some accordion pleated, some plain. She asked children how they thought these were made, and suggested that they might try some of these ideas and think of others in order to make a sculpture.

Marti Wilson introduces activities carefully to her Explorers (18 to 30 months), in order to inspire them to reason. For example, she brings to grouptime a small container of paint, a sheet of paper on which she had made some potato prints, and a blank sheet of paper. She suggests the technique as follows.

> In the Art Center, I made this picture this morning. Look. You know how I made these pictures? I took this potato and put it in the paint and I pushed it on my paper (demonstrates two prints and holds paper up to show the result to children). We have potatoes and paints in the Art Center. If you want to make a picture, what do we need to wear? (Children chorus "Smocks!")

Then Marti shows the children a container of cut-out animals, some laminated and some felt.

> I have some animals in here (tilts container to show contents to children). Some of these animals will stay on the board when you put them up here (puts felt animal on flannel backed board). Some of them will not stay up (puts laminated picture of animal against felt; it falls). Some of them fall down when you put them up (tries another laminated animal). See if you can figure out which ones will stay on our board and which will fall off. There are lots of different animals here to try.

Conduct Discussion of Children's Ideas

In some cases, it is fruitful to conduct a short discussion of children's ideas about a physical phenomenon with which they will be experimenting. This serves a diagnostic purpose for the teacher to find out how children reason at the beginning of experimentation. It also serves to make children conscious of their own and others' ideas. At the beginning of a 10-week project on shadows, Coreen Samuel conducted a discussion with her 5-year-old Inventors. Announcing mysteriously, "Today, we're going to Shadowland," she invited children's ideas about shadows. "What is a shadow?" R said, "It's a thing who comes on your body when you're walking around." B said a little wooden horse "might get to make a big shadow if it wants to," but the big horse makes a big shadow because "That's what it wants to do." Some children predicted the shadow would show the dots on a large die, but others disagreed. Coreen then encouraged an experimental attitude: "*You* get to see what happens."

Allow Children to Choose Activities

We cannot emphasize too strongly the importance of allowing children to move freely about the classroom, pursuing activities of their own choosing. This is important for children's developing autonomy in all domains. The child with solid experience in regulating the pursuit of interests is also more likely to be active in self-regulation through cooperation to settle disputes fairly.

We mention in chapter 4 our disagreement with the practice of some teachers in assigning children to activity centers and rotating groups after a certain period of time. We object to this practice because it does not respect children's interests or promote children's purposes. Even if a child is interested in an assigned activity, interest must stop at the moment determined by the teacher for moving to the next center. In response to this kind of management, some children simply do not invest themselves in the activities because they know they will be forced to leave them.

In chapter 1, we noted that the Manager of the Factory classroom allowed children to choose activities only after they completed their worksheets or other work. We disagree with this practice because it also fails to respect children's interests. It reflects the teacher's interest in academics as the highest priority. While some value may be attached to center activities, they are used as rewards for academic work, and little effort is invested in making them appealing and challenging.

We do not mean to imply that constructivist teachers should never have periods of time set aside for privileged activities. For example, at Sunset-Pearl Elementary School, teachers were concerned that children were not reading enough on their own. Partly, this seemed due to the noise level during activity time. After much discussion with children, they decided to institute a school-wide reading time called SQUIRT. Solitary Quiet Uninterrupted Individual Reading Time happened every day (usually after lunch). The length of time for SQUIRT varied according to the age of the children, but during SQUIRT everyone engaged in quiet reading, even the adults. Children could choose anything they wanted to read. They could read at tables, desks, or even sprawled on pillows on the floor. The only requirement was that they read alone. SQUIRT became a popular time of day for the entire school.

The logical consequence of allowing children the freedom to choose their activities is that teachers have very little control over what children choose. This rarely presents a problem if teachers set out attractive, interesting, and appealing activities. However, occasionally teachers may be faced with situations when they would like to influence children's choices. For example, in a class of 3- and 4-year-olds, one teacher noticed a group of three girls who spent all their time in the pretend center with the baby dolls. The teacher wanted to interest these girls in other activities without being coercive. She decided to begin by expanding pretend activities. Removing everything from the pretend center, she engaged the class in discussing the types of pretend centers they would like to have. Over the course of about 3 months, they had a restaurant, a doctor's office, a travel agency, a florist shop, a museum, an office, a beauty shop, a library, and a grocery store. Pretend play was enriched, and the pretend center became linked to other centers. For example, the travel agency led to making passport books in which they put their picture and wrote about and illustrated imaginary travels. The museum led to creating art objects to display. When the teacher finally brought the baby dolls back into the classroom, the girls still played with the dolls, but their interests had been widened to the pursuit of many other activities as well.

Encourage Reasoning

Throughout this book, we try to point out that the sociomoral atmosphere that promotes moral development also promotes intellectual development—and *vice versa*. Essentially, this atmosphere is characterized by respect. That is, the teacher's acceptance and openness to children's ideas encourage children to have ideas and to express them. To foster reasoning, we suggest four considerations. These are to respect preoperational reasoning, consider the kind of knowledge involved, assess developmental level in children's activities, and intervene in terms of children's reasoning. We discuss these briefly below. (For guidance with regard to intervention in two types of activities, the reader can consult previous books by Kamii and DeVries: *Group Games in Early Education*, 1980, and *Physical Knowledge in Preschool Education*, 1978/1993, provide useful principles and examples of how to teach in these contexts.)

Respect Preoperational Reasoning

In chapter 2 and throughout this book, we describe children's reasoning that is qualitatively different from the reasoning of older children and adults. Adults often laugh when children say, for example, that the weatherman made it rain or that their shadow sleeps under their bed at night. These ideas, however, are the product of children's honest reasoning. To dismiss children's preoperational reasoning as just cute is to devalue children's thinking and, therefore, to devalue children as thinkers. The sociomoral atmosphere is enhanced when the teacher respects children's ideas and reasoning.

Consider the Three Kinds of Knowledge

Constructivist teachers use the distinction among the three kinds of knowledge to help them respond to children's wrong ideas. If a child's wrong idea is arbitrary conventional knowledge, the teacher does not hesitate to correct the child. For example, if a child incorrectly says he is painting with blue paint, the teacher may say teasingly, "I thought that was green paint." If a child's wrong idea is physical or logico-mathematical knowledge, the teacher refrains from correcting. If an erroneous idea can be tested by acting on objects, the teacher can arrange for this opportunity. For example, if children think that water can flow up a hill as well as down, then physical-knowledge activities involving the movement of water in tubes might offer children an opportunity to experience conflict between their expectations and their actions. If an idea is logico-mathematical, the teacher does not correct, but plans for more opportunities for children to go on reasoning about the issue. For example, if a child makes the logical error of addition in a board game (counting as "1" the space occupied at the end of the last turn), the teacher makes a die with only 1's and 2's, so that the child will experience more frequently the contradiction of counting "1" and going nowhere. Wrong ideas about physical knowledge and logico-mathematical knowledge are not corrected because, being unable to understand the correction, children may experience this as a negation of themselves. They may learn to mistrust their own thinking and look to adults as the sole source of knowledge. We want children to be confident in their ability to be thinkers and learners.

Assess Children's Developmental Level

We have emphasized that children construct many wrong ideas in the course of moving toward advanced reasoning about the world of objects and the world of people. While observing and engaging in activities with children, the constructivist teacher continually assesses how children reason.

We often state that constructivist education takes development as its aim (see, for example, DeVries, 1992). Essentially, this means that when possible, constructivist teachers think about children's progress through sequential and qualitatively different stages. However, Piaget's descriptions of developmental stages are often not helpful because the content is not appropriate for classroom activities. We do not, for example, try to teach children to conserve substance (see chapter 3) because this is an example of knowledge that, as Eleanor Duckworth (1987) put it, "Either we're too early and they can't learn it, or we're too late and they know it already." We need more research that will help us recognize development in classroom activities, but some research exists. Examples are stages in children's practice of rules in marbles (Piaget, 1932/1965), stages in children's play of Tic Tac Toe (DeVries & Fernie, 1990) and Guess Which Hand the Penny Is In (DeVries, 1970), and stages in children's conceptions of shadow phenomena (DeVries, 1986). The reader may want to see a summary of these (DeVries, 1992). Here, we give a brief overview of Piaget's stages in the practice of rules because these apply to all games.

In his research on children's play of marbles, Piaget found four stages in the child's practice of rules. At the first stage of motor and individual play, the child's practice of rules is not even social. The child simply plays with the marbles, dropping them one by one onto a carpet, throwing them, or pretending with them.

The second stage of egocentric play is definitely social because the child tries to follow rules, feeling an obligation to play according to the authority that comes from others. However, the social character of play lies more in the child's intention than in practice. That is, children practice rules egocentrically—without realizing when their ideas about rules are different from those around them. In Marbles, for example, children may sometimes keep the marbles they knock out of a square and may sometimes replace them. Children imitate the observable features of others' play in a way that is correct in general but incorrect in detail. At this stage, children may play with others without trying to win. No competition exists, and "winning" means simply following some rules or having fun. Children playing together may even play by different rules without noticing it.

The third stage Piaget called incipient cooperation, characterized by the appearance of a competitive attitude. Children try to win and are concerned with cooperating by playing according to mutually agreed upon rules. Competition at this stage thus exists within a broader framework of cooperation to agree upon, accept, and abide by the rules. Competition is not the primary motivation for playing the game. Rather, the motive is to play together at a game in which everyone has an equal chance of winning. At this stage, children do not know all the rules, and their incomplete rule system results in a simplified game.

The fourth stage involves codification of the rules. Children are interested in cooperating to anticipate all possible instances of conflict of interest and in providing a set of rules to regulate play. When disagreements occur, players see the issue as one that can be settled through negotiation. Rules can be whatever players decide.

This research on children's play of games helps the teacher assess children's developmental level. A child's effort to play by rules is progress in feeling obligation to a social system of rules coming from outside himself or herself. This attitude develops before children have a good understanding of rules and before they play competitively. Research shows that the emergence of a competitive attitude is developmental progress and should not be discouraged (though some children need special help in developing a cooperative perspective on competition). This is but one example of how it is useful for the teacher to think about developmental stages in assessing children's activities.

Intervene in Terms of Children's Reasoning

The way to deal with children's incorrect reasoning is to accept it and then, when possible, set up a situation in which it is necessary for children to call into question their own ideas. The main thing to keep in mind is that children construct many wrong ideas in the course of moving toward advanced reasoning about the world of objects and the world of people.

We have noticed that the most successful constructivist teachers pay close attention to the details of children's activity. They try to figure out what children think in order to understand and decide how or whether to intervene. In a boat making activity, for example, Rebecca Peña provides 3-year-old Experimenters with a variety of materials on a table next to the water table. She asks, "What do you think would make a good boat?" Children select and try many materials, and Rebecca converses with children individually as they try cardboard, Styrofoam, and wood. When A tries a strawberry basket several times (appearing surprised that it sinks), Rebecca asks, "Is there anything you could do to make that float?" Eventually, A triumphantly sets the basket on a piece of Styrofoam.

Playing group games with children provides an excellent opportunity for assessing and promoting children's reasoning, both moral and intellectual. For example, when children all want to go first, it is an occasion to help children confront the fact that others have similar desires that conflict with their own. This can also be the occasion for helping children begin to realize the value of negotiating an agreement satisfactory to everyone. In playing a game of strategy such as Tic Tac Toe, the teacher can verbalize strategies that lead children to become more conscious of temporal and spatial relations. For example, "I'm going to put my X here because if I don't, you will finish your line on your next turn. I have to block you."

Foster Social Self-Regulation and Cooperation

Social self-regulation and cooperation may be fostered by referring children to other children for help, promoting sharing without coercion, and responding to incidents of cheating by assessing intentionality. We discuss these principles of teaching below.

Refer Children to Other Children for Help

During activity time, the teacher will inevitably be barraged by requests for information, assistance, and intervention. "Hold this for me while I glue it." "Where is the tape?" "J won't let me play." Teachers cannot possibly respond to every overture and must decide which needs really require adult help. Children can learn to see each other as resources and not depend solely on the teacher. "I'm helping S right now. Maybe you can ask L to hold it." "I think I saw K with the tape. Why don't you ask him where it is?" "Try saying to J, 'I want to play. When can I have a turn?'"

In Korea, constructivist education is managed by one teacher with 40 children. Ms. Young-Ae Choi, Director of the Moon Kyung Kindergarten in Seoul, points out that one advantage of this teacher-child ratio is that children must depend on each other and cooperation reaches a higher level than in classrooms with fewer children or more teachers where the teacher responds more frequently to children's appeals. While we do not advocate putting 40 children in a room with one teacher, we respect our Korean colleagues' ability to successfully implement a constructivist program with this ratio.

Support Negotiation

Opportunities to foster children's negotiation abilities abound during activity time. Chapter 5 provides guidance on dealing with conflicts.

Here we discuss a general approach to dealing with problems of sharing materials and turns with activities.

We would like to point out that we do not advocate forced sharing in constructivist classrooms. Especially if the item in contention belongs to one child (for example, a child-made boat) or has been chosen first by one child (for example, a puzzle), forced sharing is coercive and disrespectful to children. We believe that individual rights should be respected and that the teacher's interventions should focus on negotiation. "Did you ask D if he wants to use the boat with you or if he wants to use it by himself?" "You can ask P if he wants help with the puzzle. He doesn't? Well, maybe you can do one by yourself, too, or find another friend to help you." If an item in contention belongs to the entire class, teachers can still facilitate sharing without being coercive. The way to do this is to give children the responsibility for regulating fair use of materials. For example, at the art table, a single stapler can lead to conflicts. The teacher can support children's rights and foster cooperation through negotiation. "I see that K is using the stapler now. Why don't you ask her to give it to you when she finishes?" (See chapter 5 for more guidance on conflict resolution.)

The problem of how to share limited resources can often be handled informally with children who want turns. For example, Mary Wells once brought a real parachute in a back pack to her kindergarten class, and the children had the chance during activity time to try it on. In this incident, Mary (T) helps N negotiate with A in order to get a turn with the parachute.

N: He won't give me it.
T: You haven't had a turn, N? (To A who has the parachute) Have you had a turn yet, A?
A: No.
T: Well, then you need to tell N that he can have it when you are finished.
N: He won't.
T: A, what did you say to N?
A: I said after I get through.
T: Okay. (To N) Come listen to his words. He says when he gets through. (To A) When will you be through, A? Let's look at the clock and see when you're going to be through. N, let's look at the clock, and let's see when A's going to be done, so you'll know. Okay, it's on the two right now.
A: I'll give it up on four.

T: On four, okay. (To N) When the big hand is on the four, he'll give it to you. Okay?

N: Okay.

T: So watch for it to go to the four.

Mary shows respect for A's right to use the parachute while acknowledging N's desire for a turn with it as well. She treats A as a reasonable person who will give the parachute to N as soon as he is through using it. She also treats N's desire to try on the parachute as reasonable and asks A to respond to N. With Mary's help, A and N negotiate a resolution.

Other ways of dealing with the issue of sharing include using sign-up lists and choosing rhymes such as Eeney, Meeney, Miney, Moe (discussed in chapter 5). When an activity is particularly popular, a sign-up-list procedure is one fair way to regulate turns. Children sign a list if they want a turn at the activity, and children and the teacher consult it to see who is next after someone finishes. The list removes some of the arbitrariness from deciding who gets a turn next and allows children to predict when they will get a turn, avoiding pleas such as "When do I get a turn?" "Can I be next?" "But I asked first." The teacher simply answers, "We're going down the list. Look to see where your name is."

Promote Shared Experience

Children's interactions during activity time include shared experiences as well as negotiations. As discussed in chapter 2, friendly shared experiences occur when there is no disequilibrium or tension to be resolved in an interaction. Children engaging together in absorbing activities have many opportunities for companionable sharing. It is the pleasure of shared experiences that provides a prime motivation for the kinds of interactions that lead to progress in sociomoral development. When children experience special friendships and the satisfaction of playing with others, they are motivated to prevent and work out conflicts. For example, in chapter 5 we describe an intense argument between two 5-year-old friends over whether a jump in checkers was legitimate. It was a misunderstanding in which both boys were absolutely sure they were right. The strength of the friendship may be credited for the fact that they did not come to blows. However, the conflict became so intense that they screamed, cried, swept the checkers onto the floor, put their hands over their ears, and could not listen to or talk with one another. When her efforts to mediate proved unsuccessful, the teacher asked them to separate until they could listen and talk. Within a few minutes, K was trying to catch J's eye, and when he did, he blew on his arm to make rude "raspberry" noises. This amused J, and the two boys approached each other. The teacher asked if they wanted to talk first or clean up the checkers. Grinning with relief, they began to pick the checkers up off the floor. K continued to blow "raspberries" while J shook with laughter. This illustrates the role shared experience can play in conflict resolution.

For young children, this kind of level 0 shared experience serves a bonding purpose and should not be dismissed as mere silliness or discouraged. We have to remember that preoperational thought is also expressed in child humor that is very different from that of adults.

As they play, children engage in all levels of shared experience, from burping and other funny noises, to reciting together a naughty bathroom rhyme, to sharing a secret, to reflecting on how best friends fight "but then we get over it, don't we?"

Respond to Cheating by Assessing Intentionality

The problem of cheating is most often encountered in group games (see Kamii & DeVries, 1980). The issue of cheating is a delicate matter because it is easy to misjudge a child's behavior as cheating. Cheating is an intentional violation of rules in order to benefit the self. Young children often violate rules, however, without intending to cheat. Unintentional rule violations are often due to inadequate understanding of rules which reflects what Piaget (1932/1965) terms the child's egocentric practice of rules, discussed above. We give some clues for assessing intentionality and provide some guidelines for dealing with rule violation.

Clues to assessing intentionality. To determine whether a child is cheating, the teacher must consider various clues to the child's intention. Sneaky violation is definitely a sign of intentional cheating! For example, a child may surreptitiously turn the die to a 6 and pretend it was a fair roll. Blatant rule violation however, is often not cheating. It is probably not cheating if the child makes no attempt to conceal a violation. For example, unselfconscious turning of the die may simply reflect an intelligent approach to succeeding in the game. Figuring out that getting a 6 is an advantage is cognitive progress!

The teacher should also be aware of a form of cheating that is midway between innocent and sneaky cheating. We have in mind those occasions when a child knows that turning a die to 6, for example, is against the rules, but does it openly without seeming to realize or care that others may notice. Similarly, in card games children may go through the "draw" pile until they find the card they want. Such violations can reflect the child's failure to appreciate the idea that respect for rules is necessary to fair and satisfying play. Intellectual and moral aspects are not coordinated into a system. At times, a conscious decision to violate a rule wins out as an intelligent way to succeed.

Children often violate rules because they have not yet constructed an understanding of them. Breaking a rule you do not understand is not cheating. Therefore, it is important for the teacher to figure out how children understand rules. In the board game Candyland, players can take a shortcut if they land on the shortcut's beginning space. Children sometimes, however, misunderstand the rule to mean that you take the shortcut every time you touch it, no matter on what space you land.

Mistakes are not cheating. In games involving counting, children often make mistakes that simply reflect lack of construction of numerical or logical notions. For example, in counting, a child may recite the sequence of numbers incorrectly. The correspondence may be imperfect between the spoken numbers and pointing to dots on a die or spaces on a board. A child may make the logical error of addition (counting the space occupied as "1" rather than moving forward on the count of "1"). A child may skip the space occupied by another player, failing to count it because of lack of the logic that all spaces must be counted on the path to the final winning space. One clue suggesting these behaviors are not cheating is that they sometimes operate to the player's disadvantage. The teacher can only determine whether counting errors are cheating by observing the child's counting throughout a game. If the child always counts correctly except when the mistake benefits him or her, then the child is probably cheating.

It is important to assess whether a child has a competitive attitude. As indicated above, sneaky efforts to cheat indicate progress in this aspect of game playing. Though adults often see a different kind of competition for resources, such as calling "Me first!" young children are not naturally competitive in games. They often think, for example, that the goal of a path game is to get to the end. When everyone reaches the end, everyone wins. For these noncompetitive children, no race occurs.

It is curious that children having a competitive attitude often play in what seems to be a noncompetitive manner. A competitive attitude often coexists with noncompetitive strategies. For example, in card games they may openly show their cards or look at another's cards.

Before concluding that this is cheating, the teacher can observe whether or not knowing an opponent's hand helps the child play. Strategies may not be developed to the point that a child can understand how to use this information. In the absence of being able to use the information to advantage, there is no reason either to hide one's own hand or not to look at the opponent's hand. Children may want to win without knowing what strategies will produce a win. The competitive attitude is often the inspiration for a child to figure out strategies to win.

Guidelines for dealing with rule violations. So what should the teacher do when a child violates rules? We suggest four guidelines.

1. Make sure the child knows what the rule is. This can be done by referring to the rules. "Oh, I thought the rule said to roll the die like this (demonstrating). Let's check. Yes, it says to roll the die." If the child continues to violate the rule, he or she is either cheating or lacks the ability to understand the rule. Keep in mind that children often lose track of where they are on the board, and that going in turn can involve complex spatial reasoning. With three or more players, we often observe that children have difficulty in following the order of turns. For example, one 4-year-old saw her position as "next" in relation to both of the other players. She therefore explained, "It's S, me, T, me, S, me, T, me." When the children do not feel there is a problem with inconsistent ordering of turns, it is best to allow them to regulate turns, even when they make errors.

2. Find out if other players object to the violation. "Is that right? Is that what we are supposed to do?" If all children are happy playing by a particular rule, or if children do not even notice that they are all playing by different rules, then the teacher probably should not insist on the conventional rules. However, the teacher can emphasize the rules in his or her own play and try to make children conscious of the rules.

3. If there is a dispute among children about the rules, uphold the value of mutual agreement. "D thinks we should play it this way, and N thinks we should play it that way. What shall we do? We have to agree on what the rule is."

4. As a player in the game, protest rule violations. This is especially called for when children protest as well but can be done when the teacher thinks a child should be confronted with a different point of view. "If you can set the die down on 6, then can I do that, too?" If the child answers, "No," then the teacher can go on to question the fairness of this. "It doesn't seem fair that you get any number you want, but I have to roll the die. If you get to do it, then I should be able to, too." If the child says "Yes," then the teacher should play by the child's rule and eventually point out the disadvantage of all players moving 6 on every turn. The teacher can also model correct game playing by stating, "I like to roll the die around in my hand and let it land on any number. I think it's more fun when I don't know what number I'm going to get. I like to be surprised."

When a child tries to be deceptive in cheating, the teacher should protest, but keep it light. "Are you trying to look at my cards? Oh, no you don't! I'm going to hold them real close so you can't see them. J, better look out. L is looking at our cards." If a child cheats consistently, the teacher may want to point out to that child privately that the logical consequence of cheating is that other children will not want to play games with him or her.

In summary, cheating reflects cognitive developmental advance in young children. It requires an understanding of how to play and how to win. What is missing, of course, is recognition that cheating violates the rights of others and that winning by cheating is not really winning. In the course of play, children gradually construct these fine points. When children are cheating and no one seems to mind, the teacher should not make an issue of it. But when children cheat and others object, the teacher should uphold fairness and reciprocity. "N doesn't like it when you skip her turn. You wouldn't like to have your turn skipped, either."

Be Flexible

One key to a successful activity time is to be flexible. Children often do not do what you expect, and you have to shift your focus. For example, kindergarten children in Mary Wells's class were testing in water the boats they had made. Most children experimented in the expected ways. Then some children put pecans on their boats to represent people, and Mary asked how many they could put and still keep their boats afloat. This led one child to try to make her boat sink! Seeing that it popped back up when the child held it on the bottom, Mary shifted to the child's goal. "How could you make it stay down? What would you have to put on it to make it stay down?" A child suggested a brick, and the search was on for ways to make boats sink.

It is also important to be flexible when children do not want to engage in a planned activity. Sometimes an activity falls entirely flat. When this happens, the constructivist teacher tries to figure out why the activity did not appeal to children. Sometimes modifications are possible to salvage the activity, but sometimes the teacher just scraps the idea. Sometimes an activity that appeals to one group of children does not appeal to another. The constructivist teacher takes an experimental attitude and tries to learn from these experiences.

THREE SOURCES OF DIFFICULTY IN IMPLEMENTING ACTIVITY TIME

Over the years, we have observed that teachers' difficulties in implementing activity time fall into at least one of three patterns.

One pattern is to spend such a large proportion of time in classroom management that the teacher has little opportunity to observe children's reasoning. When the teacher's preoccupation remains solely with cleaning up, keeping the paint jars filled, and making sure that the "five-ring circus" is going, he or she does not become intimately involved in the activities themselves.

A second pattern is to provide few activities that inspire children's reasoning. When children do not have intriguing possibilities, their reasoning remains at a low level.

A third pattern is to relate to children in an authoritarian way so that children are oriented to figuring out what the teacher wants them to say. Authoritarian engagement with children cuts off or circumvents the flourishing of their spontaneous honest reasoning.

SUMMARY

Activity time is perhaps the most important period of the day in a constructivist classroom. It is a time when children choose to engage in group games, pretend play, physical-knowledge activities, reading and writing, blockbuilding, or art. The objectives in activity time, intellectual, social, and moral, can be summarized as "The having of wonderful ideas." Constructivist teachers use Piaget's distinction among physical, logico-mathematical, and conventional knowledge in thinking about planning and intervening in activities. Constructivist activities appeal to children's interests and purposes, challenge their reasoning, and appeal to their self-regulation and cooperation.

During activity time, the teacher also fosters children's negotiation and shared experience. Sources of teachers' difficulties in implementing a constructivist activity time include too much time devoted to classroom management, providing few activities that inspire children's reasoning, and relating to children in an authoritarian way.

12

Clean-Up Time

Preschool and early childhood teachers we have known regard clean-up time as one of the most difficult times of the day. Some teachers solve this problem by doing all the cleaning in their classrooms themselves. Unquestionably, it is much easier for adults to clean up than to try to get young children to do it. However, we hope to convince the reader that children's involvement in clean-up is an important part of the constructivist sociomoral atmosphere. In this chapter we outline the objectives for clean-up time and discuss how to present the issue of clean-up to the class. We consider the problems inherent in clean-up time, and, finally, we describe how four teachers handled problems with clean-up in their classes.

OBJECTIVES

First, the objective of clean-up is *not* to get the room clean. Our objectives for having children clean (as the reader can probably predict by now) involve children's developing sense of moral necessity and responsibility and developing self-regulation.

Our first goal of promoting feelings of moral necessity for classroom upkeep is part and parcel of the sense of community we discuss in chapter 6. We want children to think about the care of their class environment in terms of consideration and fairness toward everyone in the class community. This involves the ability to decenter to think about how others feel about messy classrooms, misplaced or damaged materials, dirty tables, and so forth. We hope that children will experience requirements to clean, not as heteronomous dictates from above, but as a moral necessity emerging from a feeling of belonging to the community.

Our second goal, to promote feelings of shared responsibility for classroom upkeep, is related to the first and comes out of it. That is, if children feel the moral necessity for taking care of their environment, then they will also feel a sense of personal and group responsibility to care for it. This sense of responsibility has specific long-term benefits in that children who care for their immediate environment may be expected eventually to care for their larger environments, from the local park to the planet. We hope that children who feel a sense of moral necessity for caring for their class will grow up to be adults who do not take lightly oil spills, toxic waste dumps, and overflowing landfills. We think the development of environmental awareness and responsibility begins with the classroom as a microcosm for the larger society.

Finally, our third goal to promote self-regulation underlies the other goals. By encouraging children to take responsibility for the care of their classroom environment, we aim to reduce the exercise of adult authority and turn this authority over to the children themselves. Children can exhort each other to care for the classroom, require each other to participate in cleaning, and chastise each other for failure to participate. This in turn reminds children that the moral authority of the class comes not from the teacher but from the children themselves.

HOW TO PRESENT CLEAN-UP TO THE CLASS

Problems with clean-up lead to good opportunities for children to discuss and decide on rules (see chapter 7). Such discussions are also opportunities to help children become aware of natural and logical consequences of failure to care for the physical environment (see chapter 10). In such discussions, children can construct for themselves the necessity for cleaning up. In order to avoid a situation in which children feel nagged into compliance, the teacher can emphasize practical and moral necessities, discussed below.

Practical Necessities

The teacher must introduce to children the practical reasons for cleaning up so that they will understand why the teacher is asking them to do it. It is not enough to tell children that they need a clean classroom; young children do not accept this as a given. Teachers must be specific in their explanations. For example, at the HDLS, children bring their lunches to school and eat in their classrooms. Therefore it is necessary to clean off the tables after activity time so that children have a place to eat lunch. Teachers emphasize this problem, asking children, "How do you feel when you sit down to lunch and the table is dirty? Do you like to set your sandwich down on glue? Isn't that yucky?"

Teachers can also emphasize the need to pick materials up off the floor so that they do not get destroyed. A broken toy or a torn piece of children's art can be a good illustration here. "Oh, look what happens when things are not picked up. They get stepped on, and sometimes they get broken. What can we do to make sure this doesn't happen again?"

Another practical issue that teachers can present to children is the need to know where materials are so that children can get them when they need them. If children are to be able to use the materials in the class, then the materials need to be put back in the same place every time they are used. Teachers can enlist children's help in deciding where things are going to be kept. That way, when materials are not put back properly, teachers can say, for example, "I see that there is glue in the pretend center. Where did we decide to keep the glue?"

Moral Necessities

Once the teacher has presented the practical issues of clean-up to the class, the stage is set for moving the focus to the moral issues. These are harder for children to understand because they involve the ability to decenter to see a situation from someone else's perspective. However, most children have at least a rudimentary understanding of what it means for something to be fair or unfair so the teacher can start with this idea.

The moral issues of cleaning up revolve around one person's actions causing everyone to suffer. When someone leaves a toy on the floor and it gets broken, everyone in the class is deprived of that toy, not just the person who left it on the floor. When one person leaves the caps off the markers and they dry up, everyone is deprived of markers. When one person makes a huge mess, everyone has to live with it, not just the person who made the mess. The teacher can gently draw attention to the unfairness, without being blaming. It is usually better to do this before the materials are actually ruined so that no one will be blamed. For example, if markers are left out without caps, the teacher can bring them to circle and say, "Look what I found in the writing center. These markers don't have caps. Do you know what happens when we leave the caps off? They dry out, and then no one can use the markers. That would be very sad. What should we do?" Usually children will reply that the people who were using the markers should put the caps back on and put them away. The teacher can then follow up with, "Good idea. Then everyone will be able to use the markers."

Another moral issue revolves around whether it is fair that only a few children clean up for the entire class. The teacher can enlist the help of the cleaners here. They can come to circle and tell the others how they feel about doing all the cleaning. The teacher can also state his or her own feelings about this, saying, "I don't like to clean all by myself. It doesn't seem fair that I clean up stuff and other people do not help."

PROBLEMS WITH CLEAN-UP

We have noticed a number of problems with trying to get children to take responsibility for cleaning up. These fall into three categories: coercion, transition, and distraction.

The Problem of Coercion

One of the big problems of clean-up is that unwilling children feel coerced into doing it. Young children's understanding of clean-up is frequently that it is something they are forced to do, even when they have participated in making clean-up rules. When children lack the understanding of the necessity for cleaning and caring for their class, they feel the requirement to be heteronomous. This is why the teacher must continually emphasize the reasons why we clean up. The challenge for the teacher is to appeal to children in ways that engender willingness to clean up.

The Problem of Transition

Another big problem with clean-up pertains to the difficulty children have in making transitions. Clean-up usually follows activity time. Even if they have been given a 5-minute warning ("We have 5 more minutes to do activities, and then we have to stop and clean up"), children will still find it very hard to switch gears and, instead of playing with materials, put them away. The materials may be so inviting that they simply cannot put them down. Sometimes children may not be finished with what they are doing and will try to postpone clean-up. "Just 1 more minute, I just have to glue this one thing on." This can go on for a long time. The challenge for the teacher is to figure out how to facilitate letting go of activity time and shifting to clean-up.

The Problem of Distraction

The problem of distraction during clean-up derives from success in providing materials and activities that appeal so strongly to children's interests that they do not want the activity period to end. The distraction of the materials can promote new play instead of cleaning. We have also seen children make games out of cleaning, such as aiming checkers into the basket while picking them up. These games can be so much fun that children forget the goal of cleaning up and elaborate the game. The challenge for the teacher is to find a way to help children want to complete clean-up.

SOLUTIONS TO CLEAN-UP PROBLEMS

What can be done about these problems? We recognize that each class is unique and that solutions will vary with the needs of the class. We present here several teachers' solutions to their classes' problems with clean-up. We do not suggest that these solutions are best in every instance. Rather, we hope to illustrate ways of thinking about clean-up problems that may inspire teachers to figure out the best answer to the problems in their classes.

Karen's Class

In a discussion about devising consequences for instances of broken rules, Karen Capo describes an experience she had with a class of kindergarten children who had problems with cleaning up.

> Young children do not always see the need for conse-
> quences until they are actually living with broken rules. For
> example, even though one class had devised a rule stating
> that each person should clean up what they played with,
> classroom clean-up time gradually worsened until few chil-
> dren were willing to take responsibility for cleaning. I tried

reading books like *The Berenstain Bears and the Messy Room* (Berenstain, 1983) and *The Man Who Didn't Wash His Dishes* (Krasilovsky, 1950) which addressed the need for cleanliness, but I saw no generalization from the points made in the story to our classroom. When one child finally complained that he was doing most of the work at clean-up time, I suggested that we bring the problem to the group for discussion. After talking about the situation for quite a while, the group decided that consequences for failing to clean-up were unnecessary. In fact, clean-up itself was unnecessary! Consequently, we went the rest of the day without cleaning at all! As you can imagine, the room was quite a mess by the end of the day. I left a note for the custodial staff explaining what we were doing, and we started the next day in our messy room. When the children came in the next morning they found that it was difficult to start a new activity when the remains of the activity from the day before were still there. In this way they were able to construct for themselves the need to have consequences for not cleaning up. The children changed the rule to, "You can only get out one activity at a time, and you have to clean it up before you go to a new activity." I even had several comments (and thank you's) from parents saying that children had taken this rule home and used it there!

The grouptime discussion showed Karen that the children did not understand why cleaning was necessary. She knew that it would take a graphic demonstration for the children's understanding to change, and she was willing to allow children to experience the natural consequences of not cleaning up in order to bring about this change in attitude.

Peige's Class

In the following example, Peige Fuller's Lab School class of 3½ to 4½-year-olds have a particularly hard time cleaning up. Peige (T) starts second circle with a discussion about clean up.

T: Today we had plans to do some fun stuff in circle, but you know what? We aren't going to be able to do it because we have to have a talk about clean-up time. I have a question. Why do we clean up the toys? Does anybody have an idea about that? N?

N: Because children have to clean up and turn off the lights [the Special Helper turning off the lights is a signal that it is clean-up time in this class].

T: Uh-huh, children have to turn off the lights and tell us it's clean-up time. And then when it's clean-up time we are supposed to put the stuff in the boxes and on the shelves. What do you think, M? Why do you think we need to clean up the stuff?

M: So it can, so our room can be clean.

T: Oh, did you hear that? He says that he thinks that we need to clean up so our room can be clean. K, M said that we have to make sure that our room is clean. What happens when our room is not clean?

G: We step on stuff.

M: And we would break the stuff if we step on the stuff.

T: If we step on the stuff, we'd break the stuff. And if we stepped on all the toys and broke all the toys, it would be very sad. Yes, S?

S: It break.

T: It might break. If we do not clean up, the stuff might break. Yes, A?

A: Whoever played can clean them up.

T: What? Tell me again.

A: Whoever played clean them up.

T: Whoever plays with stuff needs to clean that stuff up?

A: (Nods)

T: Yes, R?

R: We've broken spoons and cups before.

T: Uh-huh, we've broken spoons and cups because they were not cleaned up. Yes, K?

K: Well, we break the stuff and then we throw it away. When we don't play with them, they get broken.

M: If we throw our toys away, we don't get to play with nothing.

T: Yeah. You know, I was thinking today, take a look at this, all this stuff. Today we had problems cleaning up Blockhead, cleaning up the mouse game, we had problems cleaning up Pick-a-Berry (as she recites these names of materials, she gathers them up and puts them in the middle of the circle). We had problems cleaning up the Nuts and Bolts. We had problems cleaning up all this stuff and all of this stuff and all of the housekeeping area. We had problems cleaning up the fingerpaints and the watercolors and all the crayons.

G: Why do you keep on taking stuff out?

T: Why do I take the stuff out? Let me show you, G. It's very important. I'm trying to make a point here. Okay, if you did a picture and used crayons, raise your hands.

Children: I did! I did! (Many hands raised)

T: Many people used crayons. If you did a picture using the water-
     color paints, raise your hands.

Children: I did! I did! (Many hands raised)

T: If you played with the Strawberry Shortcake game, raise your
     hands.

(Peige repeats this procedure with five more items.)

T: Do you remember what A was saying? If you play with something,
     you have to take responsibility for cleaning it up? A lot of children
     were saying, "Oh, I did. I played with that." "Oh, that was neat!"
     And "I did that" and "I did that" and "I did a lot of this stuff, too."

C: I did, too.

T: Does that mean that all these children played with it and nobody
     wants to take care of it?

K: I don't.

T: You don't want to take care of it? Because what we can do then is
     we can take all the stuff, all our neat stuff, pack it all up and take
     it out of the classroom.

H: No, I don't want to.

T: You don't want to take them out? We could do that, because, see,
     what I'm seeing is that you don't want these things in the class-
     room. Okay, we could take them down.

Children: No!

T: No? But see, I'm not seeing that children want them. I'm not see-
     ing that children are taking care of them. What I'm seeing is that
     people aren't interested in taking care of this stuff. And I don't
     want them to get broken. So instead of getting broken, we can
     just take them out.

M: I don't want to take them out.

T: You don't want to take them out? No? I don't want to take them
     out either. I want to take care of them.

Children: Me, too!

T: Yeah. Well, let's practice taking care of them. Let's see. C, could
     you come and take care of these two things, please? And then get
     ready to go outside.

Children: I can! I can!

T: Of course. G, could you help by taking care of these two things
     and then go get ready by the door?

M: I can, Peige.

T: Everybody will get a chance to take care. Here you go, S. Would
     you go and put these two things away? M, would you take care of
     these two things?

(Peige continues to give each child two things to put away. Soon, everyone is involved in cleaning the classroom, and the class-room is all clean.)

T: Who played with the activities in our class today, raise your hands.

Children: I did! (All raise their hands)

T: I did. Who helped to take care of our classroom today, raise your hands.

Children: I did! (All raise their hands)

T: Everybody helped to take care! All right!

Peige starts out the circle by drawing the children's attention to the problem of the materials left out. Notice that she consistently uses the term "caring for" the materials rather that simply "cleaning up." In this way she introduces the reason for cleaning from the start. Her threat (which was also a logical consequence) to take the toys out of the class, since children were not caring for them, may have seemed slightly extreme to the reader. However, it did succeed in getting the children's attention and activated their consciousness of wanting to have the materials available. The important point to note is that she did not leave the situation at the threat level. Rather, she gave chil-dren a chance to demonstrate that they wanted to care for their classroom. She transformed what could have been a very coercive interaction into a positive experience for the children. When they fin-ished cleaning the classroom, all the children had the feeling that they had contributed to the care of their class. The final "I did!" was positively enthusiastic. Before they went outside, they all joined in a big "Hip-hip-hooray!" for themselves.

Stephanie's Class

In a 3½ to 4½-year-old class at the HDLS, the teacher, Stephanie Clark, determined that their problem with clean-up was one of transi-tion. Children were just too wrapped up in what they were doing to stop activities and clean it all up. Their morning schedule started with a circle time, followed by an hour of activities. Then came clean-up, and after clean-up they came back to circle for a snack and a sec-ond grouptime. After second circle, they went outside to play on the playground. Stephanie's solution to the problem of making the tran-sition to clean-up was to change the schedule. After activities, she had children simply stop and come to circle for snack and grouptime. After the second circle, the children cleaned and then went outside.

The transition from activities to snack was easier than the transition from activities to clean-up. Children were more willing to stop activities in order to eat snack. The transition from grouptime to clean-up was easier because children had already disengaged from play. In addition, they had another incentive. "When we finish cleaning up, we can go outside." By simply rearranging the schedule, Stephanie made clean-up time much less jarring in its interruption of children's purposes in activities.

Coreen's Class

Stephanie's solution actually had its inspirational source in a child's suggestion in Coreen Samuel's (T) kindergarten class during the preceding year. The school year started with problems at clean-up time. Some children were cleaning, but other children were running around the class and playing. The children who cleaned complained about the children who did not clean, and no one was happy. The following discussion of clean-up problems takes place during the 1st week of school, after a particularly difficult clean-up.

T: Did we have a good clean-up today? What do you think?
N: I see that table. It's still a mess.
M: I see that table.
C: I see that table.
T: Okay. I noticed something, too. I noticed that there were some people who were working real hard, and there were other children who were just playing and running around the room.
C: I was. I was cleaning up.
T: I noticed that some children didn't need to be reminded but other children needed to be reminded two and three and four times. What should we do when children choose to run around and play? I did have to ask some kids to find a place to sit down because I thought it was dangerous when they run around and play and other kids are trying to clean up. They might knock you over.
C: You might slip.
T: You might slip, too. There's water in the classroom. Does it help get a room clean when you're not taking things and putting them back where they belong? S, do you have any ideas about this problem?
S: I think maybe on the next day if we have a big clean-up, I think we should quickly get it done. Really quickly. Not running, just really quickly walking to the table you want to clean and clean it up. Like

these two tables left are messy. If you guys think we should quickly get it done for Coreen when she's somewhere and when she comes to our circle, she will be surprised for that big clean-up.

T: I would like to ask you, when you're cleaning up the room, are you doing it for me or are you doing it for yourself?

E: For ourself and for you.

T: Do you like a clean room? If it makes you feel better to be in a clean room, then you're not really cleaning up for me. It just makes us all feel better to be in a clean room.

N: It makes me feel better, too.

S: I feel sad when there's two messy tables and I feel happy when there's no messy table.

T: The other thing is, we have a lunch time and if all that stuff is still out, then how can children eat at those tables when it's lunchtime?

They decide to have the Special Helper call on volunteers to finish cleaning the parts of the classroom that are still messy. This solves the immediate problem but does not address the larger problem of children feeling that it is okay to play during clean-up time.

About a month later, clean-up is still a problem in this class. Karen Amos (T), the assistant teacher, decides to have another discussion about the problem at second circle.

T: Did anybody notice that some children were just walking around during clean-up time?

C: Yeah.

T: My question is, did you see lots of children just walking around? Don't tell me what you were doing, but just answer my question. Did you see lots of children just walking around not cleaning? C?

C: E (mumbles)

T: I don't want to hear who was doing it. 'Cause I saw lots of kids, so I couldn't even begin to name all the kids. But do you think that's the thing to do, to walk around when it's clean-up time?

Children: No.

T: Did anybody have any ideas—you can raise your hand—about what we should do about clean-up time? J?

J: Uh, we should, um, have a circle before clean-up time.

T: We should have a circle? What would that do, if we have a circle before clean-up time?

J: Well, we could, the teachers could ask them, you have to clean-up. Whoever doesn't clean up gets to have, gets to sit out.

R: And not go outside.

T: So let me try to get it straight. We should have a circle before clean-up time and then what would we do in that circle?

J: Talk about it.

T: Talk about what? Cleaning up?

J: (Nods)

T: Okay. M, is your hand up? Okay.

M: Well, I think—I don't think it's fair for the other kids to clean up and kids who are walking around.

R: No, it's not.

S: I have an idea. Well, I think we should give, let them sit out and do not go outside. Just sit out.

T: Okay.

J: No. Not fair.

T: Well, that's just her idea.

S: And then we can leave some stuff and so they can clean it up.

T: So they can just stay in while other kids go out and they can clean up?

C: Yeah.

K: That's not fair.

T: Well, we need to think of something because what we're doing now is not working. So we have to think of something. Coreen?

Coreen: Well, I think maybe we shouldn't put out any messy activities, like baking gingerbread men and doing play-doh, and things like that. So kids won't have a lot of things to clean up.

G: Yeah. That's a good idea.

Coreen: How about "no messy activities"? Just simple activities that you can just put up.

E: I know. I know what we can do.

T: Okay, E, what's your idea?

E: We could, like, have circle before clean-up time. And then like if the people who don't clean up don't get to go outside.

T: I heard two people say, let's have a circle before clean-up. I've heard one person say, let's not have any messy activities. I heard someone say to let the children who don't clean up stay inside while all the other kids go out and they can clean up what's left. Okay. A?

A: You know what?

K: What?

A: Well, what I just found was that, before, because in the afternoon, you see, we have more play time, so some people didn't clean up in the mornings will have to sit out for a while during activity time and read books or color or pencils, whichever thing that isn't, that isn't messy.

T: You know, I think you guys have been doing that but has that been working? Have they been sitting out doing books and stuff like that, and then when they came back to the other activities, did they clean up then? Did it help them to sit out?

Children: No.

T: No. So that idea's not working, you think?

A: Well, maybe we should make them sit out and not let them play with any messy activities, and that way they will learn. I know you guys like to play with messy activities.

T: Okay, let's see what O has to say.

O: I think maybe some kids don't clean up, they can't have, like, um, activities.

T: At all? That day? That morning or in the afternoon?

G: That whole day.

O: (Nods)

T: L, what do you think?

L: I think that the kids who don't clean up should not play with activities because they just don't want to clean up, and it's not fair that the kids who clean up get to do all of the work and kids who don't care about cleaning doesn't get to do the work and when it's circle time, 'cause at circle, they won't get to know anything because they'll have to clean up because they didn't clean up when they were supposed to. So I think that's what we should do with kids who don't clean up.

T: Not let them have activities. I hear lots of children and teachers saying that the children who decide not to clean up, they need to not have activities for that morning or for that afternoon. So should we vote on that?

Children: Yeah.

T: I heard some children say have a circle time, and then I guess we can decide who will clean up what? Is that what you want? K and J? Okay. So we'll vote on that. If children don't clean up, they will have to sit out during activity time and read books, and just not messy activities? And that's for the whole activity time. The other choice would be where you come to circle, and I guess we will say, "Which area do you want to clean up?" and then you can go to that area. J and K and I like this idea, too. When we turn off the light, first you come straight to the rug, and then we'll go to clean-up. We'll give children the chance to decide what area they want to clean up. So if you want to come to the circle after we turn off the light for clean-up, raise your hand.

They vote between the choices of having the clean-up circle, and
   making children who do not clean up sit out of activities the next
   day. The clean-up circle option gets all but one vote.
T: Okay. So that's our rule, that we can add on to our rules. So when
     the lights go off, we'll come to the circle and then you can choose.
S: What if they forget our rule?
T: Well, maybe I can write it down, and teachers can remind you,
     and other kids can remind you, too.
Child: What if the teacher forgets?
Coreen: We won't forget.
T: I hope I don't forget it, but if we do, maybe you guys can remind
     us. I don't want to forget it because I think it's a good rule.

Karen starts off the discussion by exhorting children not to tattle.
She knows that as soon as she broaches the subject, children will
say things like, "I saw C playing!" "I saw R, and he wasn't cleaning
up!" "I cleaned up!" "I did!" She wants to go straight to the issue of
how to solve this problem and avoid all the blaming and tattling.
She has to struggle, but she manages to keep the focus of the discussion on solving the problem. She is particularly skillful at drawing J's idea out of him. He is fairly vague at first, but she questions
and elaborates on what he suggests. She finally makes sense of his
suggestion and sorts out the options so that they have two clear
solutions to vote on. We think it is significant that, given the choice
between a punishment solution and a solution involving trying
something new, the children overwhelmingly choose the experimental solution.

   It turns out that the idea of having a clean-up circle was brilliant.
At clean-up time, the children stopped what they were doing and
came to circle. At first, the teacher asked children individually which
area of the classroom they wanted to clean, and the children went to
that area and cleaned it. After a few weeks, they decided that the Special Helper would take over responsibility for running clean-up circle
and making sure the room was cleaned properly. This made clean-up
even less heteronomous for teachers since the Special Helper called
on teachers, too, and teachers stated which area they wanted to
clean. This was also a good opportunity for children to decenter to
discover how it feels to try to lead a circle and have children not listen. This experience made them more sensitive to the teacher at
other group times.

   The next innovation was to make necklaces with the names of the
areas on them (pretend center, block center, art table, etc.). When
children called for a particular area, they wore that necklace. The

Special Helper took seriously the job of making sure the room was clean. If the Special Helper saw someone walking around or playing during clean-up, he or she would look at the necklace and say, "I see you are supposed to be cleaning up the blocks. They aren't picked up yet. You need to go back and finish."

Two things happened as a result of doing clean-up this way that we found very interesting. One was that children thought it was good to be called first to clean-up and argued over fair ways to decide the order of calling people. They never did figure out that if you are called near the last, you end up cleaning less. The other thing was that children competed for the opportunity to clean the bathroom. They loved this responsibility with its special pail and squirt bottle.

The end of this story is that clean-up time was never again the problem that it had been at the beginning of the year. Minor problems still occurred occasionally, but most of the time clean-up went smoothly. Even better, clean-up was freed from adult coercion. Children took responsibility for cleaning their classroom, both individually and as a group.

SUMMARY

Constructivist teachers use clean-up time to promote the development of children's feelings of moral necessity and responsibility. Care for the classroom is sociomoral when it is motivated by attitudes of consideration and fairness toward everyone in the community. By encouraging children to take such responsibility, teachers reduce their authority and turn the moral authority over to children, thereby promoting the development of children's self-regulation. Problems with clean-up inevitably provide opportunities for teachers to lead discussions that help children reflect on the practical and moral reasons for clean-up. Three problems frequently arise in clean-up: Unwilling children feel coerced, children often feel reluctant to end activities, and, in the course of putting materials away, they may begin new activities. The solutions of four teachers to these problems are presented.

13

Lunch Time

Lunch time in a constructivist classroom is not merely a time to meet children's nutritional needs. It is at least equally important as a time for shared experiences for children as it is for adults. We adults share meals with special friends and enjoy these times in which we acknowledge friends and feel acknowledged and understood in unique ways. So it is with children.

In most schools, especially elementary and secondary schools, lunch time is considered necessary but not important to the institution's educational mission. The mind-boggling logistics of feeding children in a large school keep educators focused on lunch time management rather than its educational potential. Administrators try to promote school spirit with athletics, not realizing that school spirit (or its lack) is located in children's interpersonal relationships. Putting the emphasis on accomplishing feeding in minimal time and with minimal noise operates against the possibility that lunch time can contribute in a positive way to the sociomoral atmosphere of the school and to children's sociomoral development. Perhaps lunch time in large schools cannot be organized differently. Yet perhaps creative educators can figure out how to avoid the destructive effects of lunch time in which children are policed and punished for engaging in shared experiences with classmates. Perhaps architects must design buildings differently. Perhaps school size in itself constrains the possibilities for achieving a positive sociomoral atmosphere.

In preschools and day care centers, lunch time usually occurs in the classroom and therefore offers an excellent opportunity to promote children's peer relationships and the sociomoral atmosphere. Trying to be unobtrusive, we videotaped some of children's lunch

time conversations in the HDLS. These observations led to our for-
mulation of the following eight guidelines for promoting the constructivist sociomoral atmosphere during lunch time. We present
these guidelines, illustrated with examples from our observations,
following a brief explanation of our objectives for lunch time.

OBJECTIVES

Lunch time is an excellent opportunity for children to engage in
relaxed shared experiences with their friends. We discuss in chapter
3 how shared meaning is basic to human survival and how the capacity for intimacy (or connection with others) in relationships is a developmental achievement. (See also the discussion in chapter 2, on Selman's conceptualization of the development of interpersonal
understanding.) Childhood peer relationships are therefore of central
importance for eventual advanced development of the capacity for
relationships with others. Our objectives for lunch time, therefore,
are that children will eat a nutritious lunch while enjoying the intimacy of shared experiences with peers as well as with the teacher.

GUIDELINES FOR LUNCH TIME

1. Establish routines for lunch time.

Predictable routines that children know will occur every day help children to be self-regulating. They relieve children of the stress and anxiety of wondering what will happen next. The most important routine
to establish is a set time for lunch. Lunch time should occur at the
same time every day. Place is not quite so important. At the HDLS,
teachers like to keep open the possibility of taking lunches outside for
impromptu picnics on beautiful days, after first consulting children
and if necessary, voting on whether children want to eat outside.

One routine procedure that children at the Lab School know to
expect before lunch is handwashing. Children eat lunch after a period
of outside play. When they come inside, the teacher greets them at
the door with a bottle of liquid soap, squirting soap in each child's
hand. The children go straight to the bathroom to wash their hands.
Children respond cooperatively to this familiar routine, so teachers
do not have to go around the classroom to remind children to wash
their hands. As we mention in chapter 4, children do not always

understand why adults tell them to wash their hands, and this rule is best handled as a familiar ritual.

Other routines can include how drinks (and food, if the school provides lunch) are distributed, whether or not music is played during lunch, how children are notified that lunch time is over (see guideline number 5), and the handling of clean-up (see guideline number 7).

2. Allow children to sit where and with whom they wish.

Lunch is a highly social, relaxed time of day. Just like adults, children enjoy eating with their friends. In constructivist classrooms, children choose with whom they will lunch. In the HDLS, children do not have assigned seats, and although children's partners tend to be fairly stable, some shifting occurs. Aware of their freedom to choose, children are overheard saying, "Will you eat with me?" and "I'll sit with you, too." Sometimes, children reserve seats for friends, prompting discussions about the fairness of saving seats. This can be a good topic for a moral discussion (see chapter 9).

Should the teacher sit with children and participate in lunch time conversations? We think there is no one right answer. Conversations are slightly different when the teacher participates and when children are left on their own. However, both can contribute in positive ways to the sociomoral atmosphere. We describe lunch time conversations both with and without adults present, under guideline number 6.

3. Provide assistance where necessary.

While our overall goal for children is self-regulation, we recognize that sometimes children are going to need assistance with containers, lunchboxes, and drinks. Especially with very young children, this will take up a large part of the teacher's time during lunch. We suggest that the teacher try to limit help to only those things that the child cannot do alone. Lab School teachers tell us, for example, that they do not peel children's bananas for them (although they will start them for very young children).

4. Remind children of good health, hygiene, and nutrition habits.

As stated above, Lab School teachers have solved the problem of handwashing before lunch by greeting children at the door with a bottle of liquid soap. Other issues of health and hygiene revolve around food sharing (we have seen children take food out of their mouths and give it to other children) and eating food that has been dropped on the floor. Teachers must stay on guard during lunch time, watching for incidents that might compromise children's health and intervening when necessary. A great deal of instruction in health occurs during lunch time.

Teachers should encourage children to eat an adequate lunch, but should not force children to eat. Young children's appetites are highly variable. Sometimes children are simply not hungry, and to force them to eat would be both coercive and (probably) ineffective. Likewise, teachers should respect children's food preferences. If the school provides lunch for children, it is inevitable that there will be days that children do not like what has been served. One way to deal with this problem is to keep peanut butter, jelly, and bread in the classroom, so that any child who does not like what has been served can make himself or herself a sandwich. In this way, food struggles are diffused, and children's nutritional needs are met.

If children bring their lunches from home, it often happens that children do not like what their parents pack for them. Packing a lunch can be tedious, and busy parents can easily get into lunch ruts. If a child complains, for example, that he or she is tired of peanut butter and jelly, the teacher can offer to help the child write a note home, asking for something different. Perhaps also the school can put together a list of tried-and-true lunch box suggestions that are nutritious, appealing to children, and easy to fix.

Carol Olson, the Experimenters teacher at the Lab School, upon noticing one child having difficulty eating all of her yogurt, suggests, "You know, I noticed when you bring yogurt in the big cups that you don't eat very much. Do you think that maybe we need to write a note to Mommy and Daddy about the yogurt, so maybe they will send a smaller cup?"

5. Allow adequate time for lunch, and help children anticipate the end of lunch time.

Lunch time can be such an enjoyable time of the day that some children forget to eat. The teacher should give reminders to children periodically, letting them know how much time they have left. At the Lab School, teachers give a 10 minute warning, a 5 minute warning, and when lunch time is almost over, call out, "Last bites!"

6. Encourage children's interactions.

As we state above, social interaction at lunch time is at least as important as eating. Children in the HDLS bring lunches from home and are often curious to see what others have and eager to show something special in their lunch. We hear children saying, "Guess what's in here," "Do you have drinks today?" "Look what I got," "I got some, too." "Don't you love pizza?" "You have the same juice carton!" A child's discovery that another has something just like his or hers establishes a mutual bond.

M: I have grapes, too, A! We have the same!
A: Yeah (smiles at M).

Consider also the following conversation.

J: I got two sandwiches.
L: Look, I got strawberries.
J: I know, but I got two sandwiches.
C: And I got a sandwich.
L: I don't know how to open this. (She leaves the table.)
E: Sweet pickles! Yummy! Sweet pickles, yummy!
J: Mom-eee (as she strains to open thermos)!
(The teacher, passing by, opens it for her.)
J: (Circles the table) I'm gonna open L's for her. (She tries, cannot, and returns to her place.)
L: (Returns to her place)
E: Do you know what, L? J tried to open it for you.
J: I tried to open it for you, but I couldn't.

Thus begins a companionable lunch time for four kindergarten children in the Inventors classroom. Later, they share food.

J: You want some of these granolas? Do you want any?
(All three children raise hands.)
J: 1, 2, 3 (counting the hands). I think I have 3 in here. I have 5, I mean 6, I mean 7. You guys can have seconds.
Children: Yeaaah!
J: Who wants it now?
(All three chorus Me! Me! Me!)
J: Okay (distributes two to each child). That's all. That's all you get. I'm gonna choose just one more person. Eenie, meenie, miney, moe. Catch a tiger by the toe. If he hollers, let him go. Eenie, meenie, miney, moe. My mother told me to pick the very best one, and it is you. (J waves her hand from side to side without pointing systematically; ends by pointing to L.) Put it in your milk (teasingly threatens to drop the granola bit in L's milk, then gives granola to L).

Lunch is a time for sharing secrets and dreams, and pledging friendship. We could not hear the whispered secrets, but we heard one Inventor confide, "When I get big, I'm going to live in a beautiful, big, *giant* house." At another table, K says, "I have some cookie cutters. My mommy has some and then we're gonna make cookies." As to friendship, consider the following conversation.

S: (Points to A) You're my best friend.
L: I have three best friends.
S: I have two best friends (points to A and E).
N: Are you my friend?
S: You're a friend (points to N) and you're a friend (points to L), but they're best friends (points to N and E).
N: (Points to E, S, and L) You are my friends.
E: You're my best friend, and you're my best friend.
N: You know what? You (S) are my friend, and L's my friend.
A: N, do you know what? I pointed to you because you're my best friend because I love you.
S: We're just going to be friends.

We have also found in our research that lunch time is prime time for child humor. Child humor is qualitatively different from that of most adults. One game children at the Lab School have been heard to play involves thinking of outrageous things to put in sandwiches ("Have you ever had a toenail sandwich?").

In the Inventors class, a group of children engage in nonsensical word play that they regard as very clever and funny.

L: It looks yummy, doesn't it?
T: And my tummy.
L: And my bummy.
T: Yummy in my tummy.
C: Mummy.
E: Yummy for my tummy.
T: Or my tummy or my cummy or my fummy or my lummy.
E: Lummy? (Laughs)
T: Lummy.
L: Lummy.
C: Lummy.
E: Lummy, cummy, fummy, tummy.

Another group of four children talk for awhile about how to spell words, and this leads into similar nonsense play with words.

A: How do you spell dog?
N: Dee-Oh-Gee.
S: Dod.
A: Ded.
A: Dod is a (unintelligible).
N: Dart!
(All laugh, and from this point on, children shout with shared laughter at each new contribution.)
E: Fart!
(All laugh, and N covers her mouth in shock.)
S: Cart!
A: Eat and don't play!
N: Sandwich!
A: Eat and don't play!
N: Bowl!
A: Go!
N: Trashcan!
A: Bathcan!
S: Bat!
N: Beeper bag.
S: Lunchbox!
N: How about sandwich bag? How about lunch kit head?
A: Baloney pig.
N: She said, "Baloney pig!"
A: Hot dog pig!
N: How about stinky pig?
S: My turn! How about ugly pig?
L: How about dog pig?
A: What about dog fish? There's really dog fishes.
N: How about apple pig?
S: Let me do it. My turn.
N: Do a pig, okay?
S: Okay, no, no, I'm gonna do a (unintelligible).
N: I want to do a pig, okay, sandwich bag pig!

While we find it difficult to comprehend what is so hilarious about all this, what is important is that the children are finding each other the source of such pleasure.

The above conversations take place among children. However, the teacher can also sit with children and engage in friendly conversation. Stephanie Clark (T) sits with six Investigators (4-year-olds) while they eat.

J: I got an apple (shows everyone his apple). This my mama's.
T: That's your mama's apple?
J: (Nods)
T: (Teasing) Why is it in your lunchkit?
J: She put it in here.
T: Do you think she's giving it to you, or does it still belong to her?
J: She (unintelligible) some apples.
T: Oh, she bought you an apple, too?
J: (Nods)
A: This is my mommy's sandwich.
T: (Mock shocked expression) That's your *mommy's* sandwich? (Teasing) What's it doing in your lunchkit, if it's your mommy's?
A: I put it in there.
T: You put it in there?
L: This is my mom's pizza.
T: That's your mother's pizza? Well, why did your mother give you her pizza?
L: 'Cause she wanted to.
T: (Teasing) Well, what's your mommy going to eat for lunch?
L: Nothing.
A: I'm tall.
T: How tall are you, A?
A: I'm 2 pounds.
T: You're 2 pounds tall?
H: I'm 4.
M: Look how tall I am, Stephanie (stands up).
T: You're very tall. M, we sure missed you for 2 days. Where did you go?

Stephanie thus steers the conversation to something that a child can share with the entire group. The danger of sitting with children at lunch is that children will talk to the teacher instead of to each other.

Later, children compare sandwiches. H holds his jelly sandwich for all to see. Jelly is dripping out the sides.

M, A, and J: Eewwww (scrunched-up faces)!
T: Looks like it has a lot of jelly coming out of it. Does it have peanut butter in there, too, H?
H: No.
L: (Unintelligible) made out of blood, right?
M: That's made out of blood.

T: You think there's blood in there?
M: Yeah.
J: No.
H: No.
T: You know what, guys? H has jelly in there. Do you think that looks like blood?
All: Yeah! (Laugh)

7. Involve children in clean-up.

We discuss in chapter 12 the rationale for giving children responsibility for keeping their classroom clean. Lunch time is an especially good time to practice this, in part because messes inevitably occur during lunch. Lab School teachers remain calm and matter-of-fact when children spill food and drinks. When one Investigator announces to Stephanie Clark, "It spilled," Stephanie answers, "What do you need to get, sweetie? You can get a paper towel. Can you get one for the rug, too?"

When lunch time is over, children pack up their lunch boxes, throw away their trash, and wipe off the tables. One way to motivate children to wipe off tables is to provide them with spray bottles of water and large sponges. The children enjoy spraying water on the tables and wiping them off.

8. Provide transition to naptime or to the next activity.

We advocate allowing children to leave the tables when they finish eating, rather than requiring that children remain until everyone is finished. This means that there needs to be something available for children to do while they wait for lunch time to be over. The ideal situation is for children to be so interested in the lunch time conversation that they remain at their tables, but this does not always happen. Children who finish eating early can be invited to the book center to look at books until lunch time is over, or they can be invited to help set up for nap time (if nap time follows lunch time). In the Investigators class at the Lab School, when children finish eating, the routine is for them to go to the bathroom, get their nap time blanket (or stuffed animal, or whatever they sleep with) and then find their mats and lie down. The teachers find that going straight from lunch time to nap time works very well, in part perhaps because it eliminates one extra transition. That is, if children get involved in doing something after lunch, they will be reluctant to leave it and will resist nap time (see chapter 14 for more on nap time).

SUMMARY

In a constructivist classroom lunch time is more than just a time to meet children's physiological needs. It is a situation rich in potential for the shared experiences that are so central to children's development of interpersonal understanding. Child humor is particularly prevalent during lunch. Teachers can enhance the educational value of lunch time by establishing routines; allowing children to sit where and with whom they wish; providing assistance; reminding children of good health, hygiene, and nutritional habits; allowing adequate time for lunch; helping children anticipate the end of lunch time; encouraging children's interactions; involving children in clean-up; and providing transition to nap time.

Nap Time/Rest Time

Anyone who teaches preschool or kindergarten children must deal with nap time. Even first and second graders may profit from a rest period. Many constructivist teachers tell us that this is the time of the day in which they feel the most coercive. Telling children who insist they are not sleepy that they must rest or take a nap is very difficult to do without sounding heteronomous. In this chapter we address common problems encountered during nap time and discuss guidelines for the constructivist teacher to keep in mind, making some suggestions about how nap time can be made less stressful for both adults and children.

PROBLEMS OF NAP TIME

The primary problem with nap time is that most children do not enter into it willingly, especially if the teacher has succeeded in creating an environment in which children enjoy stimulating activities pursued out of their own interests. It is not surprising that children are reluctant to leave these activities and take a nap in the middle of the day. Young children often find transitions difficult. Nap time is a particularly difficult transition because, from the child's perspective, he or she is going from doing something fun to doing nothing at all. The teacher can smooth other classroom transitions by emphasizing the appeal of the next activity, but there is no way to convince a child that he or she is going to enjoy a nap.

This means that the teacher is in the position of insisting that he or she knows what the child needs better that the child does. This attitude feels very coercive and runs contrary to constructivist teachers' accustomed ways of thinking about how to promote self-regulation in children. However, the fact remains that young children need to take naps. Not only are naps a physiological necessity for most young children, but they are required by day care licensing laws. The challenge for the teacher is to approach nap time in a way that respects children's autonomy while at the same time meeting their needs for rest.

The problem of children not wanting to sleep is complicated by the fact that sometimes a child really will not need sleep. This is more common with older children such as kindergartners with spring or summer birthdays. We have also seen it at HDLS with children whose families allow them to go to bed very late and sleep late. These children are brought to school well past the start of the school day. To force children who have only been awake for 2 or 3 hours to take a nap would be not only coercive and unnecessary but also nearly impossible. While the best solution, from the teacher's perspective, might be for the family to change its schedule to adapt to the needs of the school, this is often not an option. In these cases, we suggest that the teacher be open to the possibility that some children do not need naps and make other plans for them, such as arranging a place (away from the nappers) where they can engage in quiet activities.

GUIDELINES FOR A LESS STRESSFUL NAP TIME

To make life easier during nap time, we have eight suggestions.

1. Establish a quiet, peaceful environment.

The atmosphere of the classroom should be one of quiet and calm during nap time. (It helps if the entire school can be quiet during nap time, but that is not always possible.) Try to minimize the chance for interruptions, especially during the time when children are just beginning to fall asleep. A "Do not disturb" sign on the door may be in order during nap time.

The room should be as dark as possible while still allowing the teacher to be able to see well enough to intervene in problem situations. The teacher should move about the classroom slowly and avoid abrupt movements. Communication should be in low whispers, spoken close to the child, not from across the room. Soft music can be helpful, but it must be very peaceful, calm music played softly (no hard rock music or Wagner operas, please). Music that the children are accustomed to singing along with is not a good idea, for obvious reasons.

2. Make the napping environment as comfortable as possible.

The children need to be able to lie down comfortably. It is not enough for children to place their heads on tables and nap in a seated position. This is uncomfortable and not conducive to resting. While mats are best, and should be high on the list of budget priorities (indeed, mats are often required by day care licensing laws), not all schools can afford mats for nap time. In these cases, blankets on the floor will work. Children can be asked to bring a blanket or large towel from home.

3. Establish specific nap time rituals.

Teachers at HDLS tell us that nap time can be especially difficult in the first one or two months of the year. The toddlers' teacher, Marti Wilson, describes her Explorers class as a "wailing room" for the first month. As rituals are established and individual children's needs discovered, nap time will get better. Be patient.

Nap time rituals at school are just as important as bedtime rituals at home, and should be established at the beginning of the year (with, of course, the possibility for adapting rituals always left open). The regular routine of rituals makes it possible for young children to organize time. Rituals serve as self-regulating cues to children that, "Now is the time to ____ (eat, go to the bathroom, clean-up, lie down, relax, etc.)." Music, stories, and backrubs can all be part of the nap time ritual. You, your staff, and your children may think of other ritual elements. Keep in mind that the role of the ritual is to facilitate the transition to the quiet mode of nap time.

If nap time follows the noisy exuberance of lunch time, sometimes a story or poem can move children into a less active mode. We have noticed that groups of young children often have their quietest times when the teacher reads. A story may give the children a focus that will help them be quiet and still. However, the teacher must exercise caution in choosing the story. Appropriate nap time stories should not be exciting or funny (nothing disrupts nap time more than a case of the giggles); they should be relaxing. They should be stories for which the pictures are not necessary because the goal is for children to lie down and close their eyes in preparation for sleep. Suggestions might include well-loved children's books such as *Mooncake* (Asch, 1983) or poetry books such as *Half a Moon and One Whole Star* (Dragonwagon, 1990). We suggest resisting the temptation to show a video. Since children want to watch videos (as opposed to simply listening to a story), they will move around, trying to find a good place to be able to see, and they will not close their eyes. Also, keep in mind that reading a story (or showing a video) before nap time means that there will be two transitions—from whatever came before nap time to story time, and from story time to the actual nap time—instead of only one. If the class does not do transitions well, a story may do more harm than good in terms of helping children begin to rest.

4. Emphasize that children need rest in order to be healthy and happy Children.

It is appropriate for the teacher to state that children need rest, and that it is his or her job as the teacher to make sure that children's needs are met. The teacher can explain in age-appropriate language children's need for rest ("Children's bodies need rest so that they can grow strong"), the effects of lack of rest ("When children don't rest during nap time, they are tired and unhappy in the afternoon, and they fall asleep during activities"), and the rules that teachers must follow concerning nap time ("There is a rule at our school that children must rest, and I would not be doing my job if we did not have rest time").

5. Empathize with children's struggles in falling asleep.

The teacher should affirm children's feelings by letting them know that he or she understands how difficult it is to stop playing and rest. The teacher can then reassure children that there will be fun things to do after nap time.

6. Respect children's physiological and emotional needs.

Children vary widely in the ways in which they fall asleep. For example, some children need to fidget for 5 to 10 minutes before they fall asleep. Telling these children to be still does not help them to fall asleep. For some, the physical contact of a gentle backrub helps them relax and fall asleep, while for other children this is too stimulating.

A teacher at HDLS told us about a 4-year-old who always needed to go to the bathroom 10 minutes after he lay down for nap, regardless of when he last used the bathroom. The regular staff all knew about this particular child and his bathroom needs, but new staff always had to be warned so that they would not cause him great stress and anxiety by refusing to allow him to get up.

Some children need something familiar to hold when falling asleep, to comfort them. As far as this is possible, taking into consideration issues of hygiene and security, teachers should try to accommodate these needs by allowing children, for example, to bring an item from home specifically for nap time. A soft toy such as a stuffed animal, rag doll, or blanket is best. However, items from home can become distractions if used as toys rather than as comforts. Children can be reminded that the item is for sleeping with, not for playing. Teachers can invoke logical consequences (see chapter 10), telling children, for example, that, "Your rabbit is keeping friends awake. If rabbit can't be still, maybe he (she) should nap in your cubbie." Very young children can be coaxed by saying, "Rabbit needs rest, too."

Placement of children's mats or cots can be a problem. Some children relax best when near a friend, while other children are too distracted to fall asleep when near anyone else. One child at HDLS had to be separated from the other children by a barrier, such as a low bookshelf, and even then she tried to find a way to talk to other children. However, when the teacher found a way to remove her from any possibility of contact with another child, she always fell asleep almost immediately.

The teacher should talk to individual parents about their children's needs and idiosyncrasies concerning sleep. If children are accustomed to falling asleep with a parent lying beside them, for example, they will find it difficult to fall asleep alone at school. Teachers should speak with these parents about the goal for their child to become able to fall asleep alone and should cooperate with parents to achieve this goal. However, in the short-term, it may be necessary to have an adult lie down beside the child until he or she is asleep, at least for the first few weeks.

These individual differences highlight the importance of having consistent staff during nap time. Whenever possible, the same person should be responsible for nap time every day. This person will provide predictability in routines and will be familiar with each child's particular idiosyncrasies. Teachers and day care directors should try to avoid scheduling new staff during nap time unless absolutely necessary and, when necessary, should take care in instructing new nap time staff about individual children's needs.

7. Take the attitude that you are there to help the child rest.

Until the children are all resting quietly, the teacher's job is to help the children relax. Therefore the teacher should be engaged with children, assisting each child in whatever way necessary. This is not the time for the teacher to eat his or her lunch, catch up on paperwork, redo a bulletin board, or read, for example. One way to do this is to move around the classroom, rubbing children's backs or simply lying next to children, placing a hand on their shoulders and patting them gently.

It is very important to avoid conveying the message that the teacher is there to force the child to rest. A coercive attitude turns the teacher's role from facilitator to police officer. Interactions with children during nap time should reflect the desire on the teacher's part to do whatever it takes to help the child rest. Teachers can ask children, "Would it help if you put your head on the other side of the mat?" "Would it help if I rubbed your back?" "Would it help if we moved your mat to another spot in the class?" "What can I do to help you fall asleep? What do you think would help?" or even, "What can you do that will help you be able to rest?" These are all ways that teachers can help children rest while encouraging them to be self-regulating.

Teachers should neither bribe nor threaten children during nap time. We have seen an otherwise very good constructivist teacher, who would never think to use threats and bribes in other situations, say she will rub the backs of children who are being quiet. This reflects lack of recognition of the fact that it is usually the children who cannot be quiet who need backrubs the most. Offering rewards tells children that they should engage in certain behaviors in order to please the teacher. This message runs counter to the goal of self-regulation and contributes to an atmosphere of coercion rather than one of mutual respect.

8. Use problems at nap time as opportunities to help children take the perspective of others.

When asking children to be quiet, teachers should remind children that noise and talking will disturb the other children. Quiet is necessary for nap time, not because the teacher says so, but because other children are trying to rest, and noise will prevent them from sleeping. Noise at nap time can provide the topic for discussion at grouptime and children can be invited to make rules that they feel will help make nap time better (see chapter 7).

If a child is seriously disruptive during nap time, the logical consequence is that the child must leave the room (see chapter 10). The teacher might make arrangements with another teacher in the school to exchange problem nappers. When children are taken to another place, away from their friends, they usually go right to sleep. Again, this must not be presented to the child in the form of a punishment. The attitude should be one of pointing out to the child that his or her behavior is keeping other children from sleeping, and that the teacher is taking the child to another place so that everyone will be able to rest. Sometimes a child is relieved to be in a situation that makes it easier to rest and prefers to continue the special arrangement. If the child prefers to rest with his or her own class, the teacher can assure the problem napper that he or she will be allowed to try to nap with the class the next day. The child can be encouraged to change his or her behavior in order to be allowed to stay with the class.

In the HDLS, the younger classes begin their nap while the Inventors' kindergarten class plays outside. When the noisy return of the kindergartners to their classroom disturbed the younger classes the younger children wrote notes to the Inventors, asking them to be quiet on their return to their classroom. This inspired the Inventors to take the perspective of the younger children and regulate their actions out of consideration for others.

SUMMARY

Nap time is particularly difficult for many children who do not willingly let go of interesting activities in order to sleep. Nap time is one of the rare situations in which the constructivist teacher is faced with having to make children do what they do not want to do. The challenge is to do this in a way that conveys caring and respect to children. Guidelines for a less stressful nap time lead the constructivist teacher to establish a quiet, comfortable environment, establish routines, emphasize the reason for rest, empathize with children's struggles in falling asleep, respect children's physiological and emotional needs, take an attitude of helpfulness, and use problems at nap time as opportunities to help children take the perspective of others.

15

Academics

One misconception about constructivist education is that, because it includes play, it does not include academics. We want to correct this misconception. The perceptive reader may have already noticed references and anecdotes involving academics in many earlier chapters. Constructivist educators are serious-minded about children's literacy, number and arithmetic, science, social studies, and fine arts. However, in this chapter, our goal is not to provide an exhaustive account of the constructivist approach to academics. Our limited aim is to illustrate how academics influence and are influenced by the sociomoral atmosphere.

We have noticed that a number of teachers who have seen the list of chapters in this book ask first for this chapter on academics. This reflects teachers' overwhelming concern for this part of their responsibility as well as their puzzlement over how to help children learn academics in a constructivist classroom. This chapter will not satisfy all curiosities on this matter. However, we hope to help the reader conceptualize the teaching of academics in ways that do not impede intellectual and sociomoral development. Fearing that readers will begin with this chapter, we caution that it is not possible to understand the constructivist approach to academics without first understanding the constructivist sociomoral atmosphere, described in earlier chapters.

For many people, the principal goal in early education is literacy. The "common-sense" view is that children must learn to read and write before they can learn anything else in school. There are several problems with this view. The first problem is that a single-minded focus on literacy can lead to a heteronomous approach that contradicts the overarching goal of development. The teacher whose main goal is to teach children to read and write falls easily into a didactic teaching mode in which the teacher has knowledge that children lack. It is difficult to respect children when they are viewed as knowing nothing.

The problem for the constructivist teacher in approaching any academic content is to distinguish what must be constructed from what must be instructed. Certainly written language, for example, is essentially arbitrary conventional knowledge. However, it has physical aspects (the form of writing) and logico-mathematical aspects (regularities of correspondences, meaning relationships).

In the following, we discuss three points. First, the teaching of academics always occurs in the context of a sociomoral atmosphere. Second, the conditions for best promoting academics are the same as those for best promoting sociomoral development. Third, academics in a constructivist classroom are integrated with children's purposes and taught in ways consistent with children's cognitive and sociomoral development.

THE SOCIOMORAL CONTEXT FOR TEACHING ACADEMICS

In chapter 1 we describe three different sociomoral atmospheres as the contexts for teaching number and arithmetic. In the Boot Camp classroom, kindergarten children experience number and arithmetic in terms of rote drill and practice led by an authoritarian Drill-Sergeant teacher who is quick to criticize and punish for inattention and incorrect answers. The goal of academics is approached directly, and children are expected to want to think about academics for academics' sake, that is, isolated from a meaningful context. In the Factory classroom, children experience number and arithmetic in didactic lessons led by a controlling and gently critical Manager teacher who carefully rehearses children on the answers to be written on worksheets. Here, the goal of academics is also approached directly but is slightly sugarcoated with, for example, the idea of counting turtles (children are somehow expected to be motivated to count turtles on worksheets). In contrast, in the constructivist Community classroom, the goal of academics is approached indirectly, and children are expected to want to think about academics in the context of personal and group purposes. Children in this classroom, for example, experience number as the means to solve an interpersonal problem with the guidance of the Mentor teacher.

These vignettes illustrate our view that the teaching of academics always occurs in a sociomoral atmosphere that may be favorable or unfavorable for children's general development. We see in these classrooms a reciprocal relationship between the sociomoral atmosphere and the teaching of academics. With *academics* as the priority and with learning considered a matter of direct transmission, teachers easily fall into a heteronomous relation to children. With *development* as the priority and with learning considered a matter of the child's construction, a heteronomous relation is not possible. As mentioned in chapter 1, our research indicates that the Boot Camp and Factory atmospheres are associated with less advanced and the Community atmosphere with more advanced sociomoral development (DeVries, Haney, & Zan, 1991; DeVries, Reese-Learned, & Morgan, 1991a). We therefore maintain that the ethical position in planning and implementing the teaching of academics is to "Do no harm." When the teaching of academics results in harm to children's sociomoral development, it cannot be defended as ethical. This is particularly the case when, as our research suggests, the didactic academic emphasis in Boot Camp and Factory classrooms does not give children in these classrooms any long-term advantage over children in the Community classroom in terms of achievement scores (DeVries, Reese-Learned, & Morgan, 1991a).

THE CONDITIONS FOR PROMOTING ACADEMICS

Our effort to define constructivist conditions for teaching academics is prompted not just by the aim to "do no harm," but by the more positive aim of optimal construction of knowledge, including academics. We argue that academics are best learned in the context of the kind of constructivist sociomoral atmosphere described in this book. In our view, the conditions that promote social and moral development are the same conditions that promote intellectual development. In other chapters we discuss the development of children's *reasoning* about social and moral issues. Thus, a significant component in sociomoral development is intellectual. Conversely, a significant component in intellectual development is sociomoral. To summarize, we remind the reader of Piaget's view that adults' heteronomous regulation of children can result in mindless conformity in both moral and intellectual aspects of the child's life. Emphasis on obedience fosters self-doubt and qualities needed for submission. Educational experience preoccupied with giving back correct information destroys curiosity and leads to intellectual dullness and knowledge full of egocentric misunderstanding—"school varnish." Authoritarian regulation of academic lessons reinforces moral as well as intellectual heteronomy. The intellectual heteronomy that accompanies moral heteronomy is reflected in a passive orientation to the ideas of others, an unquestioning and uncritical attitude, and low motivation to reason. Parents and teachers often want children to be submissive to adults' ideas but not to those of peers. However, if we want children to resist and not be victims of others' ideas, we have to educate children to think for themselves about all ideas, including those of adults.

Piaget's view is that adults' cooperative relations with children result in active reflection in both moral and intellectual aspects of the child's life. Emphasis on the child's self-regulation fosters self-confidence, an attitude of questioning and critical evaluation, and motivation to think about causes, implications, and explanations of physical and logical as well as social and moral phenomena. When the adult respects the child's reasoning and provides extensive opportunities for exploration and experimentation, intellectual sharpness results. Piaget (1948/1973) emphasized the moral and intellectual results of heteronomy and cooperation in the following way:

> In reality, education constitutes an indissoluble whole, and it is not possible to create independent personalities in the ethical area if the individual is also subjected to intellectual constraint to such an extent that he must restrict himself to learning by rote without discovering the truth for himself. If he is intellectually passive, he will not know how to be free ethically. Conversely, if his ethics consist exclusively in submission to adult authority, and if the only social exchanges that make up the life of the class are those that bind each student individually to a master holding all power, he will not know how to be intellectually active. (p. 107)

Thus, in the constructivist view, morality and intelligence are transformed in interconnected ways. Because it is not possible to influence one without influencing the other, we argue that life in a moral classroom will promote children's intellectual development.

Our discussion thus far focuses more on conditions necessary for general intellectual development than on conditions necessary for the specific learning of academics. For Piaget, however, these cannot be easily separated. Piaget (1964) discussed learning and development, arguing that it is development that makes learning possible. That is, intellectual development involves the dynamic transformation of structures of knowledge. Structures of knowledge can be thought of as the ways the child organizes what he or she already knows. Piaget argues that development of organizational structures occurs through assimilation of content to already existing structures. In this assimilation process, the child understands specific experience in terms of the organized knowledge he or she already has constructed. When experience contradicts the child's organization of knowledge, the child has the opportunity to reorganize the structures of knowledge. We should note that "structures" do not exist by themselves. They only exist in relation to specific content. Reasoning must always be about something specific. Therefore, for Piaget, learning and development are mutually dependent. A dialectical relation exists in which development makes learning possible, and in turn, learning promotes development. This is in contrast to the classical behaviorist view of learning as a stimulus provoking a response and creating an association. This difference between traditional and constructivist theory leads to very different classroom practices.

THE CONSTRUCTIVIST INTEGRATION OF ACADEMICS

While life in a moral classroom creates general conditions for intellectual development, it is possible to establish a cooperative atmosphere with inadequate attention to academics. The challenge for constructivist teachers is to incorporate academics into classroom life and to integrate developmental and academic objectives. In fact, we argue that the best teaching of academics is rooted in knowledge of developmental transformations in children's conceptions of academic content. In contrast to the traditional approach to academics that is centered on subject matter, the constructivist approach is child-centered. We offer four principles of teaching, with examples, that may be useful guides to teachers wishing to take a constructivist approach to academics. It goes without saying, of course, that the sociomoral atmosphere described in previous chapters is the general context for implementing the following principles.

Create Active Situations Related to Children's Purposes

A general constructivist principle is that the intellect develops through its exercise. Constructivist teaching of academics therefore aims to promote children's active reasoning about content. The constructivist teacher fosters an atmosphere of thinking. This is accomplished through activities that appeal to children's interests and to their own purposes for thinking about academic content. As emphasized in chapter 11, constructivist activities are rooted in children's purposes. This is practical in teaching academics because, as Dewey (1913/1975) pointed out, people always invest more attention and effort in what interests them. We agree with advocates of the Whole Language approach to teaching literacy that the best activities are authentic rather than contrived (Manning, Manning, & Long, 1989). For example, when a child's purpose is to play a board game, interest is spontaneous in written rules, counting and number, and writing words and numerals. When children want to cook, they are inspired to try to figure out what the recipe says. In order to make sure that his friend gets to do a water activity with his group, 4-year-old C writes K's name on the sign-up list, going to the Special Helper list six times to copy the spelling one letter at a time. K, a 5-year-old, consults the numbered list of Special Helpers by counting in order to find out how to write "12" on the calendar. Children are also inspired by interest to attend to the writing in stories and song and finger play charts.

In chapter 11 we discuss the essential role of action for the construction of knowledge and intelligence, presenting the argument that young children are more mentally active when they are physically active in trying to figure out how to do something. Active purposes involving literacy and number are described above. Physical-knowledge activities involving the movement of objects (elementary physics) and changes in objects (elementary chemistry) inspire children to construct knowledge about the physical world. For example, using a ball on a string (as a pendulum bob) to knock down a target inspires children to construct specific spatial and causal knowledge about the reactions of a pendulum. Experimenting with many objects in water inspires construction of specific knowledge about the relations among properties of objects, their propensities to sink or float, and eventually, understanding specific gravity. Experimenting with using different amounts of flour, water, and oil to make play-dough inspires children to construct specific knowledge about the influence of each substance on the play-dough's consistency. Knowledge about changes in objects is elaborated in cooking activities as children have the opportunity to experiment, for example, with different amounts of baking powder or salt in cookies. Systematic experiments with different amounts of water given to plants gives children opportunities for constructing feelings of necessity and understanding about causal relationships involved in changes in these objects. Experimenting with shadows inspires children to construct specific knowledge about the nature of light and causal and spatial relations among light source, object, and shadow. In each of these activities, children learn specific academic knowledge while also increasing their general intellectual capacity for reasoning in terms of logico-mathematical relations.

Foster Social Interaction Centered on Academics

The study of academics in a constructivist classroom is a very social affair. The general atmosphere of vitality and energy invested in the experience of life together suffuses academics as well as all other aspects of the program. Many of the examples given above of academics in children's purposes are also social in nature. In previous chapters, we give examples of constructivist teachers integrating academics into rule making and decision making, voting, conflicts, and social and moral discussion, activity time, and clean-up. Academics are often involved in children's needs to communicate and desires to collaborate. Social or moral motivation can prompt revisions of academic knowledge. We discuss these ideas below.

Appeal to Children's Needs to Communicate and Desires to Collaborate

Social life is replete with communication needs. Oral language flourishes in the interactive life of the constructivist classroom. For example, in pretend play, children must use language to enact ideas and negotiate the specifics of play. In group games, children must use language to discuss rules and negotiate when rule violations are recognized. These kinds of communicative and collaborative interactions are multiplied many times over during the day.

The constructivist environment continually supports writing and reading as necessary for children's purposes. For example, when a 4-year-old Investigator writes a note to his teacher, Kathy Saxton, she emphasizes to the group, "He used his writing to tell me something." When children want to leave a block construction up overnight, they dictate a note to leave for the custodian asking that she clean around the structure.

Children in our constructivist classrooms believe writing to be a powerful tool in interpersonal negotiations. In chapter 6, we describe S's consultation with the group on how to solve her problem of not getting to school in time to be Special Helper. The first suggestion by a child is to write a note to S's mother. In the same classroom, E dictates a note to give his mother with suggestions for his lunch because he does not like what she has been preparing. He also painstakingly copies a cupcake recipe to take home so that he can enjoy the shared experience of making cupcakes with his mother.

Writing and reading numerals, counting, and calculating are necessary in a variety of activities. Needing a menu for their pretend restaurant, Inventors write items and prices: "Pepsi 4, 1 pizza 6, 2 pies 2." Inventors keep score in Uno, and Investigators keep score in bowling. When S returns from a vacation trip, she brings postcards and has to count to see if she has enough for all 18 children. Kindergarten children are motivated to write and memorize phone numbers in order to know how to call each other. In the Piggy Bank card game, children figure out how to collect sets of cards that add up to 5, and later, to 10. In this context, children are more motivated to add than in worksheet tasks, and they are learning arithmetic without having to deal with formalisms such as equations. As Kamii points out, it is dangerous to introduce formalisms before children have constructed the numerical operations. (See Kamii's [1982, 1985, 1989, 1994] books as a rich resource of practical ideas on how to facilitate children's construction of number and arithmetic prekindergarten through grade 3.)

Academic collaborations and peer support of academics often occur in constructivist classrooms. For example, J reads Thomas's name as Timmy, and K corrects him. When the kindergarten Special Helper has difficulty figuring out how to write the numerical date on the calendar, he or she asks a friend to help. In this classroom, children are heard to comment to one another, "That's a good 10," and "I like your 15."

Promote Academics in Moral Contexts

Several examples in previous chapters involve academics in moral contexts. For example, in chapter 5, Peige discovers that a physical conflict stems from one child's protest over the other's writing "2" on her score when she only knocked down one in an aiming game. In chapter 7, children reason about the optimal number of days for block constructions to remain in place. As they experience the temporal meaning of their decision to keep them up for 5 days, they revise their reasoning about what is fair. They come to realize that when one structure is left for this period, an insufficient number of blocks is left for other children. Further, the children whose structures are left up do not wish to use them for 5 days. As recounted in chapter 10, the children consider the problem of someone urinating on the floor, and the teacher provides information on the health implications.

Encourage Children's Reasoning

To encourage children's reasoning, the constructivist teacher begins with what children know, respects constructive error, and teaches in terms of the kind of knowledge involved. These strategies, discussed below, reflect respect for the child's intellectual work of excluding, ordering, categorizing, reformulating, confirming, forming hypotheses, and reorganizing their knowledge.

Begin with What Children Know

Basing activities on what children already know reflects the constructivist teacher's respect for children as constructors of their knowledge. We keep in mind the Piagetian idea that the child interacts with and transforms the object of knowledge. To appeal to children's purposes and inspire reasoning about academics, we must begin with what children already know or know how to do. For example, we can assume that children in the United States have experienced written language. The ground-breaking research of Ferreiro and Teberosky (1979/1982) has shown that before instruction children have ideas, and even hypotheses and theories, about written language, and that they continually test their ideas as they encounter print in their environment.

To find out what children know about academics, constructivist teachers can make inferences from observations of children in activities that embed academic content in children's purposes. For example, with children's names on cubbies, children have the opportunity to learn the meaning of each piece of writing, then, gradually, to notice similarities and differences among names, and construct certain regularities. Contrary to the belief that ideas about written material begin with phonics, Ferreiro and Teberosky have shown that children recognize quantitative properties of print (for example, the number of letters and the length of text) before they construct qualitative properties (names and precise forms of letters, and letter-sound correspondences). For example, Coreen Samuel, the Lab School kindergarten teacher, recounted that when some valentines were addressed with first and last names, M thought these should go to Mary Theresa because he knew her name had two separate parts.

After children learn to recognize one another's names, Coreen uses name cards to challenge children to notice details and begin to construct regularities of print. The attendance ritual provides a context in which she gives children opportunities to predict names from just the first letters. With a dramatic flourish, she creates suspense as she brings from behind her back a namecard. With only the first letter visible, she asks, "Whose name do you think this is?" At a certain point, children recognize their own first letter and call out "Mine" when they see this letter. When more than one child's name begins with the same letter, the situation is ripe for further construction of knowledge. Children are already quite sophisticated when they restrict guesses to names having the same first letter or the same first sound. Carol's name is predicted to be Colin, Chad, Coreen, Karen, and Kendal. Uncovering the second letter enables some children to know that it is Carol. Carol herself is the resource who confirms that her second letter is "a." To figure out whether a name is Sanna or Sara, many children quickly learn, with the help of Sanna and Sara, that they must see the third letter in order to know for sure. When children find it easy to predict names from first letters, Coreen challenges them by covering all but the last letters. As each name is guessed, it is placed on the floor in groups of present and absent. Children base predictions on logic as well as specific knowledge. S guesses the name Colin from the first letter, saying, "It *has* to be Colin because all the other C names are already there (on the floor)."

Respect Children's Errors

Perhaps the most distinguishing characteristic of a constructivist approach to academics is the teacher's respect for children's errors. Respecting children means accepting the meanings they construct, even when these are wrong. As we note in chapter 11, this attitude reflects respect for children as thinkers. This attitude contrasts with the direct traditional teaching of truth as straightforward facts to be regurgitated. When learning is reduced to verbalisms, these are often meaningless to children.

When young children are actively engaged in thinking their own honest thoughts, error is inevitable. In this book, we have discussed children's errors as not only an inevitable result of preoperational reasoning but as an intelligent effort to understand experience. When the child experiences a feeling of contradiction, errors can lead to construction of more adequate knowledge. Constructivist educators are convinced that only in a sociomoral atmosphere of acceptance of *all* children's efforts to reason can academics become truly understood.

In a sociomoral atmosphere that respects children's ideas, children feel more free to express their honest reasoning, and teachers therefore have more opportunity to assess children's knowledge. In constructivist classrooms, the nature of error is open for the teacher to see. For example, when in a board game children count as "1" their starting space, the teacher knows that children lack the logical capacity for the rule. At a more elementary level, teachers can observe whether children understand the cardinal meaning of counting. In our Investigator classroom, 4-year-olds count correctly as the teacher, Peige Fuller, points to the 12 namecards of children present. Not assuming their correct recitation of number names to imply understanding of cardinal value, Peige asks, "How many children do you think we have in our circle?" The Special Helper, N, begins to count the children. Peige interrupts to ask, "Would you take a guess before you count?" N says, "Five." "You think so. Okay, why don't you count and see." When N counts to 12, Peige simply comments, "How about that? Twelve cards and 12 children!" In this experience, Peige hopes that children will feel at least a dawning idea of what one-to-one correspondence means in counting.

At the beginning of the year in our kindergarten class, Coreen Samuel raises the question of how many children are in the class. She suggests numbering the Special Helper list and begins by writing a "1" by the first name. Children tell her the sequence of numbers, with some disagreement and discussion, and those who know instruct her as to how to write the double-digit numbers. Some of children's comments during the numbering process suggest they understand neither the ordinal nor the cardinal meaning of the numbers on the list. Rather, they give the numbers more personal meanings. W complains, "I don't want to be a 4. I'm 5 (meaning 5 years old)." T thinks he can choose the number he likes to be by his name. J sees the "8" by his name and says to P (who has "6" by his name), "I'm bigger than you." After completing the numbering of 22 names, Coreen asks, "So how many people do we have in our room?" Children call out, "I think 12," "11," "5," "18," "100," "59," "24," and, finally, "22." Coreen asks C (who suggested 22), "Can you tell us how you figured that out?" C points to the last number on the list, but J protests passionately, "No, that's not how you could tell because that's just the way you count the children's names." Coreen keeps the focus on the issue. "Oh, so that doesn't tell us how many people are in the room?" N argues, "Yes, it does." Realizing that the logic of both the ordinal and cardinal use of number is beyond most of the children, Coreen says, "I hear a lot of 20s. Maybe you can count and check by tapping heads."

Teach in Terms of the Kind of Knowledge

We explain in chapter 11 Piaget's distinction among three kinds of knowledge—physical knowledge, logico-mathematical knowledge, and arbitrary conventional knowledge—and how this conceptualization helps the constructivist teacher plan and teach. From the constructivist perspective, one of the problems in many traditional approaches to academics is that physical and logico-mathematical knowledge are treated as if they are arbitrary conventional knowledge that can be learned through direct instruction. In our view, such approaches fail to respect the ways in which young children learn and develop and thereby create a sociomoral atmosphere that falls short of promoting either general intellectual or specific academic development.

Consideration of the kinds of knowledge and respect for children's errors leads constructivist teachers to emphasize construction and deemphasize instruction. Especially with regard to physical knowledge and logico-mathematical knowledge, the constructivist teacher knows that he or she must not get too far ahead of children's constructive process. That is, the teacher must keep the challenges in activities at the leading edge of children's ability to reason.

Let us simply reassure the reader here that constructivist teachers do not hesitate to correct misinformation and present children with conventional information. They teach vocabulary, conventions of writing (such as the capitalization of the first letter in a proper name), conventions of books (such as its parts and types of literature), and human culture (such as who made inventions such as the telephone, what astronauts eat and how they take showers in space, and what Martin Luther King did). Constructivist teachers teach children about nature (such as characteristics and habits of animals and how recycling helps the environment). Constructivist teachers also give children certain information that is not arbitrary but can only be understood by children as arbitrary, yet is important to their daily lives (such as dental care and facts about nutritious and junk food). In addition, constructivist teachers take children to art museums and show them slides or reproductions of great art. In the Investigators class at the HDLS, children looked at reproductions of paintings and talked about the differences between abstract and realistic art, and discussed the differences among the primary colors of Picasso, the yellows and browns of Van Gogh, and the pastels of O'Keefe. At three painting stations equipped with these colors, they created their own art. A visit to an art museum was the occasion for learning about museum rules. This was followed by setting up a museum in the classroom, creating exhibits, and posting written rules and names of artwork and artists.

All of this teaching is integrated with children's interests and purposes. For example, the meaning of "inventor" is introduced in con-

junction with children's entry into the kindergarten classroom called
"the Inventors classroom." The teacher plans an Invention Convention theme in which children create their own inventions and hear
stories about famous inventors. They visit NASA, see spaceships, and
eat food made for use in space.

Allow Sufficient Time for the Constructive Process

Learning academics involves general intellectual development as
well as specific learning. Constructivist educators therefore expect
the learning of academics, especially in its beginnings, to take considerable time for the constructive process. In most cases, the construction of correct knowledge is a matter of years. Errors must be
constructed, recognized as inadequate ideas, and new ideas (that
may introduce new errors) constructed.

SUMMARY

A misconception about constructivist education is that, because it
includes play, it does not include academics. We correct this misconception by describing the constructivist integration of academics
in a program characterized by the sociomoral atmosphere described
in this book. The teaching of academics always occurs in the context
of a sociomoral atmosphere that may be favorable or unfavorable for
children's development. In our view, the constructivist sociomoral
atmosphere best promotes long-term academic development
because it emphasizes self-regulation that leads to understanding,
self-confidence, and an attitude of questioning and critical evaluation. It also promotes motivation to think about causes, implications,
and explanations of physical and logical as well as social and moral
phenomena. We therefore see morality and intelligence being transformed by the child in interconnected ways and argue that life in a
moral classroom promotes children's intellectual development. We
caution, however, that it is possible to establish a cooperative atmosphere with inadequate attention to academics. The best teaching of
academics is rooted in knowledge of developmental transformations
in children's conceptions of academic content.

 To promote children's construction of academic knowledge,
teachers create active situations related to children's purposes, foster social interaction centered on academics, encourage children's
reasoning, and allow sufficient time for the constructive process. To

encourage children's reasoning, constructivist teachers begin with what children know, respect children's errors, and teach in terms of the kind of knowledge involved.

This chapter is not an exhaustive account of the constructivist approach to academics. We simply illustrate how academics influence and are influenced by the sociomoral atmosphere.

16

The Difficult Child

Rheta DeVries
Kathryn Saxton
Betty Zan

In chapters 2 and 3, we sketched aspects of the Piagetian view of the child's gradual construction of a social world and his or her place in it. It is normal for young children not yet to have constructed a stable self-system of feelings, interests, values, and social reactions. It is normal for young children to have social difficulties stemming from an inability to take the perspectives of others and to think beyond the observable surfaces of events. With any group of children, the teacher deals with a broad, yet normal, range of self-regulating competencies. Children come to school with varied backgrounds of opportunities for constructive activity. In particular, they come with varied experiences of coercion and cooperation in relation to adults and peers. Coercive teachers and parents can create a difficult child by frustrating the child's need to be active. Sometimes a high-energy child considered difficult in a traditional coercive classroom is not viewed as difficult in a constructivist classroom where children are encouraged to be active.

All children have moments when they are difficult. However, every teacher is familiar with the special anguish and frustration of dealing with the unusually difficult child. By "difficult child," we refer to the child who regularly endangers self and/or others or who regularly disrupts the activities of others by aggressive and careless behavior. Daily confrontations, upset classmates, and frequent interruptions of planned activities are not uncommon experiences of the teacher who must cope with the difficult child. Some of these children have experienced such intense rejection and disapproval that they have constructed a self with feelings of inferiority and ill will toward others. Some children have had little in the way of positive shared experiences with others and thus have little basis for attachment to the teacher or the group. While children with severe emotional problems can profit from experience in a constructivist classroom, children in extreme circumstances may need additional help from school psychologists, guidance counselors, and family therapists.

Much of what has been written about how to manage the difficult child has its origins in a behaviorist perspective. In this chapter, we review the behaviorist approach to dealing with the difficult child before presenting the constructivist approach. Our approach to dealing with the difficult child is in most ways no different from dealing with the normal problems of normal children. Therefore, our approach to the difficult child includes the guidelines discussed in all previous chapters, and especially those discussed in chapters 2 and 3 for encouraging the development of moral autonomy. Nevertheless, because of the frustrating problems teachers often encounter in working with difficult children, this chapter will elaborate on constructivist theory (integrating constructivist theory with psychodynamic theories of maladaptive behavior) and discuss additional principles of intervention consistent with constructivist theory and philosophy.

THE BEHAVIORIST APPROACH

In this section, we discuss commonly practiced behaviorist techniques and present a constructivist critique of these practices.

Description of Behaviorist Techniques

The behaviorist approach to dealing with difficult children places the emphasis on the teacher's *management* of the child's behavior. Behaviorist techniques usually include the systematic recording of specific behavioral observations that provide the basis for evaluating the child's behavior and giving feedback. In this way, the child can be made aware of his or her progress toward some behavioral goal the teacher has set. For example, if the goal is "The child will remain seated at all times," then a star may be affixed to a chart for each hour that the child remains in his or her seat. This behavioral progress chart is then used as the basis for prescribing rewards and punishments. The child may receive a reward (such as a sticker or trinket) at the end of the day if he or she has acquired a certain number of stars. Often regular behavioral evaluations are sent home to be signed by a parent. These techniques require a significant amount of time and effort by the teacher in order simply to keep up with charting progress, writing evaluations, applying rewards and punishments, and following up to get parental signatures.

A well-known structured management approach is Assertive Discipline, developed by Lee and Marlene Canter (1976) especially to deal with "problem children." The basic premise of Assertive Discipline is that the teacher is the boss who takes charge of the classroom by spelling out clear expectations for behavior, punishing children when they behave inappropriately, and rewarding children when they behave as the teacher wants. We have seen in numerous Assertive Discipline classrooms posted regulations such as the following:

Rules

1. Listen and follow directions.
2. Keep hands, feet, and objects to yourself.
3. Bring school supplies always to class and be prepared to start working on time.
4. Stay in your seat.
5. Raise hand before speaking or leaving seat.

Negative Consequences

1st time:	Name on board and a warning
2nd time:	15 minutes of isolation in Sad Chair
3rd time:	Time-out during recess
4th time:	Note home to parents
5th time:	All of above and require conference with parents
6th time:	Send to office and require conference with parents

Classrooms using this approach also post lists of rewards children receive for good behavior. Typical rewards include praise, stickers, good behavior certificates, special treats, special activities, games, and positive notes to parents.

Critique of the Behaviorist Approach from the Constructivist Perspective

Our criticisms of the behaviorist approach to dealing with difficult children center on its psychological assumptions and its failure to address the origins and causes of misbehavior.

Questionable Assumptions of the Behaviorist Approach

We see two major assumptions of the behaviorist approach that contrast with the assumptions of the constructivist approach. The first broad assumption of the behaviorist approach is that environmental stimuli shape and control individual behavior responses. This assumption reflects the view that the child's interests and purposes are irrelevant and leads to teacher-centered power assertion in relation to children. This is in contrast with the constructivist view that the individual must actively construct knowledge, including stimuli and responses. The reader will recognize the practical implications of this behaviorist assumption as contradictory to constructivist cooperation in relation to children.

The second behaviorist assumption, corollary to the first, is that behavior is controlled through reward and punishment. This is in contrast with the constructivist assumption that such external regulation operates against the development of autonomy or self-regulation and against the meaningful construction of all knowledge, including the sociomoral.

Our view is in agreement with that of Hitz (1988) who states that Assertive Discipline operates against development of moral understanding by making children dependent on external regulation. We also agree with Render, Padilla, and Krank's (1989) critical review of Assertive Discipline in which they argue that "students should not have 'automatic respect' for anyone's authority over them" (p. 620) and that Assertive Discipline miseducates children to believe that those with power have the right to force others to do what they want. In addition, we agree with these authors that "one of the major goals of the school is to teach students to question and to resist controlling methods that lead to blind following of authoritarian demands and orders" (p. 620).

Failure of the Behaviorist Approach to Address the Origins of Misbehavior

The behaviorist teacher focuses on structuring classroom pressures to invoke change in behavior, without particular attention to the causes and origins of misbehavior. The behaviorist effort simply to change the child's behavior does not work in the long run because this approach is not informed by an awareness of the nature of the self that is constructed by the child. Behaviorist management strategies can make the difficult child consolidate a heteronomous notion of self as "managed" by others. (See chapter 3 for the three unfortunate effects of heteronomy.) In our opinion, the behaviorist emphasis on management of behavior exacerbates an already difficult situation by setting up a power struggle between teacher and child that ignores the child's motivation to misbehave.

The constructivist teacher, in contrast, tries to understand the internal causes of misbehavior in order to develop strategies to promote the child's construction of new motivations and new behaviors. In Piaget's (1954/1981) theory, all behavior has purpose and meaning. We extend this idea to say that even misbehavior is to be respected, just as all cognitive processes are respected, even those that produce wrong answers. Effective strategies for promoting behavior change require the constructivist teacher to identify the underlying belief system governing the difficult child's behavior and look for opportunities to challenge that underlying system by encouraging the child's observation and reflection on his or her experience. The question, "Why do children misbehave?" is extremely important to constructivist teachers. To answer this question, we integrate Piaget's theory with that of psychodynamic psychology.

INTEGRATION OF PSYCHODYNAMIC AND CONSTRUCTIVIST THEORIES

A basic assumption of the psychodynamic theory with which Piaget (1954/1981) agreed is that the underlying mechanisms of human behavior (in both cognitive and affective aspects) are largely unconscious (Freud, 1900). That is, the child (and often the adult as well) is unlikely to have any idea about why he or she feels or behaves in a certain manner. Thus, we suggest that it is just as ineffective to ask the child, "Why do you do this?" about social activities as it is to ask "why" questions in activities involving objects (Kamii & DeVries, 1978/1993).

One way to conceptualize this is to say that children are born with a set of needs and drives that their human nature compels them to satisfy. These needs and drives include those for physical survival and comfort and for social validation. In Piaget's (1954/1981) discussion of self-esteem, he refers to Adler's (1917) emphasis on the "will to power" and to the feelings of inferiority that result when the will to power is defeated. Central to Adler's (1927) conceptualization is his proposal that the human need for significance is the most compelling of psychological needs. According to this proposal, striving for significance is a lifelong struggle to obtain recognition, acknowledgement, and belonging. According to Adler, this urge will take precedence over other needs and drives, sometimes including those that are necessary for survival (for example, the anorexic's dedication to gaining significance through the self-denial of starvation).

The need for validation of a feeling of belonging compels the individual to seek acceptance within a community. The need for validation of a feeling of individual significance compels the individual to seek individual recognition and importance from a group. Although equally compelling, these social needs are sometimes oppositional, creating internal disequilibrium. The child will strive to create the optimum satisfaction or balance of community and individuality. However, when frustration occurs, the child might compensate by directing more energy into the expression of his or her need for recognition. For example, a child rejected by his or her peers may feel no sense of belonging to the group. This child may turn to misbehavior (aggression or acting-out, for example) in an effort to draw attention to the self, thus enhancing his or her feelings of individual significance.

Validation occurs in a social context when one elicits a response from a fellow human. What is especially important to our understanding of the difficult child is that responses need not be positive to be validating. Any reaction elicited from another "proves" one's existence and meets needs for recognition. In addition, the degree to which responses are experienced as validating reflects their emotional charge. Responses accompanied by strong emotion emphasize the effectiveness of behavior. For example, another's strong response communicates that, "You are a very powerful and influential person." When adults respond negatively and with strong emotion to unwanted behavior, this may unintentionally validate the child who otherwise receives little recognition.

Even in the first few years of life, the child is already constructing an underlying belief system about how it is that he or she belongs to a group and is significant within that group. This underlying belief system will determine what responses of others are interpreted as validating and what behaviors are needed to elicit those responses.

Although this belief system is not conscious, the child will behave consistently with this cognitive and affective structure unless subsequent experience challenges the rationale of the underlying structure and results in a reconstruction.

We want to emphasize that what the teacher views as inappropriate or dysfunctional behavior may be consistent with the child's unconscious notions about how social validation is achieved. A tragic example is the 4-year-old who witnesses his father's routine battering of his mother and becomes increasingly cruel and abusive towards his peers. His behavior is an expression of the implicit underlying view that violence is an effective means of eliciting social validation.

The first step in thinking about how to deal with the difficult child is to accept the rationality and purposefulness of the child's seemingly irrational behavior. The behavior arises from a private belief system formed early in life. (One excellent book that addresses this subject from the Adlerian perspective is the classic *Children the Challenge* by Rudolph Dreikurs and V. Soltz [1964].)

GUIDELINES FOR WORKING WITH THE DIFFICULT CHILD

In the discussion below of four guidelines we include specific intervention strategies useful in realizing the goal of each guideline. We illustrate some of these strategies by providing examples of interactions with difficult children.

Communicate Acceptance, Validation, and Faith in the Child

The difficult child has developed a repertoire of unacceptable behaviors that naturally elicit rejection from others. It is the constructivist teacher's duty to overcome this reaction by respecting, valuing, and believing in the difficult child. The teacher must recognize the difficult child's underlying need to connect and bond with others and potential ability to resolve problems. Because the difficult child will test the teacher's faith to the limit, the teacher's resolve must be certain. The difficult child may sense any faltering commitment of faith. If the teacher reacts with rejection of the child or fails to validate the child's emotional conflicts, the child will be further convinced of his or her belief system. If the teacher doubts the child's ability to resolve conflicts and cooperate with others, the child will be further persuaded of his or her own sense of inadequacy.

Communicating respect, value, and faith in the difficult child means acknowledging the child's thoughts, feelings, and behaviors. The teacher should accept what the child says, feels, and does, listen to the difficult child, and reflect back to him or her what is said. Acknowledgment may involve direct eye contact and a simple nod of the head, or an "Uh-huh," or "Oh, I see." This lets the child know that the teacher is paying attention. Acceptance also means letting the child know that the teacher does not reject or deny his or her emotional experience. Reflective listening requires repetition of what the child has said or verbalization of the feeling the child has expressed (for example, "I hear you saying that you are very angry right now."). This reflection lets the child know that the teacher is trying to understand his or her thoughts and feelings. It gives the child the opportunity to experience validation without judgement or criticism. The teacher need not agree with what is said, felt, or done in order to acknowledge, accept, and reflect the child's unique experience.

It is important for the teacher to make a verbal commitment of faith in the child. The teacher can set aside a special meeting time to discuss his or her commitment to the difficult child. Following is an example of how one might approach a difficult elementary-age child.

> I've been looking forward to our meeting this week. I wanted to talk to you about my job as your teacher. Do you know what my job is as your teacher? My most important job is to believe that you are a special, important, and capable person. My job is to believe that what you say, do, and feel matters very much. I want to do a good job of believing in you this year. Sometimes I may not agree with you, sometimes I may get angry with you, and you may get angry with me, but I want to make a promise to you that I will not stop believing that you are a special, important, and capable person to me and our whole class. Will you help me with my job? One way you can help is to tell me if you ever feel that I have stopped believing in you. Tell me if it feels like I'm not doing my job. Okay?

Underlying the communication of acceptance, validation, and faith in the child is a genuine feeling of caring for and about the child. Difficult children are usually difficult to love because their behaviors are so alienating. For the teacher to help a difficult child, the child must feel the teacher cares for him or her. This is unlikely to occur unless the teacher genuinely does care.

Understand the Child's Internal Belief System
Governing Misbehavior

Having committed to the faith in the child's unique and special individuality, the teacher must undertake the job of trying to understand the system of implicit beliefs that compels the child's misbehavior. This involves assessing the child's construction of self and others, including the schemes of social reaction (patterns of relating to others) constructed by the child. Following are several strategies to enable the committed teacher to gain insight in understanding the difficult child.

1. Assess the child's construction of self, others, and patterns of approach and response to others. Does the child show self-confidence or lack of confidence? Does the child feel competent or incompetent in specific ways? Does the child generally view others as objects, persons to command or control, persons to persuade, or persons with whom to share mutual understanding? Does the child generally approach others with an expectation of positive or negative response? When others do not do as the child wishes, how does the child construe the situation? In what ways does the child try to get others to do as he or she wishes? Is the child often resistant (actively or passively), submissive, aggressive, rebellious? Reflection on these questions will help the teacher realize how the child constructs self and others.

2. Observe reactions and emotional responses to the child's behavior. Dreikurs and Soltz (1964) (influenced by Adler) suggested that the emotions provoked in the teacher provide clues about the underlying beliefs governing the child's misbehavior. For example, if an interaction with a child leaves the teacher feeling inadequate and frustrated, then the child is likely operating under a belief in his or her own inadequacy. In our experience, we have found that a child who leaves the teacher feeling defeated without being directly confronted may be operating under a "passive-aggressive" action pattern. This unconscious pattern reflects an implicit belief that states: "In order to matter, I must be more powerful than others. Since I cannot win in a conflict with an authority figure, then I cannot be more powerful in a direct confrontation, but I can be more powerful if I keep the adult from winning." By procrastination, avoidance of responsibility, and failure to cooperate, the passive-aggressive child effectively undermines and frustrates the teacher's plans and agenda. This is one effective way to rebel against too much adult control. Thus, the passive-aggressive child may not provoke a direct confrontation or create a disruptive scene. However, the teacher who tries to motivate this child may feel frustrated and inadequate.

If the teacher recognizes a pattern of annoyance among peers, this may indicate that the difficult child feels compelled to seek constant attention. The attention-seeking child might frequently interrupt others' activities or clown around in a way that is not necessarily harmful but is disruptive. He or she may be operating with an underlying belief system that "I matter when I have the attention of others."

3. Interview the difficult child. Another important strategy is to talk to the child in order to gain understanding of beliefs underlying behavior. After a specific conflict or disruptive event, the teacher might ask the child to talk about feelings and events precipitating the misbehavior. It is ineffective to ask the child why he or she behaved in a certain way, but it can be very useful to ask about events leading up to the behavior. For example, if a difficult child has a pattern of hurting others and has just hit a peer with a block, the teacher might schedule a time to talk with the child several hours after the event occurs.

The general strategy in the interview is to help the child acknowledge feelings and identify patterned emotional and behavioral reactions. Sometimes, "What if" questions may reveal the child's underlying belief system. For example, the teacher might say:

> I can see that you were angry with J. What did he do? So he wouldn't let you build the road with him? Sometimes people feel sad, too, when that happens. What would happen if you felt sad? Some people cry when they are sad. Would you feel like crying? Or maybe you don't like feeling sad at all, so maybe you would rather feel mad?

The child may be operating under some inner belief that disallows feelings of sadness. Perhaps the child has a belief that states, "If someone hurts me, they have demonstrated their power over me. I must hurt them to feel significant by regaining a sense of my own power." Unfortunately, the child is beginning a cycle that will produce more and more anger and suppressed sadness in his or her life.

We can offer no simple formulas for understanding a child's implicit belief system. Although psychoanalytic theory has provided some good frameworks, it will nevertheless be the job of the sensitive teacher to probe for the meanings for each individual child. We would like to stress that our examples represent only a fraction of possible reasons children misbehave. The implicit belief system of each child is as unpredictable as his or her genetic inheritance and unique experience.

Challenge and Confront the Child's Implicit Belief System

Having communicated acceptance, validation, and faith and gained an understanding of the beliefs governing the child's behavior, the teacher is now ready to challenge and confront the problem behavior. As indicated above, the teacher will need to look for opportunities to validate the child's belonging to the group and his or her individual significance. At the same time, the teacher tries to confront the implicit belief system that ultimately defeats the satisfaction of these compelling inner needs. However, it is important to stress at this point that *the goal is not to change the child's behavior so much as it is to challenge the behavior.* The teacher must accept the child's ultimate autonomy over his or her own behavior and see change as a hoped for by-product to the child's development, not as an operational goal that the teacher has power to produce.

1. Help the child to consider another perspective. In the context of an interview, the teacher can challenge the child to observe another perspective in much the same way that the teacher might challenge a child's logico-mathematical reasoning. By asking the child to think about how others feel and think, the teacher fosters the child's construction of alternative views of a given event. In chapter 5 on conflict resolution we give many examples of how to do this. The conflict resolution techniques discussed there are appropriate ways of confronting a difficult child with the effects of his or her behavior on the feelings of peers. Group process can provide another opportunity to challenge the difficult child's problem behaviors and beliefs. By encouraging group members to express their feelings openly and honestly, the child will be confronted with the alienating aspects of misbehavior.

The teacher can lead the group to give feedback to a difficult child while protecting him or her from criticisms and insult by requiring elementary-age children to use a "When you __, I feel __ because __" statement. It is helpful to have the words available on posterboard cut-outs and then ask the child who is expressing feelings to hold up each phrase with that part of his or her statement. For example, if a child who is upset after having his construction project destroyed blurts out, "I hate Aaron for breaking my building!" the teacher can intervene by passing the "feeling phrases" to him and asking him to restate his feelings. The injured child is then encouraged to state, "When Aaron breaks my building, I feel angry because I am sad." The teacher can foster a widening repertoire of emotions along with a vocabulary of feelings. Experiencing and identifying the open expression of emotions challenges the difficult child to recognize the effects of his or her behavior.

It is also useful to help the child recognize and label feelings that are not conscious. For example, following the interview discussed above with a sad-angry child, the teacher could further challenge the belief in needing to hurt others to avoid personal sadness by the following suggestions.

> I have thought of an idea. Next time you feel angry about a problem, can you look inside your heart and see if there are sad feelings there as well? If you have sad feelings, I would like you to come and get me because I know that it is difficult to feel sad all alone. Maybe I can feel sad with you, and then together we can think of something to do with those feelings.

The teacher is targeting the acknowledgement and acceptance of sad feelings and offering validation of those feelings. With the teacher's acceptance of those feelings, it is hoped that the child will begin to acknowledge his or her own feelings of sadness rather than reverting to the old pattern of aggression when emotionally injured.

2. Help the child reconstruct feelings and patterns of reaction to others. The difficult child is not conscious of many feelings and patterns of reaction to others. The teacher's goal is to help the child become conscious of these and alternative ways of feeling and reacting. For example, one teacher identified a child whose passive-aggressive behavior controlled many of the classroom transition times. Because of this child's procrastination, the class often had to wait before beginning a new activity. Employing a sort of reverse psychology, the teacher asked the child to be last in this way:

> I've noticed that you have a special place in our class—did you know that you had a special place in our class? Many times you are the last one to come to our circle time and so we wait for you to get started. And often you are the last one to finish your lunch, and we wait for you to finish before we go outside. I was just thinking that being the last one is a special place in our class because then you say when we change activities. I would like to give you a special job so that everyone will recognize the impor-

tance of your being last. I am going to give you the bell to ring when it is time for our circle to begin and when lunch is over. Now, you must remember to be the last one so that you can see that everyone is ready before we begin the new activity.

This paradoxical intervention is effective when it brings to the child's conscious awareness the intention of trying to be last in order to control the group. By giving the procrastinating child legitimate control over the end of an activity, the teacher has provided a more direct and acceptable means of control. The child can then make a choice about continuing to behave, according to conscious intention.

3. Emphasize natural and logical consequences of the child's patterns of reactions to others. Natural and logical consequences have already been discussed in chapter 10 as appropriate strategies for confronting misbehavior. When the child experiences natural or logical consequences in a nonpunitive environment, he or she has the opportunity to reason about personal responsibility for those consequences. However, one must exercise caution when using consequences to deal with the difficult child who may have already included the consequences in his or her system of beliefs. For example, if a disruptive child is often isolated from the group, he or she may be gaining significance through the special status resulting from exclusion. When a logical consequence used consistently and appropriately is not working, the teacher must reevaluate the child's behavior and look for an alternative intervention that does not confirm dysfunctional unconscious beliefs.

Guide the Child in Reconstructing Feelings and Patterns of Reaction to Others

After challenging and confronting the difficult child's unconscious beliefs, the teacher must guide the child in reconstructing feelings and patterns of reaction to others. By this we mean that the child must learn new ways of feeling and reacting to others. The child who gives up the old beliefs will do so only when an alternative is constructed. We discuss below three strategies that can help the child in the reconstructive process.

1. Help the child experience others in valued ways, and help others experience the difficult child in valued ways. This will not be easy because everyone involved will have to overcome established conceptions and patterns of reaction. One way to make the difficult child more attractive to peers is to work with his or her parents and arrange for the child to bring to school a new game or a special activity that can be enjoyed by the entire class. The teacher can help the difficult child share the activity with other children (teaching them a game, for example). If this succeeds, the teacher can look for opportunities to help the difficult child become aware of his or her changed status in the group. If children have enjoyed the special activity, the teacher might suggest at grouptime that the children express appreciation for the difficult child's special effort.

Another way to begin to build friendly links between children and the difficult child is for his or her parents to invite a class member to their home for an afternoon or overnight, or to accompany them on a special trip (to a pizza restaurant or amusement park, for example). This can mark the beginning of a special friendship. The teacher may also think of ways to build friendly links through analyzing the child's strengths—what he or she likes and does well. As the difficult child begins to have more positive experiences with others, he or she attaches new positive feelings to certain interactions with others.

2. Help the child construct and conserve new values by exercising will. If efforts to help the difficult child experience others in valued ways succeed, the child already has unconsciously begun a reconstruction of the old internal meanings of social relationships. The teacher's challenge is to help the child repeatedly to have such experiences and thereby to construct the new values as permanent. This will not be a smooth, continuous path of success, as the difficult child will only gradually consolidate the new values and thereby reconstruct the beliefs guiding behavior.

Piaget (1954/1981) discussed the will as the organizer of feelings into a relatively stable system. He quoted William James' point that "the will comes into play only when it is necessary to choose between two drives or tendencies" (Piaget, 1954/1981, p. 13). Piaget therefore emphasized the role of the will in making conscious value choices concerning interpersonal exchanges in the child's construction of the world of people.

It is therefore important for the difficult child to begin to exercise will, that is, consciously to make choices in relations with others. The teacher can help the child make conscious choices in feelings and ideas about others, thereby assisting the child in constructing and conserving values and exercising will.

3. Help the child construct feelings of justice and caring for others. This principle involves everything we have written in this book about promoting children's sociomoral development. Once a teacher has implemented the other principles described in this chapter, he or she has to work with the difficult child in the same ways as with other children.

Finally, we would like to point out that the principles for dealing with the difficult child will also be useful when the teacher deals with the normal child in difficult moments. We must also point out that some difficult children cannot be helped in the average classroom where the teacher is not free to give undivided attention to one child. Some difficult children need to be in very small groups with a therapist. If the teacher's time is so consumed by work with the difficult child that other children's needs are neglected, then the situation is not fair to other children. If after several weeks of work according to the guidelines described in this chapter, the difficult child has not made progress, the teacher should refer the child for evaluation and possible referral to another setting.

SUMMARY

With any group of children, the teacher deals with a broad range of self-regulating competencies. All children have moments when they are difficult. However, the especially difficult child who endangers others and disrupts activities presents a special challenge to the teacher. Much of what has been written about how to manage the difficult child is based on a behaviorist perspective that emphasizes the teacher's management of the child's behavior. Assertive Discipline is an example of such an approach. The central behaviorist assumption is that environmental stimuli shape and control individual behavior through reward and punishment. The behaviorist teacher focuses on structuring classroom pressures to invoke change in behavior, without attention to the causes and origins of misbehavior. In contrast, the constructivist teacher, integrating psychodynamic and constructivist theory, tries to understand the child's construction of self, others, and patterns of relating to others. Guidelines for working with the difficult child (1) communicate acceptance, validation, and faith in the child, (2) understand the child's internal belief system governing misbehavior, (3) challenge and confront the child's implicit belief system, and (4) guide the child in reconstructing feelings and patterns of reaction to others. The guidelines for working with difficult children are also useful for working with the normal child in difficult moments.

17

The Sociomoral Atmosphere
of the School

It is impossible to realize fully the constructivist sociomoral atmosphere in the classroom if the sociomoral atmosphere of the school is at odds with it. Unless the sociomoral atmosphere of the entire building is constructivist, children will have contradictory experiences. The classroom does not exist in a social vacuum, and contacts with others outside the classroom form part of the sociomoral atmosphere children experience in school. In this chapter we discuss the work of Kohlberg and his colleagues on assessing the moral culture of institutions, especially high schools. In addition to studying how moral atmosphere relates to individual sociomoral development, they have conceptualized levels of moral atmosphere in institutions. Then we comment on children's and teachers' experiences of the larger sociomoral atmosphere in preschools and elementary schools and suggest principles for principals who wish to cultivate a constructivist sociomoral atmosphere in their schools.

KOHLBERG AND COLLEAGUES' WORK ON ASSESSING MORAL CULTURE

In their book *Kohlberg's Approach to Moral Education,* Power, Higgins, and Kohlberg (1989) describe the "Just Community." Implemented in high schools and prisons, the Just Community invites participation in democratic decision-making concerning the life of the group together. In this approach, teachers can be advocates of a particular point of view, but they avoid indoctrinating students. Instead, they express the perspective of the community in class meetings. They present positions that can be criticized, encourage students to formulate their own views on issues, and accept as binding the democratic judgment of the majority. Study of the Cluster School, a Just Community school within a larger high school, showed dramatic results. In addition to significant increases in the moral reasoning of individuals, racial relations improved and interracial conflict became almost nonexistent. Stealing ceased. Drug use virtually ceased. Cheating was curbed as students adopted an honor code. Educational aspirations were enhanced. In contrast, Power, Higgins, and Kohlberg commented:

> Our data indicated that the culture of the large public high school actually undermines effective moral education by subjecting students to negative peer group influences and by alienating them from adults. In such a context adult authority tends to reside more in adults' status and coercive power than in their moral persuasiveness. (p. 300)

Kohlberg and his colleagues conclude their book by saying that the experience in a Just Community leads to a responsibility orientation characterized by awareness of and concern for relationships, the welfare of others, and the public interest. This research provides further evidence, in addition to our own study of sociomoral atmosphere and sociomoral development at the kindergarten level (see chapter 1), that cooperative adult-child relations promote, and coercive relations impede, child development.

Kohlberg and his colleagues developed several ways of assessing moral atmosphere in an institution. For example, they describe five levels of teenagers' institutional valuing of the school reflecting increasing perspective taking:

- Level 0: Individuals do not value the school
- Level 1: Instrumental value (school helps individuals meet their needs)
- Level 2: Enthusiastic identification (school valued at special moments such as when a team wins a sporting event)
- Level 3: Spontaneous community (school valued for closeness or friendliness of members where members feel inner motivation to help others)

- Level 4: Normative community (school valued for its own sake where membership involves a social contract to respect the norms and ideals of the group) (Power, Higgins, & Kohlberg, 1989)

In their research on the Cluster School, Power, Higgins, and Kohlberg (1989) found change from level 1 (before the Just Community was established) to level 4 (by the second year of implementation).

Power, Higgins, and Kohlberg also discuss how norms (generally accepted rules) differ according to the sociomoral atmosphere of a school. Norms of order are the collective rules that simply safeguard the survival and orderly functioning of the organization (for example, rules prohibiting stealing library books or disrupting the classroom). Norms of fairness involve respect for the equal rights and liberties of individuals and the processes through which rules are made. Norms of community involve caring (sharing concerns and affection), trust, integration (sharing of communication among subgroups), participation (sharing time, energy, and interest), open communication (sharing knowledge about matters that affect the group), and collective responsibility (sharing obligations, praise, and blame). Research on the Cluster School showed a shift by its second year from norms of order and fairness to norms of community.

Research on prison inmates also provides data that inform our understanding of the effect of the moral atmosphere of the larger institution on individual development. Scharf (1973) showed that many prisoners reasoned at the lower level of the prison's moral atmosphere even when they were capable of higher level reasoning. Kohlberg and his colleagues realized that the moral education of inmates would be ineffective unless it also involved working with the prison authorities to change the moral atmosphere of the prison experience.

These findings suggest that in preschools and elementary schools we must be concerned with the sociomoral atmosphere of the larger school institution if we want to be maximally effective in influencing children's sociomoral development.

CHILDREN'S EXPERIENCE OF THE SCHOOL ATMOSPHERE

The larger school atmosphere can foster or impede the development of the classroom's sociomoral atmosphere. The Boot Camp and Factory classrooms of our program comparison study (see chapter 1) reflected larger school atmospheres consistent with classroom practices. The Community classroom, however, was an island within a larger school atmosphere that reflected behavioristic principles and contradicted the children's classroom experience in many ways. For example, children from the Community classroom described in chapter 1 had to walk in the halls in a straight line and without talking. In the cafeteria children were managed by a "token economy" in which they were given play money for good behavior. Children could exchange their "bucks" for trinkets in the school store. Bucks were given to children mainly for quiet behavior. According to the assistant teacher who supervised the class in the cafeteria, Community children got few bucks because of their talking. The person in charge of the token economy even yelled at the assistant teacher for not insisting that the children refrain from talking. Community children had specialty teachers for art, P.E., and music. The music teacher maintained a positive dynamic in the classroom, but this cannot be said for art and P.E. teachers. The P.E. teacher was heteronomous and promoted a negative sort of competition among children. The art teacher was extremely negative and critical toward children. She insisted that children "create" exact, perfect duplicates of her models. When children did not demonstrate skills such as use of scissors, she shamed them. Children often ended their art period in tears.

Even in this situation in which the constructivist program received ambivalent support and in which children also had non-constructivist experiences, they still made more sociomoral progress than the children in Boot Camp and Factory classrooms. We therefore suggest that a constructivist classroom atmosphere can to some extent compensate for a nonconstructivist atmosphere in the larger school. However, we should say that children in this public school classroom made less progress than kindergarten children in the HDLS at the University of Houston. This may be due to one or more of several differences in experience. First, the Lab School children had been in constructivist education for more than 1 year (in some cases, for 4 years). Second, the larger school atmosphere of the Lab School was consistent with the constructivist experience of the classroom. Third, Lab School children lived in more privileged family situations with better educated parents who had opportunities to participate in constructivist parent education offered by the school.

Assessment of the school's sociomoral atmosphere focuses mainly on rules but also on children's contacts with the adults who enforce those rules. The first question to consider is where school rules originate. If children are not consulted about what these rules should be, they experience them as coming from others rather than as self-regulating principles. It is possible for children to participate in deciding what school rules should be—for the library, for the lunchroom, for bathroom privileges, and so forth. We agree with Power, Higgins, and Kohlberg (1989) who state:

> The aim of developmental moral education has to be a change in the life of the school as well as in the development of individual students. For the teaching of justice, as the teaching of reading or arithmetic, is set in a *context* of a classroom and a school, and how the students experience the life of the classroom and school will have a shaping effect on what they learn from what the teacher teaches. (p. 20)

THE TEACHER'S EXPERIENCE OF THE SCHOOL ATMOSPHERE

The sociomoral atmosphere for the teacher includes not only relations with the children in his or her class, but relations with the administration and other teachers. The school atmosphere can reflect the attitudes of the school district administration, but school districts cannot usually be said to have a coherent philosophy. More important to school atmosphere are attitudes of the principal, discussed in the following section.

Relations among teachers can provide a network of support or its opposite, a feeling of negation and isolation. In our program comparison study the constructivist teacher of the Community classroom enjoyed a friendly atmosphere in relation to other kindergarten teachers, but first grade teachers were critical. They felt the Community teacher was too lenient and that she should not give children choices. The principal, while willing to give us a chance to try, had some doubts that constructivist education could work in a public school. Nevertheless, she supported the Community teacher after an unfavorable evaluation by the district evaluator because the room was not quiet.

The larger school and school district (or, as in the case of the Lab School, the University) environment also constitutes an important sociomoral environment for the teacher by offering supportive or antagonistic attitudes, help or hindrance, praise or criticism. The system within which the school operates determines salaries and working conditions that carry a message of respect or lack of respect for teachers.

PRINCIPLES FOR PRINCIPALS

The sociomoral atmosphere of the classroom is embedded in that of the school, the school district and state education department, and the wider community. Yet just as teachers have latitude in how they operate a classroom, principals have latitude and can influence the sociomoral atmospheres of their buildings. Many readers are already teachers or principals and may be considering how to change a heteronomous sociomoral atmosphere into a more cooperative milieu. This is more difficult than beginning a new school with teachers already committed to the constructivist point of view. Sarason (1982), in discussing the problem of change in schools, refers to the principal as having "a key role in the educational change process" (p. 184). In agreement with this view, we therefore focus here on how principals can foster a constructivist sociomoral atmosphere in their schools. In this section, we rely particularly on the experience of Deborah Murphy, former principal of Maplewood Elementary School in North Kansas City, Missouri, and currently principal of Edison Elementary School in St. Joseph, Missouri, who consciously tries to be a constructivist principal and for 4 years has worked toward influencing teachers in a constructivist direction. We present four general principles for principals wishing to work toward a constructivist sociomoral atmosphere in their buildings.

Respect Teachers

Murphy (personal communication, June 1993) expressed the following rationale for her attitude as a principal toward the teachers in her school:

> If I wanted teachers to respect kids, I had to respect teachers. If I wanted students to be free to challenge rules and ideas, I had to permit teachers that same freedom. If I wanted teachers to reflect on their educational beliefs and practices, I had to be open to the possibility that I could be wrong as well.

While not taking a specifically constructivist perspective, Sarason (1982) provides a cogent description of how teachers treat children as they are treated. He conducted research on constitutional issues (the written or unwritten rules) in classrooms by having observers in six classrooms (grades 3, 4, and 5) record every statement by a teacher or child that related to rules. The results were as follows:

1. The constitution was invariably determined by the teacher. No teacher ever discussed why a constitution was necessary.
2. The teacher never solicited the opinions and feelings of any pupil about a constitutional question.
3. In three of the classrooms the rules of the game were verbalized by the end of the first week of school. In two others the rules were clear by the end of the month. In one it was never clear what the constitution was.
4. Except for the one chaotic classroom, neither children nor teachers evidenced any discomfort with the content of constitutions—it was as if everyone agreed that this is the way things are and should be.
5. In all instances constitutional issues involved what *children* could or could not, should or should not, do. The issue of what a *teacher* could or could not, should or should not, do, never arose. (p. 216)

Sarason comments:

> What I became aware of during the discussion was that these teachers thought about children in precisely the same way that teachers say that school administrators think about teachers; that is, administrators do not discuss matters with teachers, they do not act as if the opinions of teachers were important, they treat teachers like a bunch of children, and so on. (p. 217)

Sarason's argument is consistent with our constructivist view. He argues that failures in introducing and sustaining educational change "have foundered largely because they have not come to grips with the power aspects of existing relationships" (p. 218).

As former director of a school, the first author can testify to the many positive outcomes of respecting teachers. Teachers become autonomous and take more responsibility for the education they offer children. This leads to increased creativity in curriculum planning, increased competence and confidence as professionals, more collaboration with other teachers, and higher morale.

Recognize the Necessity for a Paradigm Shift

In earlier chapters we have discussed how a teacher's world view or theoretical paradigm influences teaching. The predominant behaviorist paradigm has influenced all of us. This is why Piaget's theory is such an eye-opener for most people. Piaget's theory leads us to think in a new way about learning and development. The implications of Piaget's theory lead us to think in a new way about teaching. We can speak about these fundamental changes in our world view as a paradigm shift from behaviorism to constructivism.

To recognize the necessity for a paradigm shift is one way to respect teachers. That is, principals must recognize that just as children construct their knowledge and sociomoral convictions, so do teachers. This construction takes time because for some teachers it involves basic restructuring of fundamental beliefs and ways of being. However, many teachers already possess constructivist intuitions and tendencies. These teachers are relieved to find a scientific rationale for what they have felt all along. Still, old habits change slowly. Working with teachers who have been teaching in nonconstructivist ways challenges a constructivist principal who would like to realize the constructivist vision right away. However, short-circuiting the constructive process can lead teachers to view constructivist education as a set of tricks or methods rather than a way of thinking. Our goal is a shared vision among all staff in a school. When this occurs as it has in the HDLS, the result is a unified community of professionals who work together and work with children in ways that go beyond the vision of the director or principal.

Engage Teachers in the Long View

Murphy (personal communication, June 1993) describes this principle as "head lifting," the result of moving one's focus from the specificities of day-to-day work with children to considering "where we are going and why, versus all the other possibilities." Murphy emphasizes that "To shoot for long-term outcomes without articulated theories, beliefs, and principles that form the bedrock is shaky ground indeed. So a majority of our time together has been spent in this arena." In pursuing the long view, Murphy and her teachers have tackled the following questions:

> What do we really want our children to know, do, and value as a result of their time with us?
> What principles will guide us as we become a collaborative team?
> What do we know about child development that can inform our decisions?
> What do we believe truly and deeply about teaching/learning?

Strategies followed by Murphy and her teachers (personal communication, June 1993) in order to "flesh out outcomes and belief statements" have included conducting anonymous surveys; engaging in group process (such as brainstorming and consensus building); forming study groups; reading journals; undertaking action research; supervising in classrooms; participating in workshops and other forms of in-service; developing a professional library and media center; and encouraging individual reflection on readings.

In our work in the HDLS, the focus on the long view takes the form of articulating rationales that emphasize the continuity of development. For example, Piaget's theory (discussed in chapters 2 and 3) leads us to conclude that if we want children to grow into autonomous personalities, we must minimize the exercise of adult power and authority. While goals for activities include specific short-term objectives, they also reflect general long-term objectives.

Model and Explain Constructivist Attitudes and Practices

Modelling constructivist attitudes and practices can be summarized as treating teachers as constructivist teachers treat children and by showing how to treat children respectfully. We discuss these below in terms of governance, discipline, and shared experience.

Governance

In contrast to traditional decision-making by administrators, Murphy's Maplewood School exemplifies shared decision-making. Murphy (personal communication, 1993) describes the issue of governance in terms of who owns the school and recounts her first faculty meeting in which she asked teachers to make rules she should live by. The rules teachers suggested were: Tell the truth; keep us informed; give us specific, helpful feedback on our teaching. From recommendations by teachers through committee structures, Maplewood has evolved to decisions made by the staff as a whole, students, and interested parents. For example, they are considering how basal and workbook money could be could be used for more appropriate instructional materials and equipment.

The student council at Maplewood is unusual in its power to consider real school problems and make real decisions about issues of concern to children. For example, in a round robin when members say how they think the school is doing, what needs to change, and concerns to think about, the issue of wearing hats in school was mentioned. Murphy followed her typical procedure of getting people to dialogue before they make a decision they feel they must defend. After a straw poll, students were asked to take a position opposite the one they took in the straw poll and to give reasons for the opposite view. Murphy reports that this method was more successful with children than with teachers who tended to be polarized and to find it difficult to consider another viewpoint. Murphy asked whether other information might be obtained in addition to their initial opinions. Students suggested contacting other elementary schools and the high school they would later attend, to find out what the policy on hats was and why that policy was instituted. Eventually, students decided that hats would not be worn in common areas (hallways, gym, cafeteria) but that hats could be worn in classrooms if the class decided on this alternative.

Murphy (personal communication, June 1993) put mailboxes in strategic places in the school so that students could anonymously submit an idea, complaint, or issue for student council consideration. Students therefore did not have to be on the student council to bring up something. Teachers, too, could communicate a question, idea, or concern anonymously. Murphy notes that fewer letters are now submitted to the student council than in the beginning and that teachers use the anonymous communication less frequently. She believes this shows that the teachers are getting better at resolving issues at the classroom level, and that people in the school are developing a sense of community in which they openly discuss concerns.

Discipline and Conflict Resolution

Murphy (personal communication, June 1993) comments that the greatest challenge for a constructivist principal involves discipline. Teachers generally expect principals to resolve all situations referred to them. The principal who does not quickly fix a problem is not a good principal in teachers' eyes. In one instance, a teacher felt that a child was manipulating Murphy. Murphy invited the teacher to observe her problem-solving approach in which she listened and showed respect for the child's viewpoint. Afterward, Murphy and the teacher critiqued the process and developed shared understanding of the problem. Murphy emphasizes in her problem-solving approach that there is "no one rule or consequence that fits all situations." She explains to teachers her concern with long-term sociomoral growth and not just a "quick fix." According to Murphy, (personal communication, June 1993) "the point is to grow and not that someone wins. The long view leads to different strategies than just maintaining law and order for the day."

In our view, "discipline" is not appropriate in a constructivist school. As argued in chapter 10, alternatives to discipline focus on logical nonarbitrary consequences. The establishment of a sociomoral atmosphere actually reduces the need for discipline because children do not have to struggle against adult authority in order to maintain their self-respect.

Shared Experience

We would like to point out the importance of shared experience in the sociomoral atmosphere of the school. We do not refer to school spirit as shared pride and identification when the school team wins a football game (level 2 of institutional valuing, as previously described; Power, Higgins, & Kohlberg, 1989). We refer, instead, to students valuing the school because it is the kind of place in which people want to help each other and serve the community as a whole (level 3) and to students valuing the school as a community in which members feel an obligation to group norms and responsibilities (level 4).

Maplewood School again provides us with an example. Student Council discussion of concerns led to the idea of a buddy system in which children would help other children with academic problems, emotional problems, and conflicts with adults in their lives. According to Murphy (personal communication, June 1993), students really took charge and decided what steps to take to bring this system about. Student Council members decided that three children should be elected from each class to be buddies. They emphasized to their classmates that a good buddy would have three critical attributes: Be a good listener; be trusted not to tell; and have good ideas. Student council members emphasized that a good buddy might not be the smartest, most popular, or the best leader. After selection of the buddies, the next step was that the buddies decided they wanted high school students to train them. The Wellness Coordinator at the high school developed a group to come once a week and facilitate the buddy system. They did role playing and discussed issues such as how to identify themselves and whether to stay after school to pursue buddy activities.

THE SOCIOMORAL ATMOSPHERE OF THE
STATE DEPARTMENT OF EDUCATION

We have mentioned that the larger school and school district can support or obstruct the implementation of a constructivist sociomoral atmosphere in a classroom or school. Obviously, the more philosophical agreement within the entire culture of the school, the easier it is to establish and maintain any type of sociomoral atmosphere. We point to the state of Missouri as a model in this regard. There constructivist education (called Project Construct) has been officially adopted by the State Department of Elementary and Secondary Education for pre-K through grade one. Project Construct can be voluntarily adopted by school districts or by individual schools. A core group of educators has widened through a program of education, including Saturday workshops, summer institutes, and special sessions at the annual Conference on the Young Years, and through publication of a curriculum guide (Murphy & Goffin, 1992), a framework for curriculum and assessment (Missouri Department of Elementary and Secondary Education, 1992), and a newsletter.

Missouri teachers wishing to implement Project Construct must participate in training to which they take an administrator, a requirement that has worked to insure administrative support. Project Construct is now implemented in more than 100 Missouri schools. The Project Construct National Center, located at the University of Missouri–Columbia and directed by Dr. Sharon Shattgen, oversees continuing development of Project Construct, including development of assessment methods that are consistent with constructivist objectives. In addition, early education teacher certification requirements and teacher evaluation procedures have been developed to reflect Project Construct principles.

Changes in early education in Missouri are now systemic and continue to grow. However, the reform began with individuals concerned about providing the best possible educational opportunities to young children and their families.

SUMMARY

While it is true that children's experience of the larger school atmosphere does enhance or impede the development of a constructivist classroom atmosphere, and it is important that the sociomoral atmosphere of the entire school support that of the classroom, a constructivist classroom atmosphere can compensate to some extent for a nonconstructivist atmosphere of the larger school. The work of Kohlberg and his colleagues on assessing sociomoral atmosphere emphasizes the different ways students value the school and different types of school norms. The individual teacher's experience of the school atmosphere can support or negate his or her effort to establish a constructivist sociomoral atmosphere. There are four general principles that principals wishing to create such an atmosphere should observe: Respect teachers; recognize the necessity for a paradigm shift; engage teachers in the long view, and; model and explain constructivist attitudes and practices. However, systemic change in the direction of the constructivist sociomoral atmosphere such as achieved in Missouri will best support the development of moral children in moral classrooms.

Appendix

Rationales for General Categories of Constructivist Activities During Activity Time

The following rationales were written by the first author and Lead Teachers in the Human Development Laboratory School at the University of Houston. We post these on a parent board in our hallway to inform parents and visitors. In addition, teachers write rationales for selected activities in their weekly lesson plans.

Pretense

Pretense is the ability to think about a nonpresent object, person, or event and is a major step forward in cognitive development. Pretense involves decentering to consider the behavior and, eventually, the points of view of others. Through pretense, children experiment with situations, relationships, and emotional issues that are not well understood. In play, children are in control and can structure their experiences so as to work through personal concerns and interests. Pretense is a kind of "language" that is especially important in the years when children's verbal language is not fully developed.

Language and Literacy

The basis for language and literacy lies in general symbolic and representational development that begins in the second year of life with spoken language and pretense. Throughout early childhood language develops through social interaction in a language-rich environment that includes children's stories, poetry, rhymes, and songs. Children are encouraged to use their words to express thoughts and feelings. Teachers model effective communication and refrain from speaking for children. Through entertaining stories children acquire knowledge of book characteristics (author, illustrator, page progression), conventions of written language (separation of print and picture, top to bottom and left to right sequencing, and correspondences between spoken and written language) and elements of story (setting of scene, introduction of characters, problem, and resolution).

Through all these experiences, children are constructing semantic and syntactical rules. The constructive process includes errors such as overgeneralization ("foots," "goed") that children correct on their own in time.

Children learn to read and write in ways analogous to learning spoken language—through stumbling first approximations. Teachers support these efforts in a variety of ways: (1) encouraging and accepting writing from scribbling to pseudoletters to conventional letters, invented spelling, and conventional spelling; (2) encouraging and accepting pretend reading, recognition of important words such as names of self, family, and friends, signs and labels in the environment, beginning hypotheses about relations between spoken and written language, and eventual construction of the alphabetic or phonetic hypothesis.

Blocks and Other Construction Toys

Construction toys such as Waffle Blocks™, Legos™, Construx™, Tinker Toys™, Bristle Blocks™, Ramagons™, pop beads, wooden blocks, cardboard blocks, etc., offer many opportunities for development, including the following.

- **Physical knowledge.** Acting on objects in a variety of ways to observe the variety of reactions and to create certain effects. Examples: Creating windows and walls within a structure, balancing, bridging, stacking, and using inclines.
- **Representation and pretense.** Emergence and elaboration of representational or symbolic thought at different levels. The ability to let an object represent something else is important progress in the development of thought. With construction toys and props such as dolls and cars, children may also be

inspired to engage in pretense. *Example:* The toddler may let a block be a house, a kindergartener may make an elaborate downtown scene.

- **Spatial reasoning.** Making things fit together, interlock, define open and enclosed spaces.
- **Logico-mathematical reasoning.** Noticing similarities and differences and classifying by creating equivalences that are possible in unit blocks and in Construx™.

Group Games

Playing games with rules contribute to children's cognitive and sociomoral development. To play a game with rules, children must cooperate by agreeing on the rules and accepting their consequences. When a rule is broken or a disagreement occurs, children have the opportunity to negotiate and figure out how to continue the game. Games are an excellent context for considering issues of fairness, the beginning of ideas of justice.

We select games for their potential in promoting children's reasoning.

- **Number.** Dice and card games offer opportunities for developing an understanding of 1-to-1 correspondence; more, less, and equal, and adding and subtracting. Some are games of chance, and some involve strategy. *Examples:* board games such as Hi-Ho Cherry O™ and Sorry™, and card games such as Uno™.
- **Physical-knowledge.** Many games also offer advantages found in physical-knowledge activities. *Examples:* Bowling, Topple™, Blockhead™, target games. Number, reading, and writing are involved in keeping score.
- **Social logic.** Some games challenge children to decenter or figure out what someone else may be thinking. *Examples:* Guessing games such as I Spy, Guess Which Hand the Penny Is In, chasing games, Hide and Seek, Simon Says.
- **Non-social logic.** As children get older, they are encouraged to figure out strategies in games not involving chance. These often involve spatial reasoning. *Examples:* Checkers, Tic Tac Toe, Connect Four™, Isolation™, Blokado™.

Art

Art activities such as painting, cutting, gluing, creating with a large variety of media also offer various developmental possibilities.

- **Physical knowledge.** Acting on a variety of materials to observe the variety of effects and reactions; figuring out how different materials combine.
- **Representation.** Emergence and elaboration of representational or symbolic thought at different levels. First representations do not usually resemble the thing represented. It is the representation in the child's mind that counts! As they grow older, children feel a need to achieve a resemblance.
- **Logico-mathematical relations.** Noticing similarities and differences among textures, colors, "tools," "canvases," and media.

REFERENCES

Adler, A. (1917). *Study of organ inferiority and its psychological compensation.* New York: Nervous Disease Pub.

Adler, A. (1927). *The practice and theory of individual psychology, 2nd edition.* New York: Harcourt Brace Jovanovich.

Asch, F. (1983). *Mooncake.* New York: Scholastic.

Berenstain, S., & Berenstain, J. (1983). *The Berenstain bears and the messy room.* New York: Random House.

Bonica, L. (1990). Negociations interpersonnelles et jeux de fiction. In M. Stambak & H. Sinclair (Eds.), *Les jeux de fiction entre enfants de 3 ans* (p. 113–150). Paris: Presses Universitaires de France. (Published in English as *Pretend play among 3-year-olds,* Hillsdale, NJ: Erlbaum, 1993).

Canter, L., & Canter, M. (1976). *Assertive discipline: A take-charge approach for today's educator.* Santa Monica, CA: Lee Canter and Associates.

Colby, A., & Kohlberg, L. (1987). *The measurement of moral judgment.* Cambridge: Cambridge University Press.

DeVries, R. (1970). The development of role-taking in young bright, average, and retarded children as reflected in social guessing game behavior. *Child Development, 41,* 759–770.

DeVries, R. (1986). Children's conceptions of shadow phenomena. *Genetic, Social, and General Psychology Monographs, 112,* 479–530.

DeVries, R. (1992). Development as the aim of constructivist education: How do we recognize development? In D. Murphy & S. Goffin (Eds.), *Understanding the possibilities: A curriculum guide for Project Construct* (pp. 15-34). Columbia, MO: University of Missouri and the Missouri Department of Elementary and Secondary Education.

DeVries, R., & Fernie, D. (1990). Stages in children's play of tic tac toe. *Journal of Research in Childhood Education, 4,* 98–111.

DeVries, R., Haney, J., & Zan, B. (1991). Sociomoral atmosphere in direct-instruction, eclectic, and constructivist kindergartens: A study of teachers' enacted interpersonal understanding. *Early Childhood Research Quarterly, 6,* 449–471.

DeVries, R., & Kohlberg, L. (1987/1990). *Constructivist early education: Overview and comparison with other programs.* Washington, DC: National Association for the Education of Young Children. (Originally published as *Programs of early education: The constructivist view,* New York: Longman.)

DeVries, R., Reese-Learned, H., & Morgan, P. (1991a). Sociomoral development in direct-instruction, eclectic, and constructivist kindergartens: A study of children's enacted interpersonal understanding. *Early Childhood Research Quarterly, 6,* 473–517.

DeVries, R., Reese-Learned, H., & Morgan, P. (1991b). A manual for coding young children's enacted interpersonal understanding. (ERIC Document Reproduction Service No. PS 020123.)

Dewey, J. (1913/1975). *Interest and effort in education.* Edwardsville, IL: Southern Illinois Press.

Dragonwagon, C. (1990). *Half a moon and one whole star.* New York: Aladdin Books.

Dreikurs, R., & Soltz, V. (1964). *Children the challenge.* New York: Hawthorn Books.

Duckworth, E. (1987). *"The having of wonderful ideas" and other essays on teaching and learning.* New York: Teachers College Press.

Ferreiro, E., & Teberosky, A. (1979/1982). *Literacy before schooling.* Portsmouth, NH: Heinemann.

Freud, S. (1900). *The interpretation of dreams.* In J. Strachey, (Ed.), *The standard edition of the complete psychological works of Sigmund Freud, Vols. 4–5.* London: Hogarth Press.

Garis, H. (1947). *Uncle Wiggily's Happy Days.* Platt and Munk.

Hitz, R. (1988). Assertive discipline: A response to Lee Canter. *Young Children, 43* (2), 25–26.

Jackson, P. (1967). *Life in classrooms.* New York: Holt, Rinehart, and Winston.

Kamii, C. (1982). *Number in preschool and kindergarten.* Washington, DC: National Association for the Education of Young Children.

Kamii, C. (1985). *Young children reinvent arithmetic: Implications of Piaget's theory.* New York: Teachers College Press.

Kamii, C. (1989). *Young children continue to reinvent arithmetic: Second Grade.* New York: Teachers College Press.

Kamii, C. (1993). *Young children continue to reinvent arithmetic: Third Grade.* New York: Teachers College Press.

Kamii, C., & DeVries, R. (1975/1977). Piaget for early education. In M. Day & R. Parker (Eds.), *The preschool in action* (pp. 363–420). Boston: Allyn and Bacon.

Kamii, C., & DeVries, R. (1978/1993). *Physical knowledge in preschool education: Implications of Piaget's theory.* New York: Teachers College Press.

Kamii, C., & DeVries, R. (1980). *Group games in early education: Implications of Piaget's theory.* Washington, DC: National Association for the Education of Young Children.

Kohlberg, L. (1984). *Essays on moral development, Volume 2: The psychology of moral development.* San Francisco: Harper and Row.

Kohlberg, L., & Mayer, R. (1972). Development as the aim of education. *Harvard Educational Review, 42,* 449–496.

Krasilovsky, P. (1950). *The man who didn't wash his dishes.* New York: Scholastic.

Lickona, T. (1985). *Raising good children.* New York: Bantam Books.

Lickona, T. (1991). *Educating for character: How our schools can teach respect and responsibility.* New York: Bantam Books.

Manning, M., Manning, G., & Long, R. (1989). Authentic language arts activities and the construction of knowledge. In G. Manning & M. Manning (Eds.), *Whole language beliefs and practices, K–8,* (pp. 93–97). Washington, DC: National Education Association.

Mead, G. (1934). *Mind, self, and society.* Chicago: University of Chicago Press.

Missouri Department of Elementary and Secondary Education (1992). *Project Construct: A framework for curriculum and assessment.* Columbia, MO: Author.

Morris, W. (Ed.) (1973). *The American heritage dictionary of the English language.* Boston: American Heritage Publishing Co. and Houghton Miflin Co.

Murphy, D., & Goffin, S. (1992). *Understanding the possibilities: A curriculum guide for Project Construct.* Columbia, MO: University of Missouri and the Missouri Department of Elementary and Secondary Education.

Nucci, L. (1981). Conceptions of personal issues: A domain distinct from moral or social concepts. *Child Development, 52,* 114–121.

Piaget, J. (1928/1976). Ecrites sociologiques: I. Logique génétique et sociologie. In G. Busino (Ed.), *Les sciences sociales avec et après Jean Piaget* (pp. 44–80). Geneva: Librairie Droz.

Piaget, J. (1932/1965). *The moral judgment of the child.* London: Free Press.

Piaget, J. (1948/1973). *To understand is to invent.* New York: Grossman. (First published in *Prospects,* UNESCO Quarterly Review of Education.)

Piaget, J. (1954/1981). *Les relations entre l'affectivite et l'intelligence dans le developpement mental de l'enfant.* Paris: Centre de Documentation Universitaire. (Published in part in J. Piaget, *Intelligence and Affectivity: Their relation during child development.* Palo Alto, CA: Annual Reviews.)

Piaget, J. (1964). Development and learning. In R. Ripple and V. Rockcastle (Eds.), *Piaget rediscovered: A report of the conference on cognitive studies and curriculum development* (pp. 7-20). Ithaca, NY: Cornell University Press.

Piaget, J. (1964/1968). *Six psychological studies.* New York: Random House.

Piaget, J. (1969/1970). *Science of education and the psychology of the child.* New York: Viking Compass.

Piaget, J. (1975/1985). *The equilibration of cognitive structures: The central problem of intellectual development.* Chicago: University of Chicago Press.

Power, C., Higgins, A., & Kohlberg, L. (1989). *Lawrence Kohlberg's approach to moral education.* New York: Columbia University Press.

Render, G., Padilla, J., & Krank, M. (1989). Assertive discipline: A critical review and analysis. *Teachers College Record, 90,* 607–630.

Sarason, S. (1982). *The culture of the school and the problem of change (2nd ed.).* Boston: Allyn and Bacon.

Scharf, P. (1973). *Moral atmosphere and intervention in the prison.* Ph.D. dissertation, Harvard University, Cambridge, MA.

Scieszka, J. (1989). *The true story of the three little pigs.* New York: Scholastic.

Selman, R. (1980). *The growth of interpersonal understanding.* New York: Academic Press.

Selman, R., & Schultz, L. (1990). *Making a friend in youth: Developmental theory and pair therapy.* Chicago: University of Chicago Press.

Shaheen, J., & Kuhmerker, L. (1991). *Free to learn, free to teach.* Manhattan, KS: The Master Teacher Inc.

Shure, M. (1992). *I can problem solve.(ICPS): An interpersonal problem-solving program.* Champaign, IL: Research Press

Shure, M., & Spivak, G. (1978). *Problem-solving techniques in childrearing.* San Francisco: Jossey-Bass.

Smetana, J. (1983). Social-cognitive development: Domain distinctions and coordinations. *Developmental Review, 3,* 131–147.

Stambak, M., Barriere, M., Bonica, L., Maisonnet, R., Musatti, T., Rayna, S., & Verba, M. (1983). *Les bébés entre eux.* Paris: Presses Universitaires de France.

Steig, W. (1982). *Doctor DeSoto.* A Sunburst Book: Farrar, Straus, and Giroux.

Turiel, E. (1983). *The development of social knowledge: Morality and convention.* Cambridge: Cambridge University Press.

Verba, M. (1990). Construction et partage de significations dans les jeux de fiction entre enfants. In M. Stambak and H. Sinclair (Eds.), *Les jeux de fiction entre enfants de 3 ans* (pp. 23–69). Paris: Presses Universitaires de France. (Published in English as *Pretend play among 3-year-olds,* Hillsdale, NJ: Erlbaum, 1993).

Wood, A. (1987). *Heckedy Peg.* San Diego: Harcourt Brace Jovanovich.

Index

A

Academics, 250–263
  constructivist integration of, 254–262
  conditions for promoting, 252–254
  social interaction centered on, fostering
    of, 256–257
  teaching of, sociomoral context of,
    251–252
Active situations, related to children's pur-
    poses, creation of, 254–256
Activities, constructivist, 62–70
  categories of, 197
  choice of, by children, during activity
    time, 204–205
  classroom, decision making about, by chil-
    dren, 139–140
  knowledge reflected in, categories of,
    193–197
  rationales for, 293–296
Activity time, 192–217
  implementation of, 201–216
  objectives and rationale, 193
  planning for, 197–201
Adler, A., 267–269
Affect, 2, 63
Anger, of teacher, with child, 102
Apologies, 182
Art activities, 295–296
Asch, F., 245
Assertive Discipline, 266–267
Atmosphere. *See* School atmosphere;
    Sociomoral atmosphere
Authoritarian teaching. *See* Boot Camp
    classroom
Authority
  blind obedience to, 48
  of constructivist teacher, 50
  limits of, 26, 49
Autonomous morality, 46, 49–52
Autonomy, 31
  in peer interaction, 53, 56
  and rule making, 126

B

Barriere, M., 54–55
Behaviorist approach, 265–268
  assumptions of, 267
  critique of, from constructivist perspec-
    tive, 267–268
  failure of, to address origins of misbehav-
    ior, 267–268

techniques of, 265–266
Belief system, internal, of difficult child
  challenging of, 273–276
  understanding of, 271–273
Belonging, feeling of, need for, 269
Berenstain, J., 223
Berenstain, S., 223
The Berenstain Bears and the Messy Room
    (Berenstain), 223
Blocks, 294–295
Bonica, L., 54–56
Boot Camp classroom, 7–8
  academics teaching in, 251–252
  effect on sociomoral development, 24–25
  interpersonal understanding in, 36–38
  and neglect of emotional needs, 59
  peer relationships in, 52
  sociomoral atmosphere of, 10–14, 281–282

C

Canter, L., 266
Canter, M., 266
Celebrations, during grouptime, 120–121
Censure, 184
Cheating, response to, 212–214
Classroom atmosphere. *See* School atmo-
    sphere; Sociomoral atmosphere
Classroom organization, 58–62
  for children's needs, 58–60
  for child responsibility, 61–62
  for peer interaction, 60–61
Classroom ownership, feeling of, 59
Clean-up time, 218–232
  after lunch time, 241
  moral issues in, 220–221
  objectives of, 218–219
  presentation of, to class, 219–221
  problems with, 221–232
Coercion
  and clean-up time, 221
  effects on children, 51
  mixed with cooperation, 51–52
Coercive relationship, 46–49
Colby, A., 31, 164
Collaboration, and academics teaching,
    256–257
Community, feeling of, development of, 56
Community classroom, 8–9
  academics teaching in, 251–252
  effect on sociomoral development of, 24
  and emotional needs, 59

Community classroom *(cont'd.)*
  interpersonal understanding in, 36–38
  peer relationships in, 52–53
  sociomoral atmosphere of, 14–18, 281–282
Competitive attitude, and cheating, 213–214
Conflict, 79–103
  group discussion of, 76
  interindividual, 79–80
  intervention in, 74–75
  intraindividual, 79–80
  ownership of, 82
  role in development, 79–81
  between teacher and child, 101–102
  teacher's attitude toward, 81–82
  teaching principles in, 82–84
Conflict resolution
  by children, 55–56, 82, 99–100
  by principals, 288–289
  role of teacher in, 57
  and sociomoral atmosphere, 81–100
Consequences. *See also* Natural conse-
      quences
  inappropriate, suggested by children,
      185–186
  indefinite, avoidance of, 189–190
  logical, 185, 276
  negative, in Assertive Discipline class-
      rooms, 266
Conservation, of values, in intellectual
      development, 44, 48
Construction toys, 294–295
Constructive error, 199–200
Constructive process, allowing time for,
      262
Constructivist activities, rationales for,
      293–296
*Constructivist Early Education: Overview and
      Comparison with Other Programs*
      (DeVries & Kohlberg), 2
Constructivist education
  academics in, 254–262
  definition of, 62
  first principle of, 1
  overview of, 1–3
Conventional arbitrary knowledge, 195
  in academics teaching, 260–262
  in classroom activities, 195–197
Conventional morality, 165
Cooperation
  and conflict resolution, 55–56
  appeal to, during activity time, 201
  benefits of, 49–52
  definition of, 49, 68
  effects on children, 51
  examples of, 69–70
  importance of, 69
  incipient, 207–208
  mixed with coercion, 51–52
  motive for, 49

promotion of, 68–70, 72–78, 209–215
  between teacher and child, 70–72, 49–52
Coping abilities, promotion of, 72–74

D
Decentering, 2, 41, 69, 76
  and construction of self-concept, 44–45
Decision making
  by children, 125–126, 139–144
  by teachers, 287–288
Department of education, sociomoral atmo-
      sphere of, 289–290
Development. *See also* Sociomoral develop-
      ment
  cognitive, Piaget's theory of, 1–2
  of community feelings, 56
  intellectual, 44, 48, 253–254
  interpersonal relationships in, importance
      of, 43
  of moral feelings, 43, 45
  of moral reasoning, 164–165
  role of conflict in, 79–81
  of self-knowledge, 73
Developmental level, assessment of play
      with marbles, 206–208
DeVries, R., 2, 4, 24, 30, 36, 64, 81, 197, 205,
      207, 212, 252, 268
Dewey, J., 63, 255
Difficult child, 264–278
  behaviorist approach to, 265–268
  internal belief system, 272–276
  psychodynamic and constructivist
      approaches to, integration of, 268–270
  working with, guidelines for, 270–278
Dilemma discussion. *See* Sociomoral dis-
      cussion
Direct-instruction classroom. *See* Boot
      Camp classroom
Discipline
  assertive, 266–267
  and conflict resolution, 288
  cooperative alternatives to, 178–191
  definition of, 178
  during grouptime, 112–113
  by principals, 288–289
Doctor DeSoto (Steig), 170–171, 173
Do rules, 131–132
Dragonwagon, C., 245
Dreikurs, R., 270
Duckworth, E., 193, 207
E
Eclectic classroom. *See* Factory classroom
Egocentric play, 207
Emotional balance, construction of, 72–74
Emotional needs
  of children, and classroom organization, 59
  respect for, at nap time, 246–247
Enacted interpersonal understanding,
      assessment of, 32–41

levels of, 33–34, 34f
sociomoral development assessment, in
    terms of, 38–41
Equilibration process, in sociomoral and
    cognitive development, 2
Errors, respect for, 259–260. *See also* Con-
    structive error
Exclusion, 183–184
    of a child by other children, management
        of, 61, 189
    as logical consequence of, 183–184
    reinstatement after, opportunity for,
        188–189
Experience. *See also* Shared experiences
    of difficult child, reconstruction of, 276–277
    personal, role in sociomoral development,
        179
    of school atmosphere, by children and
        teachers, 281–283
Experimentation
    encouragement of, 66–68
    examples of, 67–68
    importance of, 66–67
Expiatory sanctions, 180–181
    avoidance of, 185
External control. *See* Authority

F
Factory classroom, 9–10
    academics teaching in, 251–252
    effect on sociomoral development, 24
    interpersonal understanding in, 36–38
    and neglect of emotional needs, 59
    peer relationships in, 52
    sociomoral atmosphere of, 18–22, 281–282
Faith, in child, communication of, 270–271
Feelings
    in conflict situation, 85
    of difficult child, 272, 275–278
Fernie, D., 207
Ferreiro, E., 258
Flexibility, during activity time, 215–216

Free play. *See* Activity time
Freud, S., 268
Friendships, among children, respect for,
    60–61

G
Garis, H. R., 202
Genetic epistemology, 1
Glass breaking, lesson incorporating, 65
Goffin, S., 290
Goodwill, feelings of, 51
Governance, by principals, 287–288
Group discussion, of conflicts between chil-
    dren, 76
Group games, 295
    children's reasoning during, assessment
        of, 209

teacher involvement in, 72
Group project, planning of, during group-
    time, 116–119
Grouptime, 104–124
    case study, 122–123
    children's ideas, for activity time, 203–204
    conducting of, 108–122
    conflicts between children, 76
    content of, 114–122
    individual problems during, 114–116
    length of, 109
    management strategies for, 109–114
    moral dilemmas during, 167–168
    objectives for, 104–106
    peer interaction during, organization for,
        60
    planning for, 106–107
    role of teacher in, 106–108
    rule-making for, 126–136
    seating arrangements for, 108–109
    voting, 150–155

H
Half a Moon and One Whole Star (Drag-
    onwagon), 245
Hand counting, in voting, 155–156
Hand washing, lesson incorporating, 66
Haney, J., 4, 24, 81, 252
The Having of Wonderful Ideas (Duckworth),
    193
Health issues
    at lunch time, 235–236
    at nap time, 246
Heckedy Peg (Wood), 169, 171, 173
Heteronomous morality, 46–49
Heteronomy, 31
    and neglect of emotional needs, 59
Hidden curriculum, 3
    of moral education, 3
    sociomoral atmosphere as, 25–26
Higgins, A., 3, 76, 165, 279–281, 283,
    289–290
Hitz, R., 267
Hygiene issues, at lunch time, 235–236

I
Ideas, children's
    for activity time, 203–204
    for rules, 130–131
Impartial procedures, for conflict resolu-
    tion, 92–93
Incipient cooperation, 207–208
Individual problems, discussion of, during
    grouptime, 114–116
Insincerity, in conflict resolution, 97–99
Instrumental purpose and exchange, 165
Intellectual development, 253–254
    and sociomoral development, 2
    Piaget's studies of, 44

Intellectual needs, of children, and classroom organization, 59–60
Intentionality, assessment of, in cheating,
  212–214
Interest
  definition of, 62
  importance of, 62–63
Interest engagement, 62–66
  during activity time, 198, 201–204
  examples of, 64–66
  during grouptime, 110–111
Interpersonal Cognitive Problem Solving
  skills, 75
Interpersonal problems
  clarification of, in conflict situation, 88–89
  decision making about, by children,
    141–144
  individual, discussion of, during group-
    time, 114–116
  rule-making discussions in response to,
    128–129
Interpersonal relationships, importance of,
  in development, 43
Interpersonal understanding. See also
    Enacted interpersonal understanding
  components of, 33
  construction of, promotion of, 74–75
  examples of, 36–38
Interview, of difficult child, 273

J
Jackson, P., 3
Just Community, 3, 76, 279–281
Justice, feelings of, construction of,
  277–278

K
Kamii, C., 2, 64, 197, 205, 212, 257, 268
Knowledge
  construction of, based on current knowl-
    edge, 258–259
  structures of, transformation of, 253–254
Knowledge categories, 193–195
  in academics teaching, 255–256, 260–262
  in activity time, 195–197
  understanding of, by teachers, 206
Kohlberg, L., 2–3, 30–32, 41, 64, 76, 164–166,
  197, 279–281, 283, 289–290
Kohlberg's Approach to Moral Education,
  279–281
Krank, M., 267
Krasilovsky, P., 223
Kuhmerker, L., 6

L
Language activities, 293–294
Leader, teacher as, in grouptime, 107–108
Lickona, T., 2, 6
Literacy activities, 293–294
Lobbying, in voting process, management

  of, 159
Logical consequences
  children's ownership of, encouragement
    of, 185
  of patterns of reaction, emphasis on, 276
Logico-mathematical knowledge, 194–195
  in academics teaching, 260–262
  in classroom activities, 195–197, 295
Long, R., 255
Lunch time, 233–242
  guidelines for, 234–241
  objectives of, 234
  seating arrangements for, 235

M
Maisonnet, R., 54–55
Majority rule, acceptance of, 160–161
Management strategies, for grouptime,
  109–114
Manning, G., 255
Manning, M., 255
The Man Who Didn't Wash His Dishes
  (Krasilovsky), 223
Mayer, R., 30
Mead, G., 44–45
Minority views, respect for, in voting pro-
  cess, 160–161
Misbehavior
  failure of behaviorist approach to address,
    267–268
  internal belief system governing, 271–273
  teacher's behavior in response to, 272
Miseducative tasks, 63
Missouri Department of Elementary and
  Secondary Education, 290
Mooncake (Asch), 245
Moral children, 28–42
  classroom observation of, 38–41
  definition of, 4, 28–31
Moral classrooms, 7–27
Moral contexts, promotion of academics in,
  257
Moral development, role of personal experience in, 179
Moral dilemmas, 166–168
  definition of, 166
  for discussion, 167–169
  hypothetical, from real-life experiences,
    175–177
  types of, 167
Moral discussions. See Sociomoral discus-
  sions
Moral feelings, development of, 43, 45
Moral intention, prosocial behavior without, 29–30
Moral issues
  definition of, in relation to social issues,
    162–164
Morality
  autonomous, 46, 49–52

bag of virtues approach to, 30
child, characteristics of, 31–32
conventional, 165
heteronomous (of obedience), 46–49
preconventional, 164–165
in relation to religion, 30
types of, corresponding to adult-child relationships, 46
The Moral Judgment of the Child (Piaget), 31, 181
Moral judgment theory, 164–166
Moral realism, 31–32
Moral reasoning
clarification of, by repeating ideas, 173
developmental stages of, 41, 164–165
Moral rules, how children think about, 31–32
Moral values, construction of, promotion of, 76–78
Morgan, P., 4, 24, 36, 81, 252
Morris, W., 178
Murphy, D., 284, 286–290
Musatti, T., 54–55
Mutual agreement
and rule violations, 214
value of, 90–92

N
Nap time, 243–249
guidelines for, 244–249
problems of, 243–244
transition to, 241
Natural consequences, 182
cause-effect relation with, understanding of, 186–187
of patterns of reaction, emphasis on, 276
selective use of, 187
Negative consequences, in Assertive Discipline classrooms, 266
Negotiation , 33. *See also* Enacted interpersonal understanding
definition of, 34–35
during peer interaction, 55
levels of, 34f, 34–35
promotion of, 209–211
Nucci, L., 162–163
Nutrition habits, and lunch time, 235–236

O
Obedience
in constructivist classrooms, 50
morality of, 46–49
motivated by affection and attachment, 29, 48–49
motivated by fear of punishment, 29, 48–49
P
Padilla, J., 267
Paradigm shift, need for, recognition of, by principal, 285–286

Peer interaction, 52–57
classroom organization for, 60–61
in constructivist classroom, benefits of, 53–56
during lunch time, 236–241
role of constructivist teacher in, 56–57
schemes of, 54
and sociomoral atmosphere, 22–23, 52–53
Personal experience, role in sociomoral development, 179
Perspective-taking
and construction of self-concept, 44–45
coordination of, 33–34, 41
development of, 32–36
in discussing moral dilemma stories, 170–171
by difficult child, promotion of, 274–275
and nap time problems, 248–249
Physical knowledge, 194
in academics teaching, 255–256, 260–262
in activities, 195–197, 294
Physical safety, teacher's responsibility for, in conflict situation, 82–84
Physiological needs
of children, and classroom organization, 58–59
respect for, at nap time, 246–247
Piaget, Jean, 1–2, 5, 25, 31–32, 34, 41, 43–54, 62–63, 68, 71, 79–81, 125, 135, 164, 179–184, 193–197, 207–208, 212, 252–254, 260, 267, 277, 285, 287
Planning
for activity time, 197–201
of group project, during grouptime, 116–119
for grouptime, 106–107
Power, C., 3, 76, 165, 279–281, 283, 289–290
Preconventional morality, 164–165
Preoperational reasoning, respect for, 206
Pretense, 293
Principal, and sociomoral atmosphere, 284–289
Prosocial behavior, without moral intention, 29–30
Psychodynamic approach, to difficult child, integration of, with constructivist theories, 268–270
Psychosocial knowledge, construction of, 2
Punishment. *See also* Discipline; Expiatory sanctions
in behaviorist approach, 267
Punitive sanctions, 180–181
avoidance of, 185

R
Rayna, S., 54–55
Real-life moral discussions, 174–175
Reasoning
appeal to, during activity time, 199–201
encouragement of, 205–209, 258–262

Reasoning *(cont'd.)*
  intervention in, 208–209
  moral, 41, 164–165, 173
  preoperational, respect for, 206
  spatial, 295
  teacher's understanding of children's, 71
Reciprocity
  in peer relationships, 53
  between teacher and child, 70
Reciprocity sanctions, 181–184
Reese-Learned, H., 4, 24, 36, 81, 252
Relationships. *See also* Teacher-child rela-
    tionship
  interpersonal, importance of, in develop-
    ment, 43
  repair of, 97–99, 101–102, 182
Religion, in relation to morality, 30
Render, G., 267
Representational thought, 294–295
Respect
  for children, 58–59, 62, 76, 253, 258
  communication of, to difficult child,
    270–271
  for errors, 259–260
  for needs, at nap time, 246–247
  for others, promotion of, 76
  for preoperational reasoning, 206
  and the sociomoral atmosphere, 1, 14–18
  for teachers, by principals, 284–285
Responsibility.
  shared, promotion of, during clean-up
    time, 219
  teacher, for physical safety, in conflict sit-
    uation, 82–84
Responsibility, child
  classroom organization for, 61–62
  in conflict situation, 93–95
  promotion of, during clean-up time,
    218–219
  and reciprocity sanctions, 183
Restitution, 182
  in conflict situation, 95–96
  opportunities for, provision of, 187–188
Rest time. *See* Nap time
Rewards, in behaviorist approach, 267
Routines, establishment of
  for lunch time, 234–235
  for nap time, 245–246
Rule making, by children, 56, 125–139
  objectives of, 125–126
Rule-making discussions, guidance of,
    126–136
Rules
  agreement on, 135
  in Assertive Discipline classrooms, 266
  changing of, 133–134
  child's practice of, stages in, 207–208
  codification of, 208
  created by children, respect for, 130–131
  dictation of, avoidance of, 132–133

"Do" and "don't" rules, 131–132
  enforcement of, 138–139
  positive, 131–132
  reason for, emphasis on, 129–130
  recording and posting of, 136–138
  for teachers, 135–1346
  unacceptable, responding to 134–135
  violations of, dealing with, 212–215

S
Safety, physical, teacher's responsibility
    for, in conflict situation, 82–84
Sanctions, 180–184
  expiatory or punitive, 180–181, 185
  reciprocity, 181–184
Sarason, S., 45, 284–285
Scharf, 281
Schemes of social reaction, 54, 276
School atmosphere, 279–291. *See also*
    Sociomoral atmosphere
  children's experience of, 281–283
  and principals, 283–289
  teacher's experience of, 283
School district, sociomoral atmosphere of,
    289–290
Schultz, L., 31
Scieszka, J., 169
Self, differentiation of, from others, through
    peer relationships, 53–54
Self-concept, construction of, and social
    interaction, 43–45
Self-construction, of difficult child, assess-
    ment of, 272
Self-esteem, construction of, 48
Self-knowledge, development of, promotion
    of, 73
Self-regulation. *See also* Autonomy
  and academics teaching, 253
  promotion of, during clean-up time, 219
  social, promotion of, 209–215
  in sociomoral and cognitive development,
    2
Selman, Robert, 31–36, 38, 41, 164
Shaheen, J., 6
Shared experiences, 33, 35–36. *See also*
    Enacted interpersonal understanding
  definition of, 35
  levels of, 34f, 35–36
  promotion of, 211–212
  importance in sociomoral atmosphere,
    289
Shared meaning, among peers, 54–55
Show and tell, 121–122
Shure, M., 74–75
Sink-and-float activity, 67–68
Smetana, J., 162–163
Social interaction. *See also* Peer interaction
  centered on academics, fostering of,
    256–257
  and construction of self, 43–45

schemes of, 54
Social issues
  definition of, 162–164
  how children think about, 31–32
Social perspective
  coordination, 33–34, 41
  and development of moral reasoning, 165
Social reaction, stable schemes of, construction of, 45
Social self-regulation, promotion of, 209–215
Social validation
  communication of, to difficult child, 270–271
  need for, 269–270
Socioaffective bonds, motivation of sociomoral development by, 2
Sociomoral atmosphere, 279–291
  assessment of, techniques for, 280–282
  components of, 22–23
  and conflict resolution, 81–100
  definition of, 1, 22
  establishment of, 22–23, 43–44
  as hidden curriculum, 25–26
  influence on development, 23–25, 43–57
  of state department of education, 289–290
  research on, 23–25
  types of, illustrations of, 7–22
Sociomoral context, of academics teaching, 251–252
Sociomoral development
  assessment of, with enacted interpersonal understanding, 38–41
  research on sociomoral atmosphere, 23–25, 43–57
  Piaget's theory of, 1–2
  role of personal experience in, 179
Sociomoral discussions, 162–177
  hypothetical dilemmas, 168–173, 175–177
  objectives of, 168
  real-life dilemmas, 174–175
Sociomoral issues
  children involved in, examples of, 38–40
  in clean-up time, presentation of, 220–221
  definition of, 162–164
  how children think about, 31–32
Sociomoral objectives, of grouptime, 104–105

Soltz, V., 270
Spatial reasoning, 295
Spivack, G., 74
Stambak, M., 54–55
State department of education, sociomoral atmosphere of, 289–290
Steig, W., 170

T
Teacher-child relationship, 45–52
  coercive or controlling, 46–49
  cooperative, 49–52
  importance of, 3
  and sociomoral atmosphere, 22, 44
Teberosky, A., 258
Transition
  after lunch time, to next activity, 241
  problem of, during clean-up time, 221–222
Turiel, E., 162–163

U
Unfairness, perception of, in teacher-child conflict, 101

V
Values
  conservation of, in moral development, 44, 48
  moral, construction of, 76–78
  reconstruction of, by difficult child, 277
Verba, M., 54–56
Voting, 145–161
  choice of issues, 146–150
  guidelines for, 146–161
  objectives of, 145–146
  procedures, 155–159
  by teacher, 159–161
Voting procedures, understandable to children, 155–159

W
Will, as conservation of values, 48
Will to power, 268
Wood, A., 169
Wording, of rules, by children, 130–131

Z
Zan, B., 4, 24, 81, 252

About the Authors

Rheta DeVries is director of the Iowa Regent's Center for Early Developmental Education and professor of curriculum and instruction at the University of Northern Iowa. A former public school teacher, she previously taught at the University of Illinois at Chicago and at the Merrill-Palmer Institute. She received her Ph.D. degree in psychology from the University of Chicago and did postdoctoral work at the University of Geneva, Switzerland. Previous publications include *Constructivist Early Education: Overview and Comparison with Other Programs* (coauthored with Lawrence Kohlberg) and *Physical Knowledge in Preschool Education,* and *Group Games in Early Education* (both coauthored by Constance Kamii).

Betty Zan is a research fellow at the Iowa Regent's Center for Early Developmental Education. She is also a doctoral candidate in developmental psychology at the University of Houston, where she received her M.A. She has coauthored journal articles with Rheta DeVries, reporting research on classroom sociomoral atmosphere.

DATE DUE

1 13 95	OC 25 '06		
MAR 18 '95	AG 26 '07		
NOV 07 '95			
JAN 03 '96	AP 11 '08		
APR 16 '96			
6 26 97			
NOV 03 97			
NOV 1 0 1998			
MAR 1 ? 1999			
APR 0 9 1999			
SEP 0 2 1999			
MAR 9 2000			
FEB 2 ? 2001			
SE 01 '01			
APR 1 2 2002			
SE 11 '02			
MY 16 0?			